IMAGES
of America

BIG PINEY AND MARBLETON

On the Cover: The Big Piney Roundup Association was formed to handle and take care of the area cattle collectively. Pictured here is the Big Piney Pool Roundup in 1897. From left to right are (first row) Archie Roberts, Ralph Friend, Al Davison, Al Osterhout, Billy Johnson, Fred Schebel, James Mickelson, foreman A.W. Smith, C.P. Budd, Ez Swan, Grant Swan, and Jim Sykes; (second row) N.W. Griggs, Frank Ball, Dozzie Edwards, cook George Edwards, wrangler Joe Andrews, and Fred Dubois. Legend has it that the riders all rode white horses on this roundup so that at night, when raiding a sheep camp, they could see and identify one another. (Courtesy of Bill and Carrie Budd.)

IMAGES
of America

BIG PINEY AND MARBLETON

Ann Chambers Noble

ARCADIA
PUBLISHING

ISBN 978-0-7385-7588-9

Published by Arcadia Publishing
Charleston, South Carolina

Printed in the United States of America

Library of Congress Control Number: 2011925402

For all general information, please contact Arcadia Publishing:
Telephone 843-853-2070
Fax 843-853-0044
E-mail sales@arcadiapublishing.com
For customer service and orders:
Toll-Free 1-888-313-2665

Visit us on the Internet at www.arcadiapublishing.com

To residents of the Big Piney and Marbleton area for their assistance in making this book possible, and to my family, for their never-ending support

CONTENTS

ACKNOWLEDGMENTS

Photographs in this volume came from many families. Thanks to those who took the time to collect their personal pictures and explain to me their stories. This includes Bill and Carrie Budd, who have preserved numerous photographs, including Pearl Budd Spencer's collection, which is very valuable for early Wyoming history. Thanks also to Nancy Budd Espenscheid, Sprout and Jane Wardell, Mike and Tara Miller, Jay and Sandy McGinnis, Abner Luman, Mardell Fear, Dan Budd, and Robert and Helena Linn. Jonita Sommer's help was critical to this book. In addition to providing and scanning many Sommer family pictures, her editorial help and research is greatly appreciated. Thanks also to Carrie Anderson with the Green River Valley Museum for her help, Clint Gilchrist's for his photograph collection on Sublette.com, and Dawn Ballou for her computer assistance. Finally, special thanks for my husband, David, and our daughters for their editorial assistance and constant support.

Introduction

Big Piney is the oldest settlement in Sublette County, Wyoming, and was named by Dan B. Budd for the Piney Creeks. In 1879, Daniel B. Budd and his partner Hugh McKay came through the area moving 1,000 head of cattle from Nevada, hoping to ship them at Point of Rocks in central Wyoming. Prior to making their destination, winter set in and the men were forced to winter their cattle in the Green River Valley. They moved the livestock to South Piney Creek to sit out the winter. When spring came, it was noted that the cattle had done well on the local grass. Budd decided to stay in the area and moved his family there.

Budd was not the first to bring livestock to the Piney Creek area. In 1878, Ed Swan brought cattle with the PL brand, and Otto Leifer brought 500–700 head of cattle branded with the Circle that same year. When these cattlemen arrived, they found Dick Fagan on North Piney Creek with horses.

During the early years, Green River Valley cattle were run on the open range and no one thought of putting up hay except a few loads, which they cut along the sloughs for the wrangle horses and the milk cows. There were no fences except for a few corrals near the ranch houses. That all changed, though, the severe winter of 1889–1890, when most of the cattle starved to death and everyone had to start over. It was called the "Equalizer Winter," as the loss from severe weather devastated prosperous and poorer ranchers alike. Cowmen began to plan ahead for winter. They grubbed sagebrush by hand, sowed grass seed, and built ditches to irrigate meadows. This was followed with growing a hay crop and fencing it in.

As more land was cultivated and fenced, grazing of livestock became more of a problem. This caused the cattlemen to change their methods of handling cattle. For this purpose, they established the Big Piney Roundup Association. The ranchers pooled their resources and ran their cattle together. Together they worked roundups, cattle drives, and brandings. Later, the Upper Green River Cattle and Horse Growers Association was formed, continuing the pooled labor efforts.

Big Piney's first post office was established in 1879, with Nicolas Swan as the postmaster. The post office was located on the Muleshoe Ranch, where North Piney Creek drains into the Green River. When Daniel Budd moved to Big Piney, he became the postmaster, and he kept the position until his death in 1902. Budd put the post office in a store he built to supply the growing numbers of settlers to the area. Above his store was a big room that was used as the first community hall. Area residents gathered for years in Budd Hall for dances and other social events.

The first schoolhouse in Big Piney was a log cabin with a dirt roof. It was later replaced with a modern schoolhouse on land donated by Daniel Budd. Schoolhouses were also built throughout the area. With travel difficult, schools were built or moved near the ranch children. A large number of ranch wives were former schoolteachers, and therefore, education has always been a priority in the community.

Big Piney was incorporated on July 5, 1913. By then, the town had a school, church, store, hotel, bar, bank, newspaper, and telephone service. The town location, though, was problematic because there were many drainage problems. The boggy area made travel difficult, especially during the wet spring time. Building foundations could also be unstable. So Charles Budd, eldest son of Dan B. Budd, hoped to move the town to the higher ground north of the original townsite to alleviate this problem. Charles established Marbleton on the bench in late 1913, and it was incorporated in 1914, but it never replaced Big Piney. The two towns are only a mile apart, but every effort to combine the two has failed.

Agriculture—mostly cattle—continued to be the main source of support for the two communities. Energy extraction has also had an impact on the towns throughout its histories. Drilling for oil started in the area in 1910s, though it was considered only marginally successful. Additional attempts to extract oil and natural gas continued throughout the 20th century, with four booms in the 1920s, 1950s, 1980s, and again starting about 2000.

Big Piney and Marbleton have been fairly isolated throughout much of their history, with the closest railroad stop in Opal, Wyoming, nearly 60 miles away. Yet locals were always impacted by world events, at times taking part in them. When the United States entered the Great War in 1917, young area men joined other Wyoming volunteers to serve in the Machine Gun Platoon, Sunset Division, in France. Tragically, one would not return when Russell Daniels was killed on November 28, 1918, leaving a wife and three children in Big Piney.

A decade later, the town was impacted by economic hard times brought on by the Great Depression of the 1930s. Pres. Franklin D. Roosevelt's New Deal programs helped the community when federal aid came with the Works Progress Administration that was used to build the Big Piney community hall. The largest federal New Deal program in the area was the Civilian Conservation Corps camp built a mile west of Big Piney. A few young local men worked with the CCCs, but most of the enrollees were from around the country. They built roads and fences on the US Forest Service land in the nearby mountains.

The towns were again directly impacted by world events when the nation went to war in December 1941. The war was felt close to home, and the townspeople raised money through war bonds, collected materials for recycling, and took war precautions. Young men—and some women—from Big Piney, Marbleton, and the surrounding area—joined the military services in great numbers and fought for our country around the world. The young soldiers returned veterans and were soon back at work building their ranches and communities.

The communities have always taken time to celebrate their heritage, especially the cowboy culture. Throughout their history, the towns have hosted hundreds of spectators for rodeos, especially over the July Fourth holiday, with its Chuckwagon Days. Local cowboys on local horses have always been featured, and for much of the 20th century, a favorite of the crowds were the chariot races.

Big Piney and Marbleton have experienced relatively small growth throughout its history, with the exception of the oil and natural gas booms. The surrounding agriculture industry has kept the towns going throughout much of the 20th century. Raising cattle continues to sustain the communities, but the energy industry even more so. Big Piney seems to have lost one claim to fame, though. Big Piney was called the "Ice Box of the Nation" when it was officially made a weather station in 1930. Big Piney had the coldest year-round average temperature of any place nationally. Additional stations have been added, and two other communities now fight over the very cold claim.

One

Birth of a Frontier Town

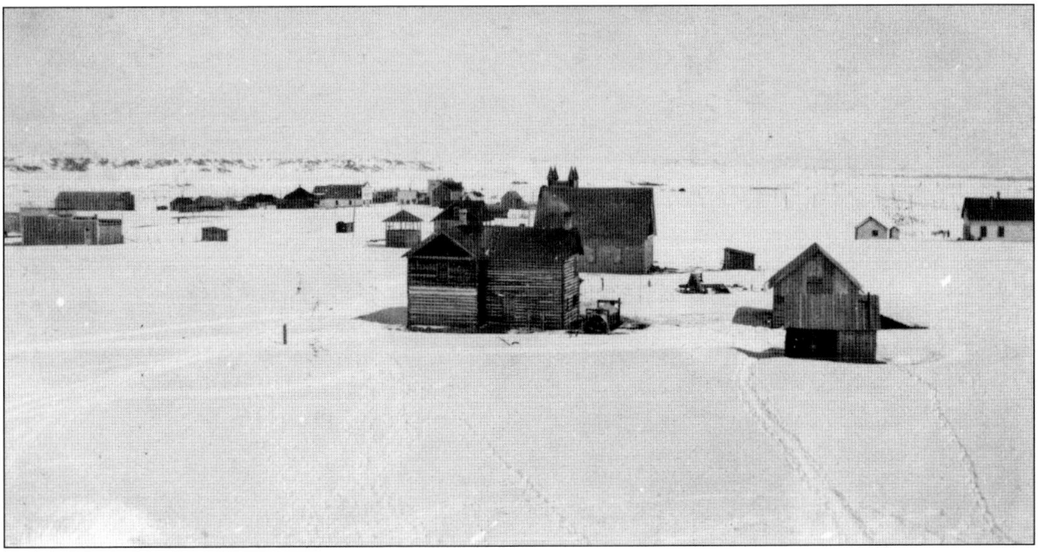

This picture was taken from the top of the school looking east at the small town of Big Piney in the 1920s. The town buildings are mostly made from wood brought from the timber in the mountains. Hoofprints in the snow suggest distant travel was made by horseback or horse-drawn buggies. The large, two-story building in the middle is the George Moffat house with the Congregational church behind it. (Courtesy of Georgia Wenz.)

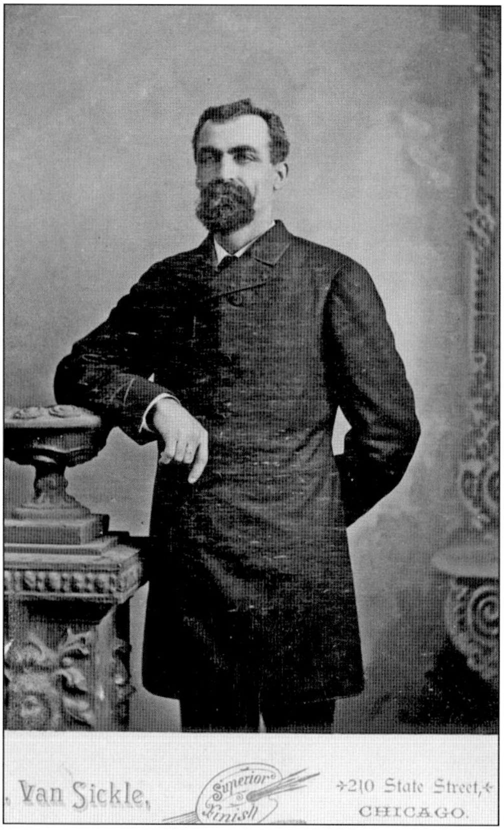

Otto Leifer was one of the first settlers to the Big Piney area. As a young bachelor in his 30s, Leifer came with Edward Swan and sons in the summer of 1878. They filed adjoining homestead claims in the broad valley of South and Middle Piney Creeks and took up cattle ranching. Leifer's brand was the O, and his place became known as the Circle Ranch. (Courtesy of Green River Valley Museum.)

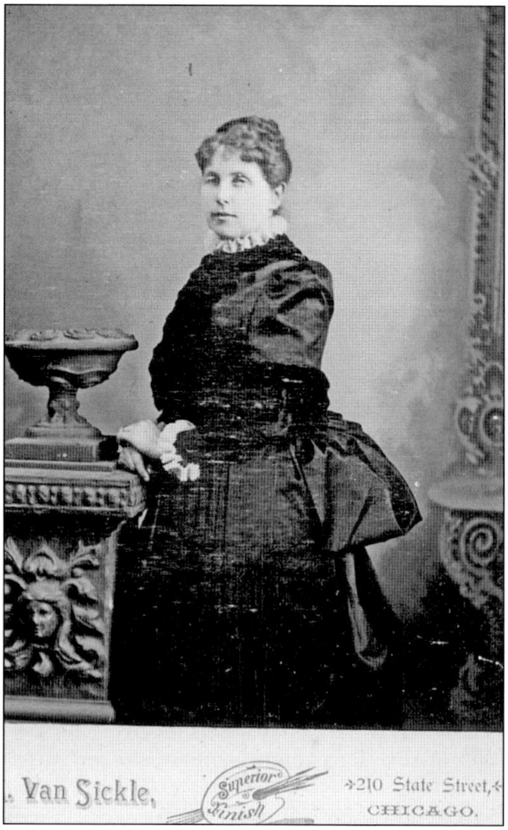

After nine years of ranching in Big Piney, bachelor Otto Leifer returned to his home in Virginia and married Delia M. Sollars. Otto brought his new wife back to his Wyoming ranch, where she was remembered for her womanly graces. After eight years of marriage, the couple moved to Salt Lake City due to Delia's failing health. Leifer sold his ranch to a young man from Denmark, James Mickelson. (Courtesy of Green River Valley Museum.)

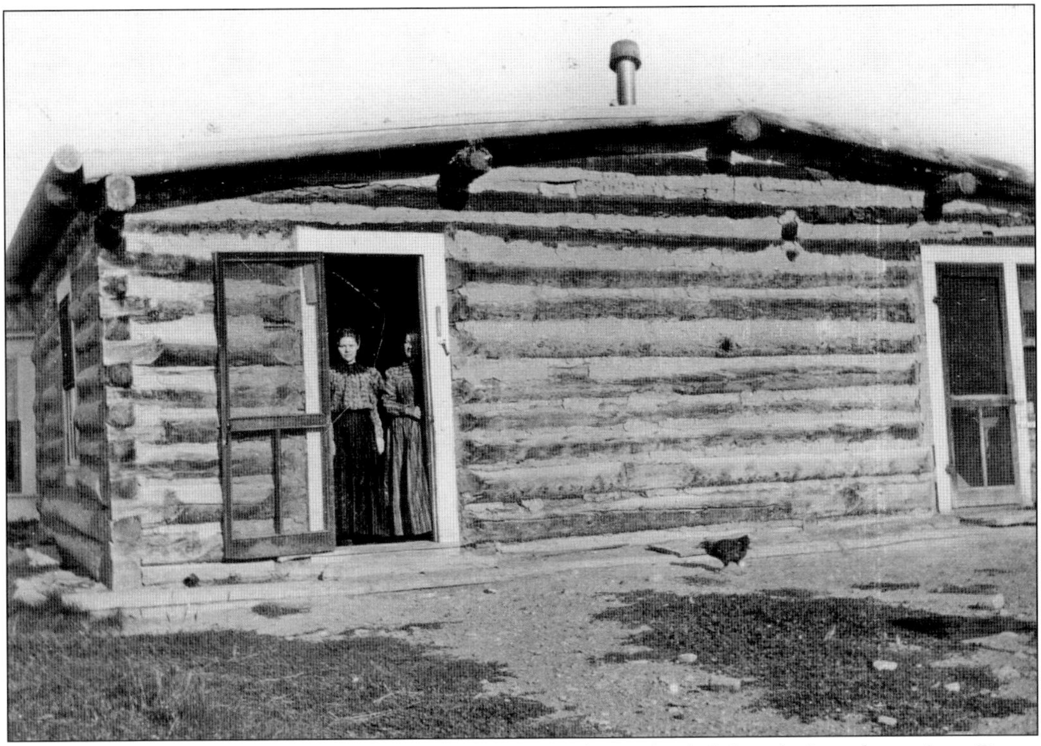

Ettie Naylor (later to marry Louis H. Hennick) stands on the left beside Josephine Ann Boyer Budd in the Big Piney Budd home about 1896. The small structure was typical of the early homes in the area in the late 19th century. Female companionship was treasured by the women in a place where the neighbors were usually far and away and travel was often difficult. (Courtesy of Bill and Carrie Budd.)

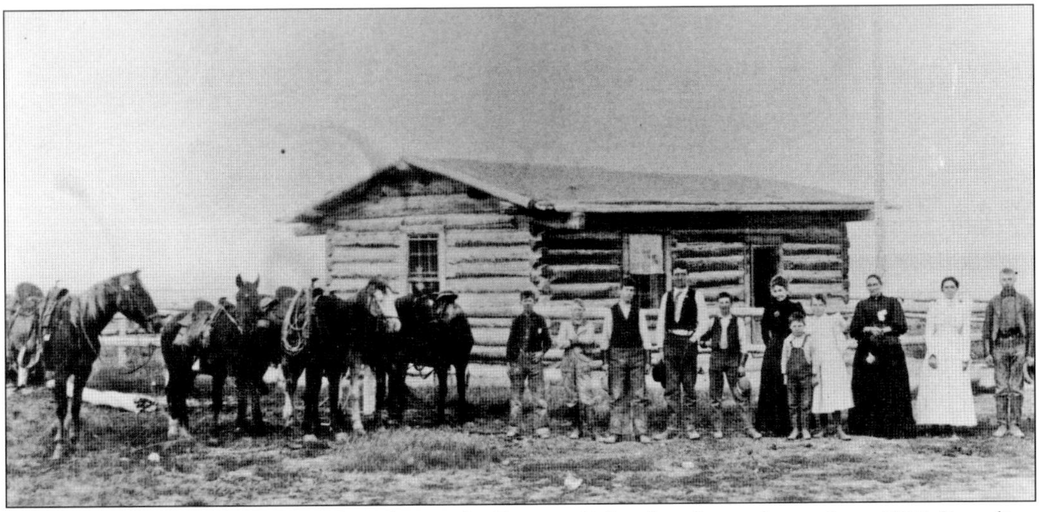

The first school in Big Piney, referred to as the Pioneer School, is shown here about 1894. Standing for the photograph are, from left to right, school members Dan Budd, Fred Beck, Henry Budd, Guy Jaycox, Billie Nichols, teacher Hittie Morris, Orlin Black, and Ida Black, and visitors Julia B. Nichols, Mabel Morris (daughter of the teacher), and Willie Swan. (Courtesy of Bill and Carrie Budd.)

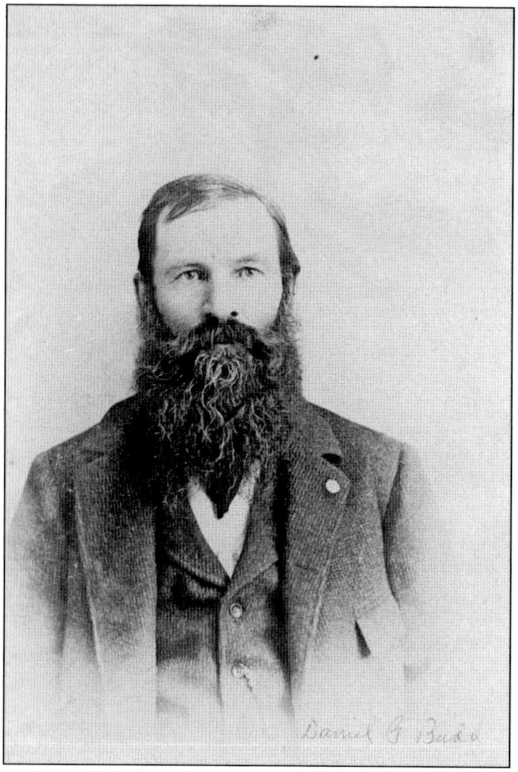

Daniel G. Budd, at left, left his wife, Josephine, below, and four small children in Kansas to travel to Nevada to settle the estate of his brother Philip. His brother had died suddenly, leaving a number of cattle and horses. Budd rounded up the animals, branded the cattle with an iron in the shape of the number 67, and left Nevada to take them to sell at market. During the long and arduous trip, he found himself snowed in for winter in the Big Piney area. Finding the feed good for the animals, he ultimately chose to stay there and raise cattle. Soon he relocated his wife and children. The family played an important role in building the town. (Courtesy of Green River Valley Museum.)

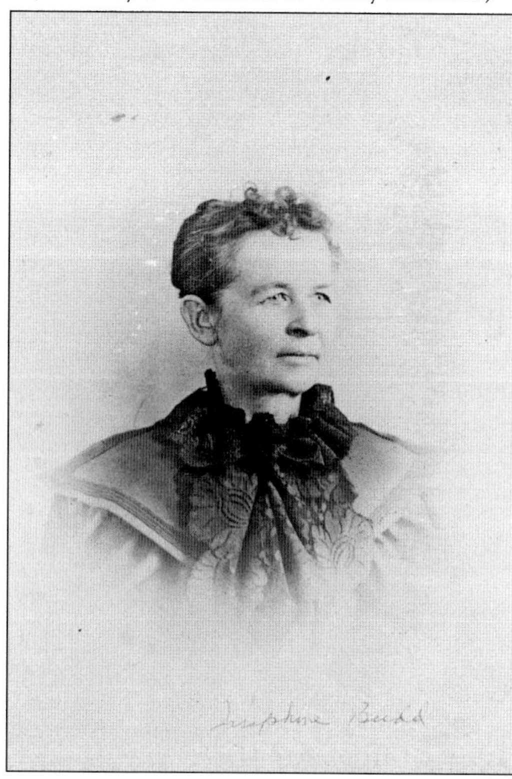

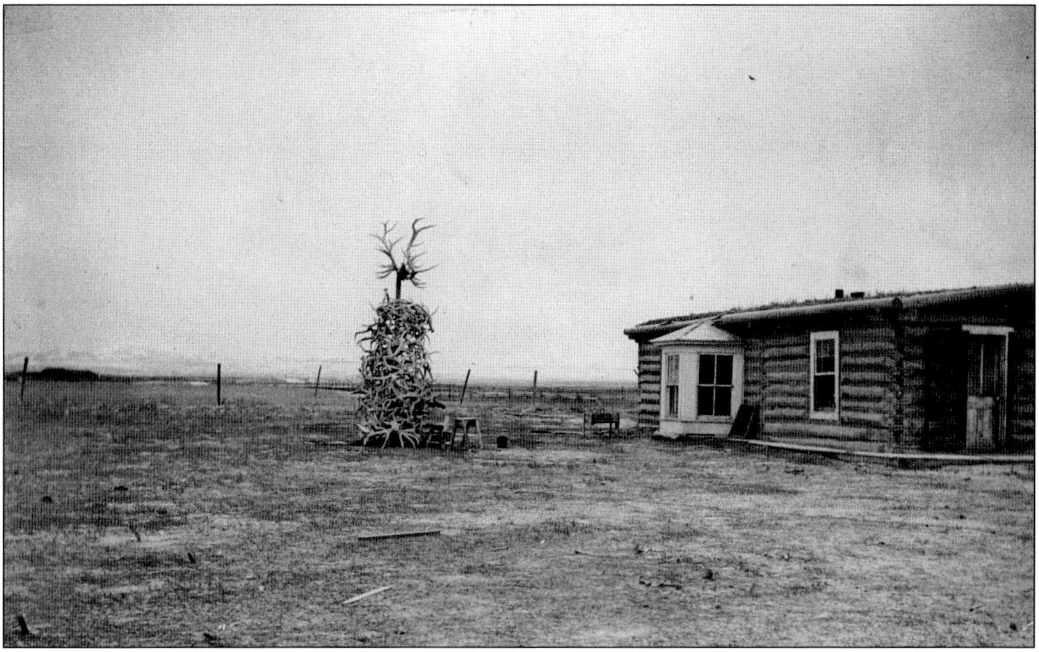

The Daniel B. and Josephine Ann Budd home, pictured here, is a simple log structure with a sod roof. It would later be the center of the town of Big Piney. Note the antler pile in the yard. It was common for ranchers to collect antlers for decorations for their yards. (Courtesy of Nancy Budd Espenscheid.)

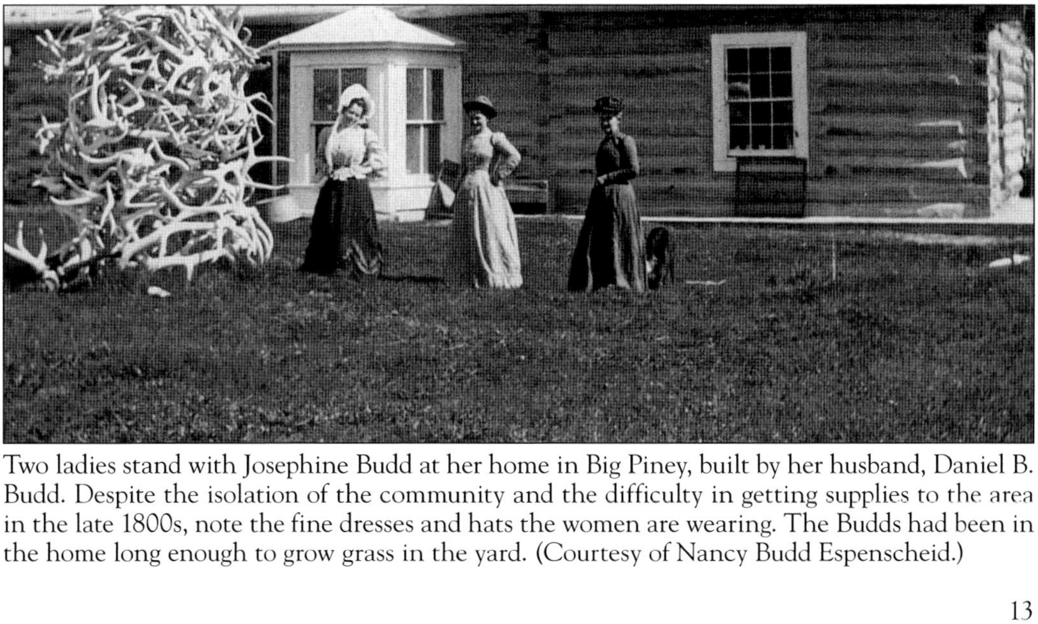

Two ladies stand with Josephine Budd at her home in Big Piney, built by her husband, Daniel B. Budd. Despite the isolation of the community and the difficulty in getting supplies to the area in the late 1800s, note the fine dresses and hats the women are wearing. The Budds had been in the home long enough to grow grass in the yard. (Courtesy of Nancy Budd Espenscheid.)

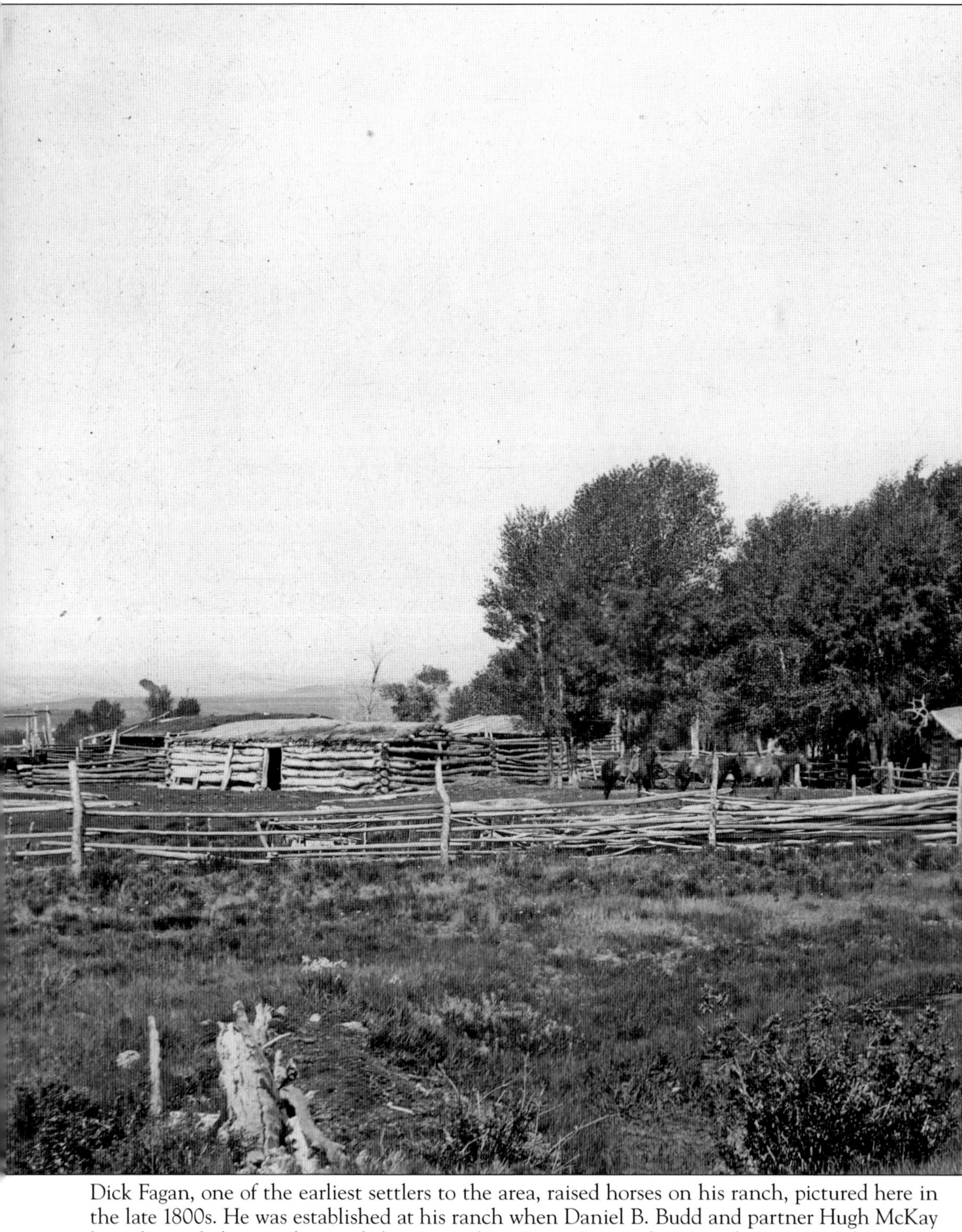

Dick Fagan, one of the earliest settlers to the area, raised horses on his ranch, pictured here in the late 1800s. He was established at his ranch when Daniel B. Budd and partner Hugh McKay brought cattle here and started the town of Big Piney. Located on North Piney Creek, Fagan's ranch was five miles up the valley and to the west from Budd's ranch and the town of Big Piney.

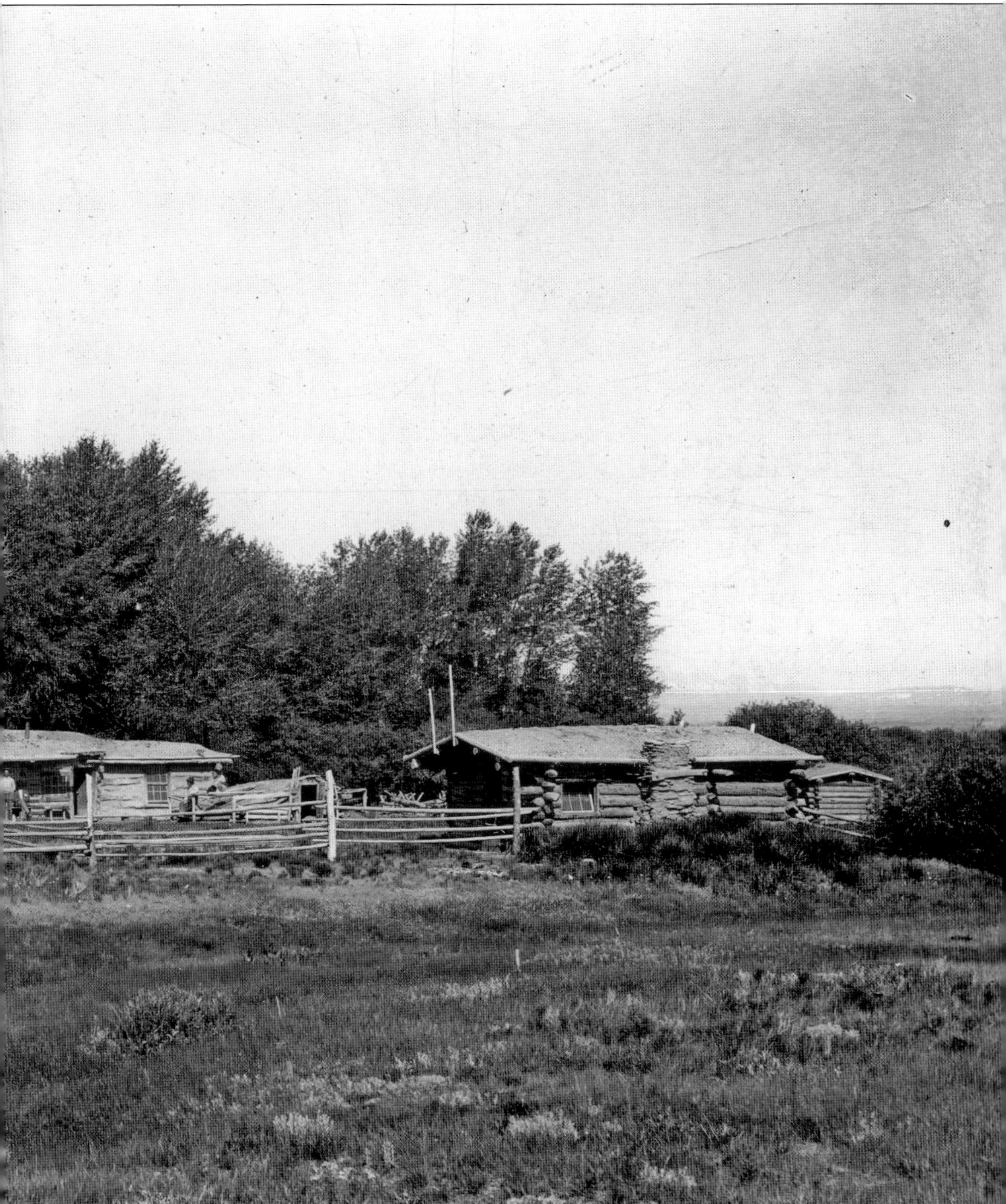

Fagan's ranch was later sold to Henry Budd. The buildings in the photograph are, from left to right, the barn, house, original cabin with the rock fireplace, and the outhouse. (Courtesy of Bill and Carrie Budd.)

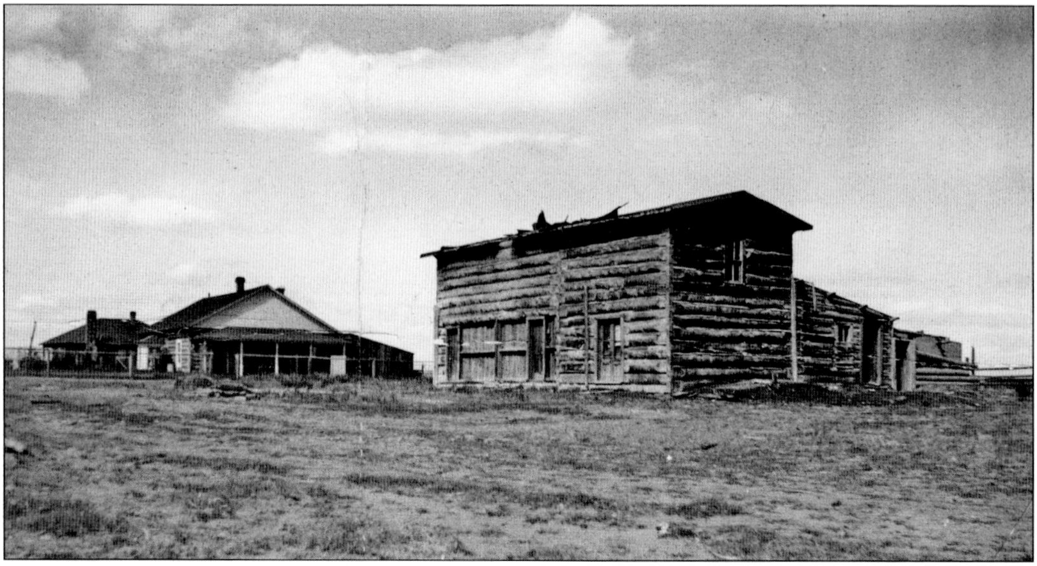

The two-story log structure pictured here was built by Daniel B. Budd in 1892 as a general store and post office. Over the store was Budd Hall, which served as a social center for Christmas parties, community get-togethers, and dances. Perhaps the most exciting incident related to the store was the holdup and robbery on August 19, 1896. Despite an all-out pursuit of the outlaws, the robbers were never caught. (Courtesy of Bill and Carrie Budd.)

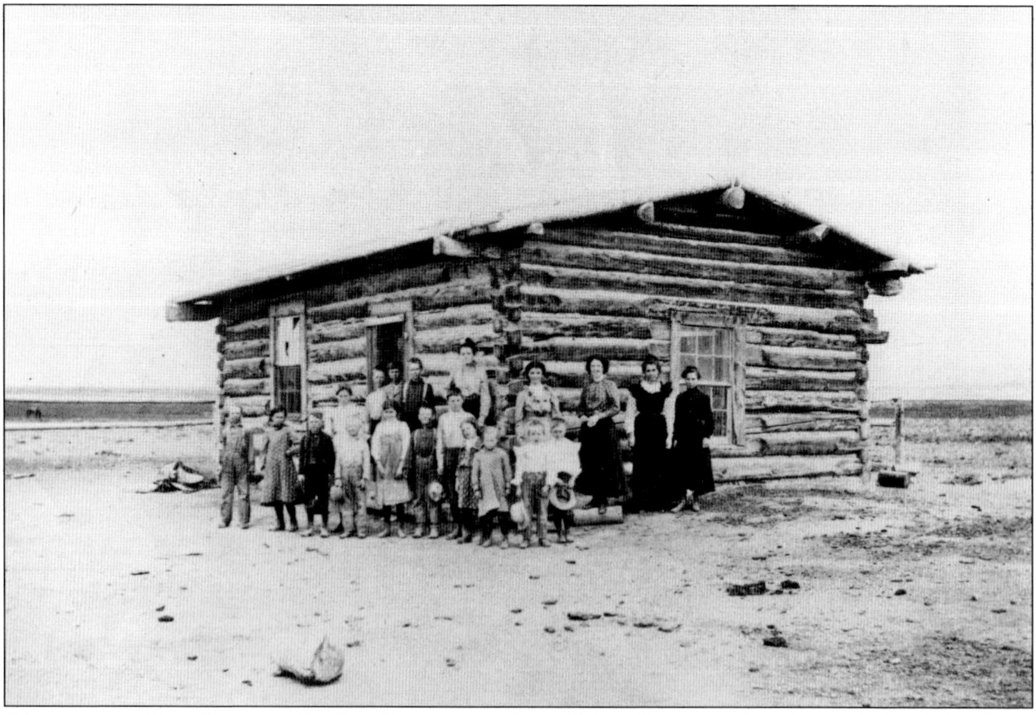

There were 20 students in the Big Piney school in 1904. Their teacher, Mary Solon Murdock, would have had her hands full with all the grades. The 14-foot-by-18-foot school was made of logs with a dirt roof. It had only one room, with windows on the west and east sides and a door and a window on the south. (Courtesy of Bill and Carrie Budd.)

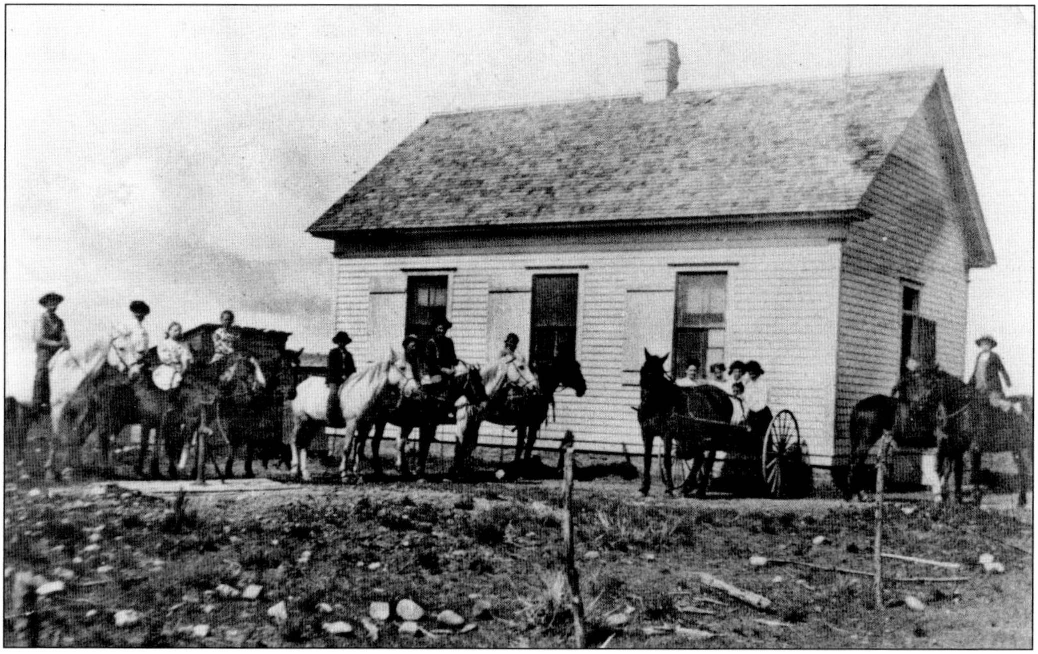

In 1902, the community built and furnished a modern framed building for the new Little White School at a cost of between $1,000 and $1,200. The land for the school site was a donation by the late Daniel B. Budd comprising two acres. Members of the community gathered in front of the building in 1907 with the teacher, Phoebe Pepper, for this photograph. (Courtesy of Bill and Carrie Budd.)

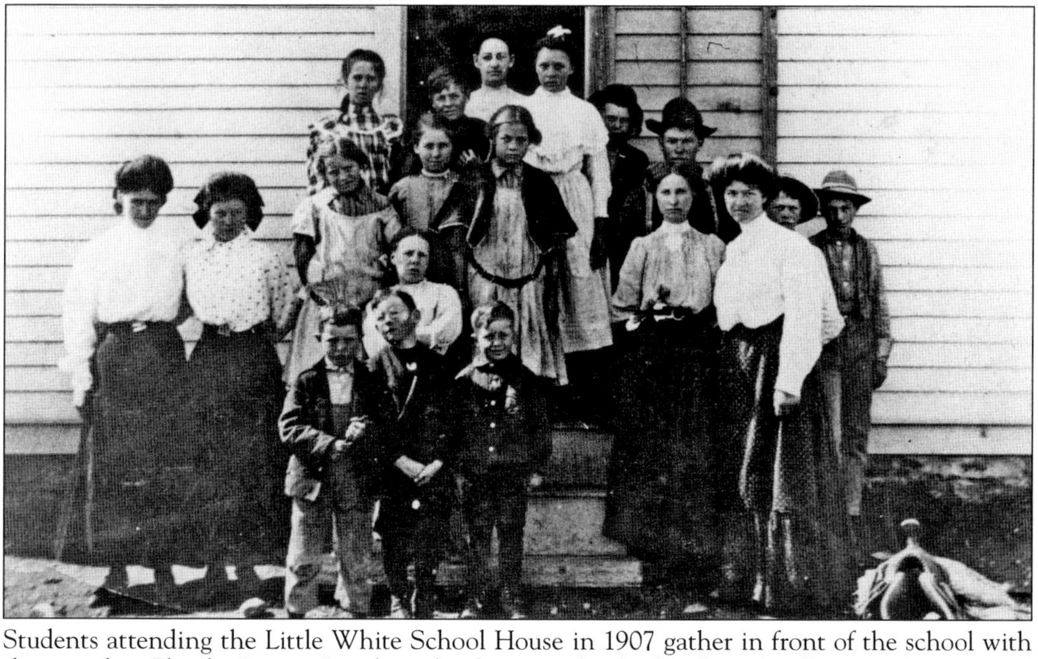

Students attending the Little White School House in 1907 gather in front of the school with their teacher, Phoebe Pepper. It only took a few years for the first log schoolhouse to be too small for the growing community, resulting in the building of this newer and bigger school. (Courtesy of Bill and Carrie Budd.)

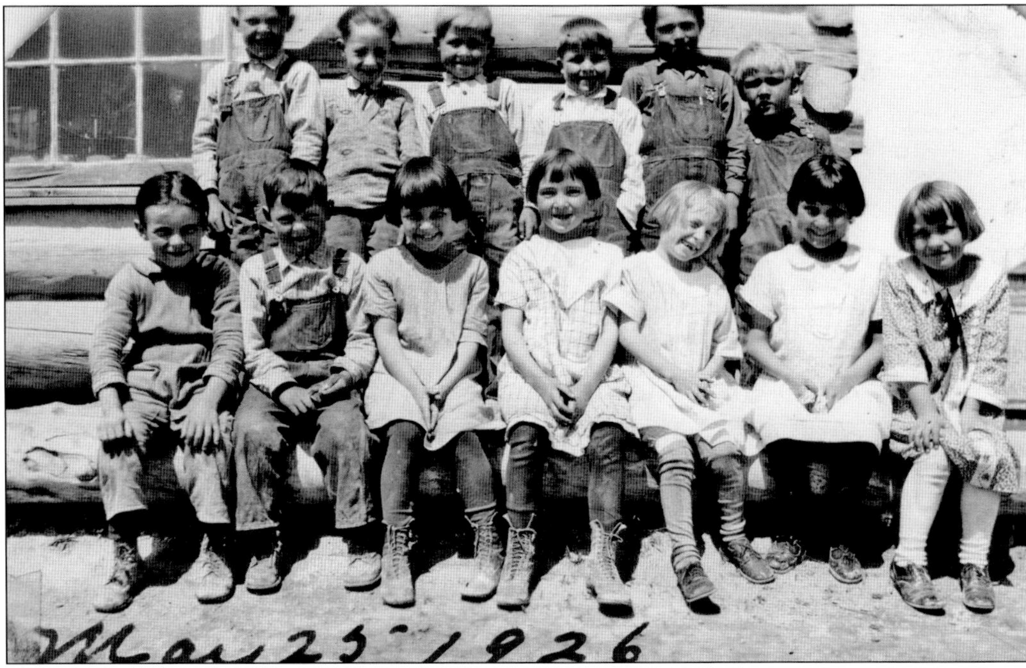

Young students appear happy in this grade school photograph taken May 25, 1926. Years later, Helen Budd Tanner wrote, "School was a privilege. I had the opportunity of attending a country 'summer school.' As I recall, we looked forward to each day. This may have been because, living on rather isolated ranches, we found extra enjoyment in the companionship of our friends. We were also very fortunate in having had very fine teachers." (Courtesy of Mardell Fear.)

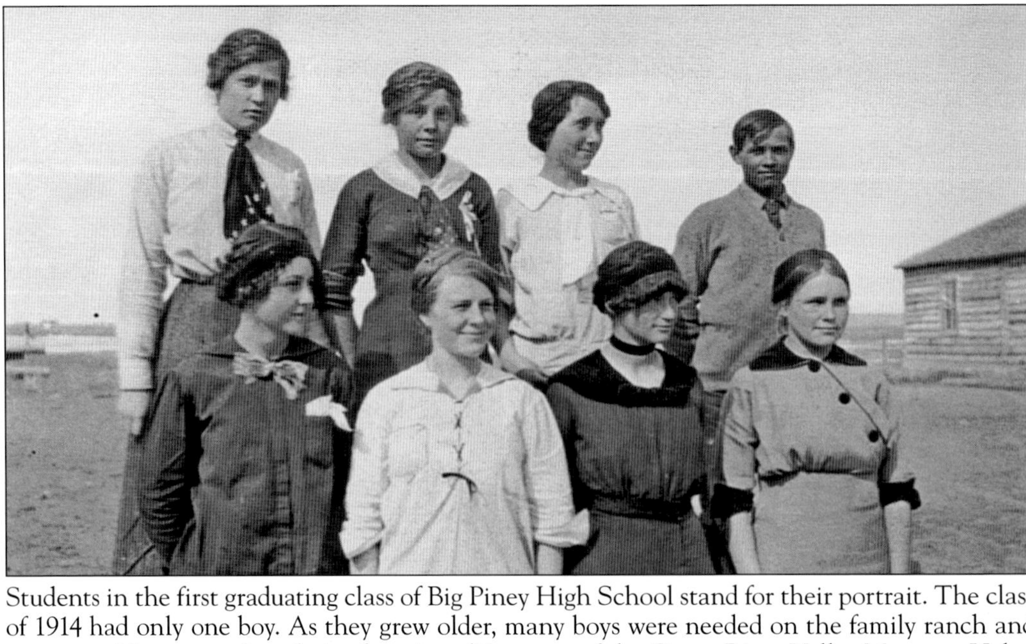

Students in the first graduating class of Big Piney High School stand for their portrait. The class of 1914 had only one boy. As they grew older, many boys were needed on the family ranch and were not able to complete their education. (Courtesy of the Green River Valley Museum, Helen Atwood Collection.)

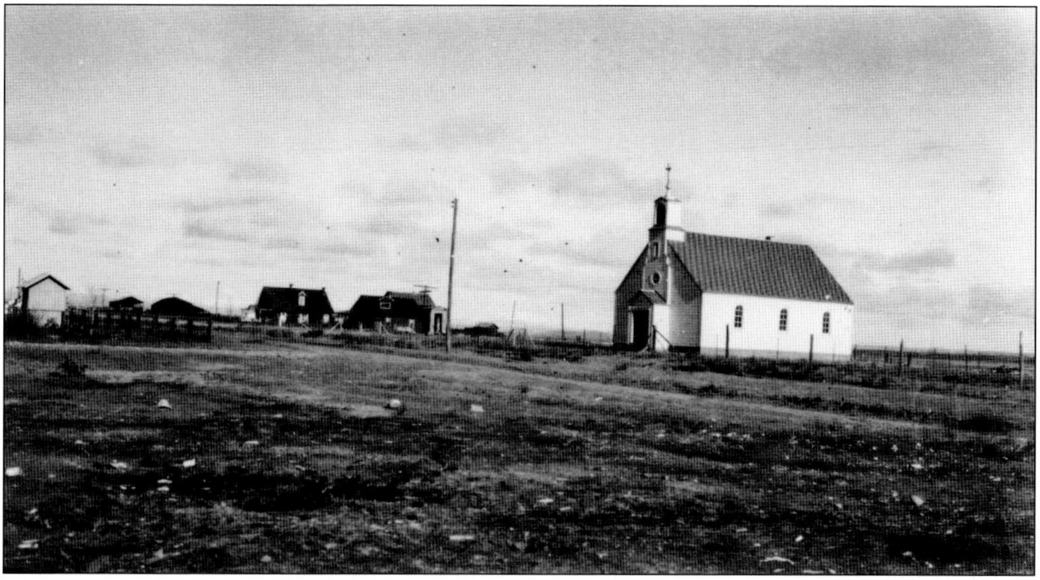

Mass was offered by visiting priests at Minnie Budd's home until 1934, when a Catholic church was built on Piney Drive in Big Piney. The church was built by the Catholic Extension Society, a group that constructed many churches throughout the West. Dedicated as St. Anne's Catholic Church, it has always been a mission church—first to a Kemmerer parish, then later to the parish in Pinedale. (Courtesy of Bill Cox.)

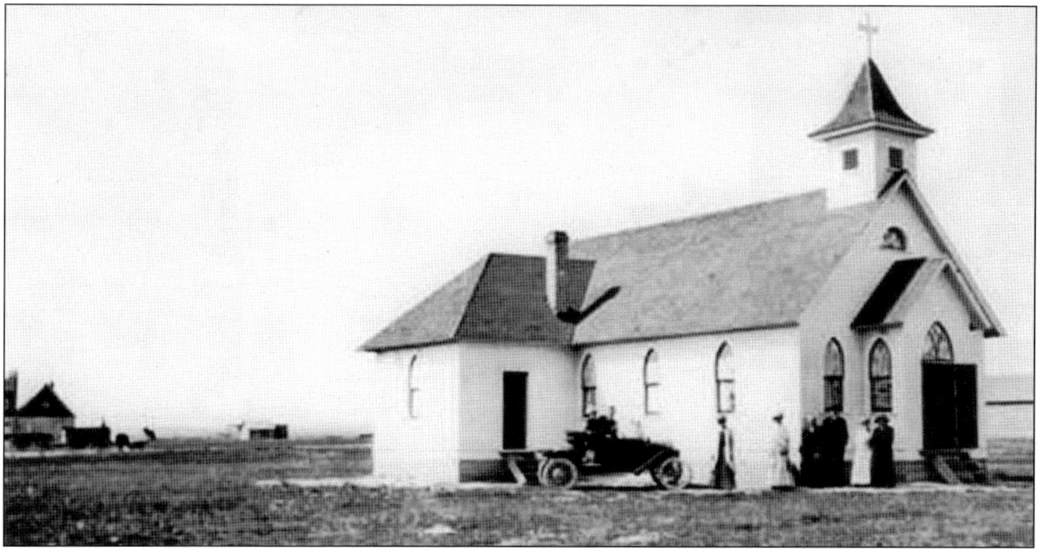

St. John the Baptist Episcopal Church, shown in its early years, was established about 1913. The First Congregational Church of Big Piney, in the background on the left, was organized in 1907 and incorporated in 1912. The Congregational church building was constructed of locally kilned bricks in 1914 and dedicated the following year. It was later called the Community Congregational Church. (Courtesy of Green River Valley Museum.)

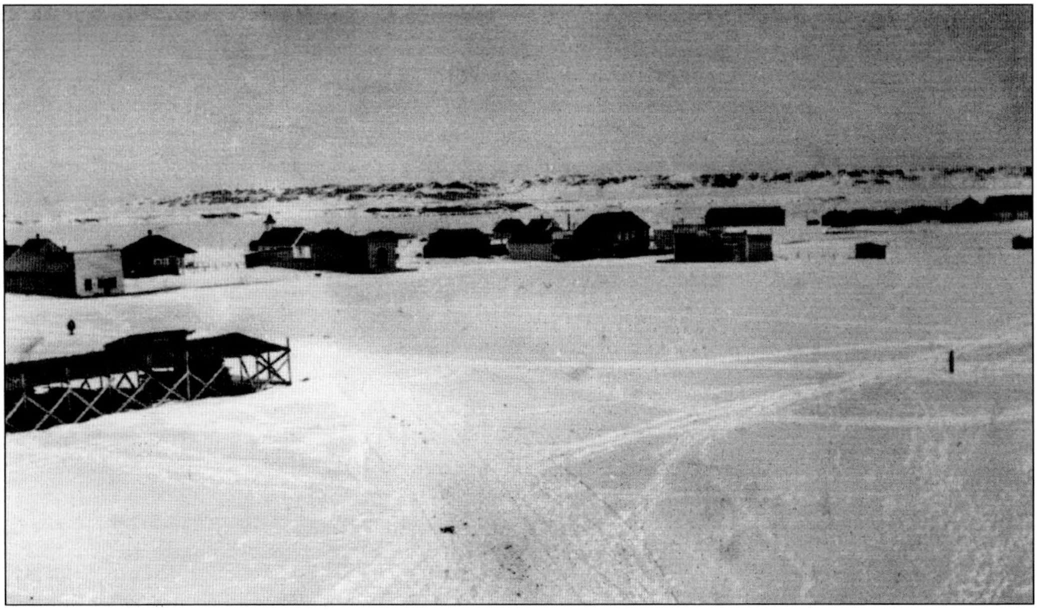

This early-1910s aerial view of Big Piney shows the shed on the left, with most of the town behind it. The buildings would be lined along Budd Avenue, the main street of the town from the beginning. Note the horse and sled runner tracks at the bottom of the photograph. (Courtesy of Mardell Fear.)

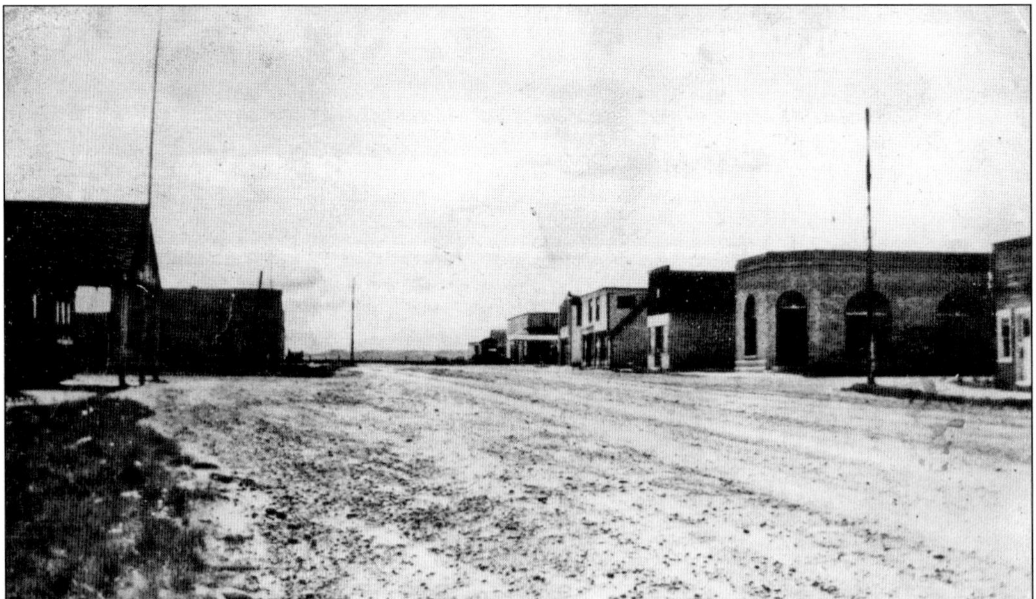

This view of Big Piney looks west down Budd Avenue in the early 1930s. At the left is the post office, and on the other side of the street are, from left to right, Burney and Company, the *Sublette Examiner* office, and Big Piney State Bank. The streets in the town had not yet been paved. (Courtesy of Bill and Carrie Budd.)

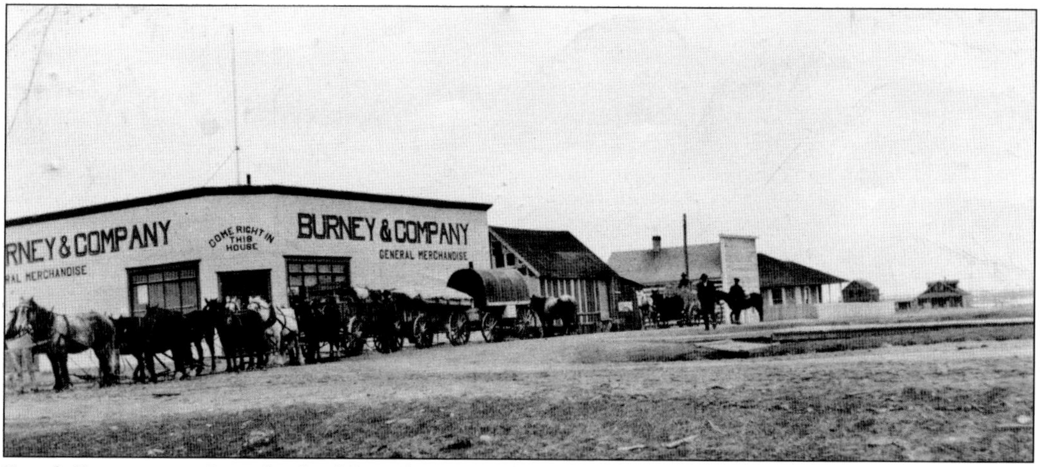

Frank Burney purchased a building from Frank Fear and ran a store there for one year before constructing his own larger structure in 1914. Located on the corner of Budd Avenue and Nichols Street, the Burney and Company General Merchandise building stood for 50 years and became one of the most stable and reliable businesses Big Piney had. Burney was remembered for greeting his customers by saying, "Come right in this house." (Courtesy of Bill Cox.)

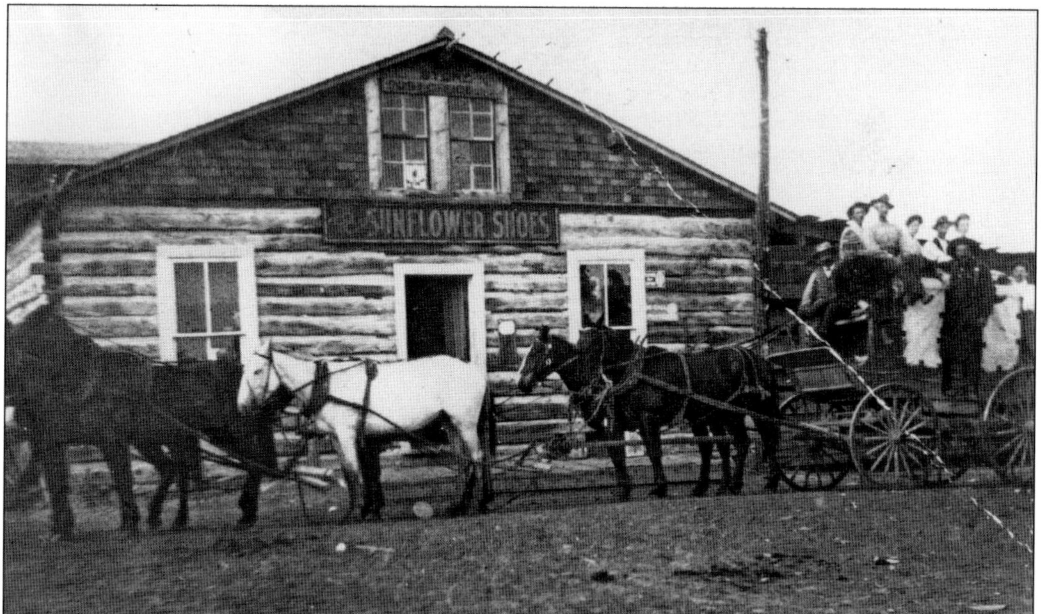

Butch Norris's stage is loaded with plenty of travelers, seated at the right. The stage is parked in front of the Budd Store, which was built when the original store was removed from Budd's ranch home. The Budd store also housed the post office starting in 1892. Note the advertisement for Sunflower Shoes on the building. (Courtesy of Sublette County Historical Society.)

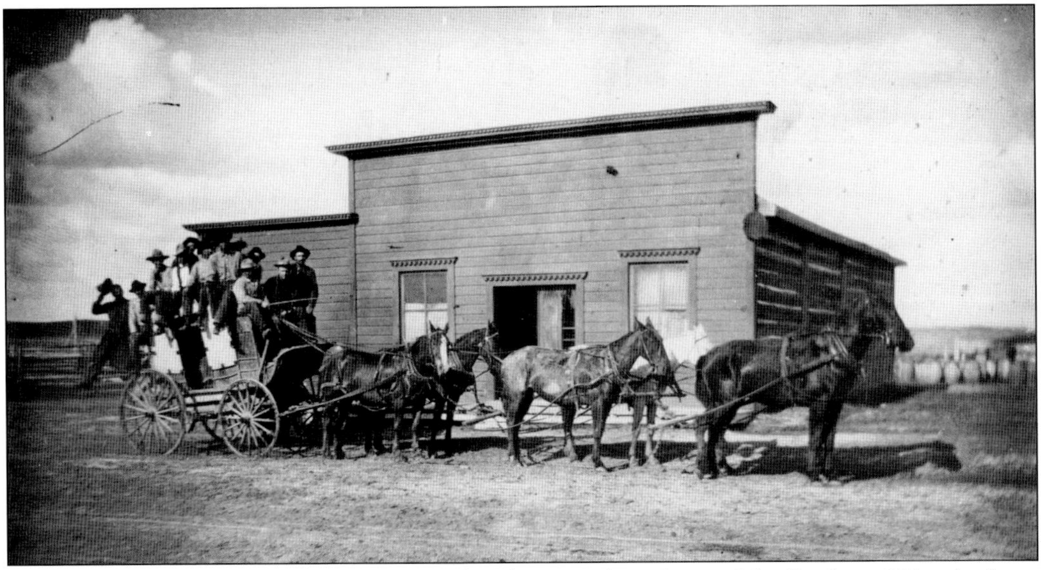

Travelers on Butch Norris's stage pose for the photograph in front of the Bucket of Blood saloon in the early 1900s. "Bucket of Blood" was a common name for saloons throughout the West at this time. In 1915, a young man became intoxicated and unruly in the bar and was shot by the proprietor, a Mr. Heitz, who was later acquitted in a jury trial on the grounds of self defense. (Courtesy of Sublette County Historical Society.)

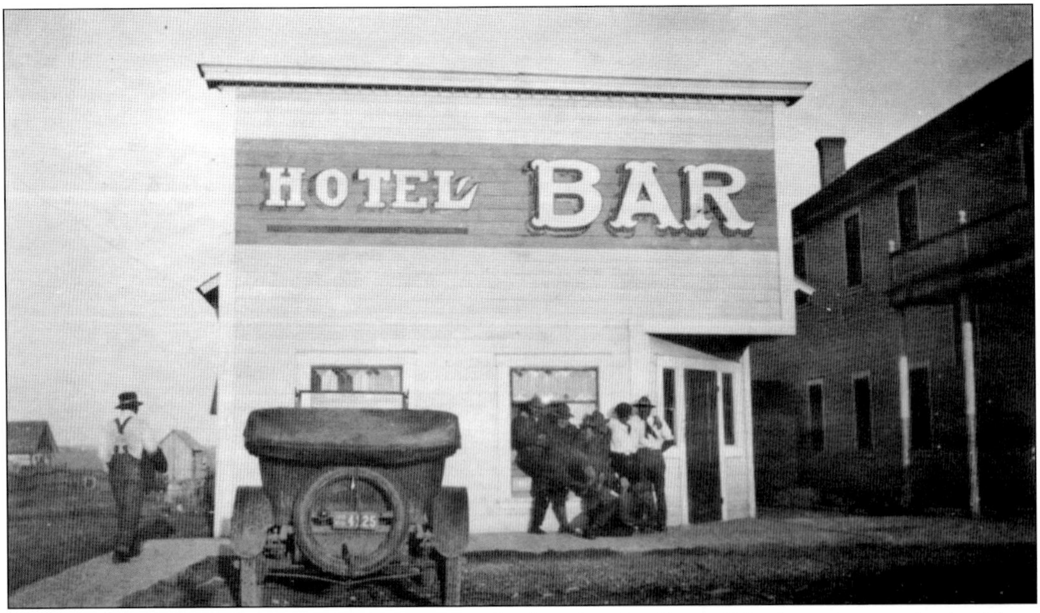

Friendly patrons stand outside the bar next to the hotel in Big Piney. The lettering on the building seems to be emphasizing the bar part of the business. Note the outhouse in the back at the left of the photograph. The vehicle in front of the business has a number four at the start of the license plate, indicating the owner is from Sweetwater County. (Courtesy of Helen Atwood.)

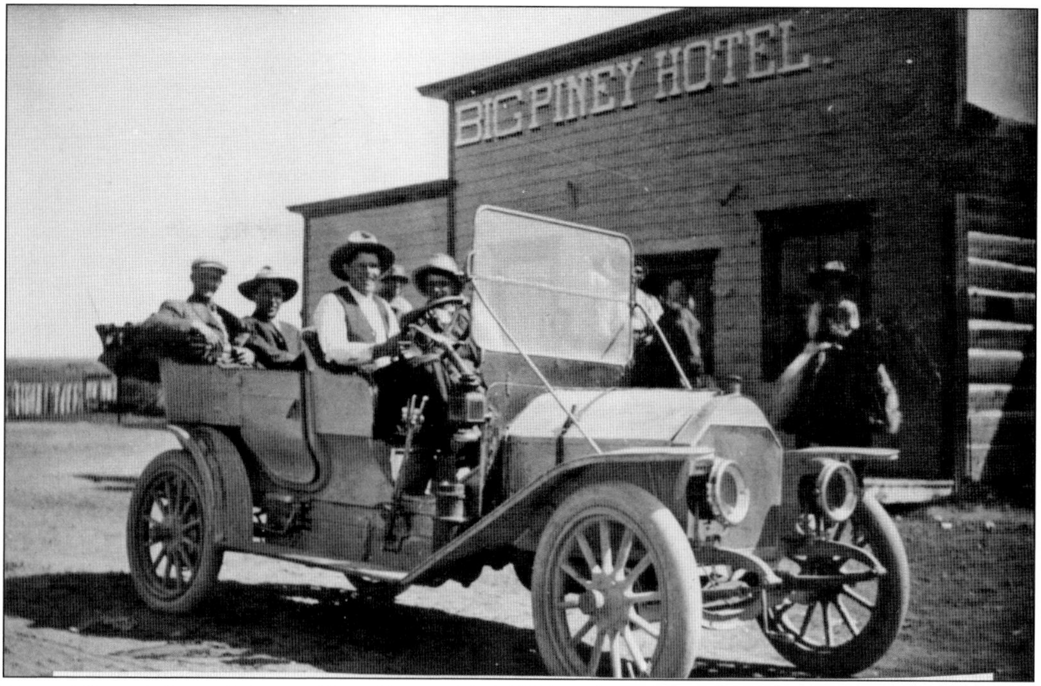

Seated from left to right are Ray Griggs, Ted Wilkes, Joe Gose, and Roy Bird; their vehicle is parked in front of the Big Piney Hotel in 1910. Next to the vehicle are men on horseback. It was common to see both vehicles and horses in the streets of Big Piney and Marbleton at this time. (Courtesy of Sublette County Historical Society.)

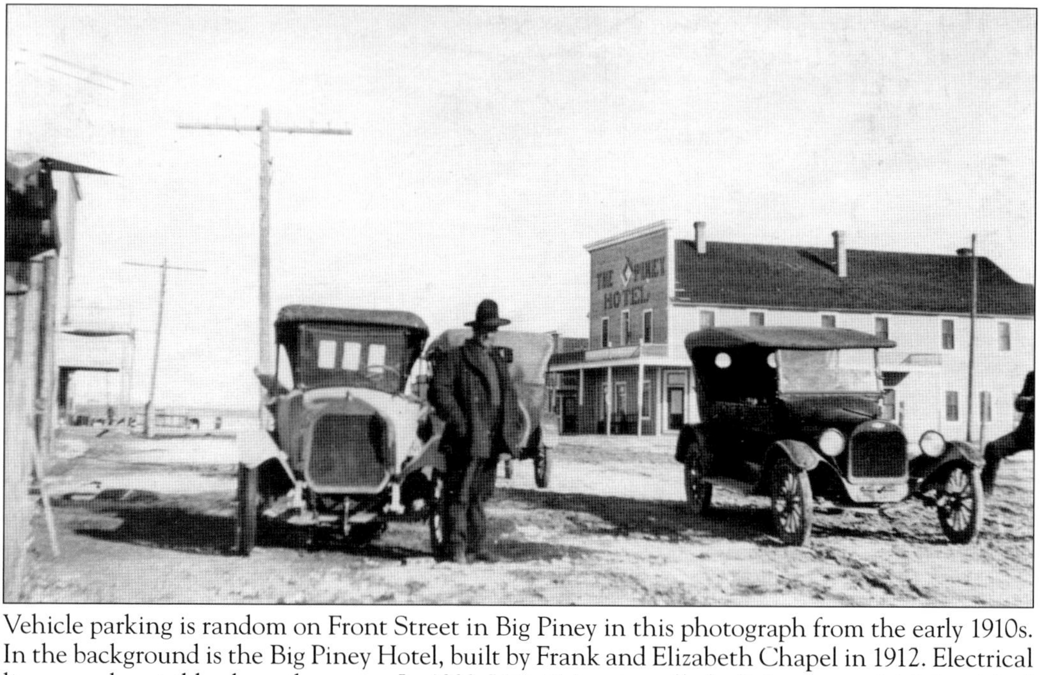

Vehicle parking is random on Front Street in Big Piney in this photograph from the early 1910s. In the background is the Big Piney Hotel, built by Frank and Elizabeth Chapel in 1912. Electrical lines are also visible along the street. In 1933, H.E. Griggs installed a light plant, which furnished light for the town. (Courtesy of Bill Cox.)

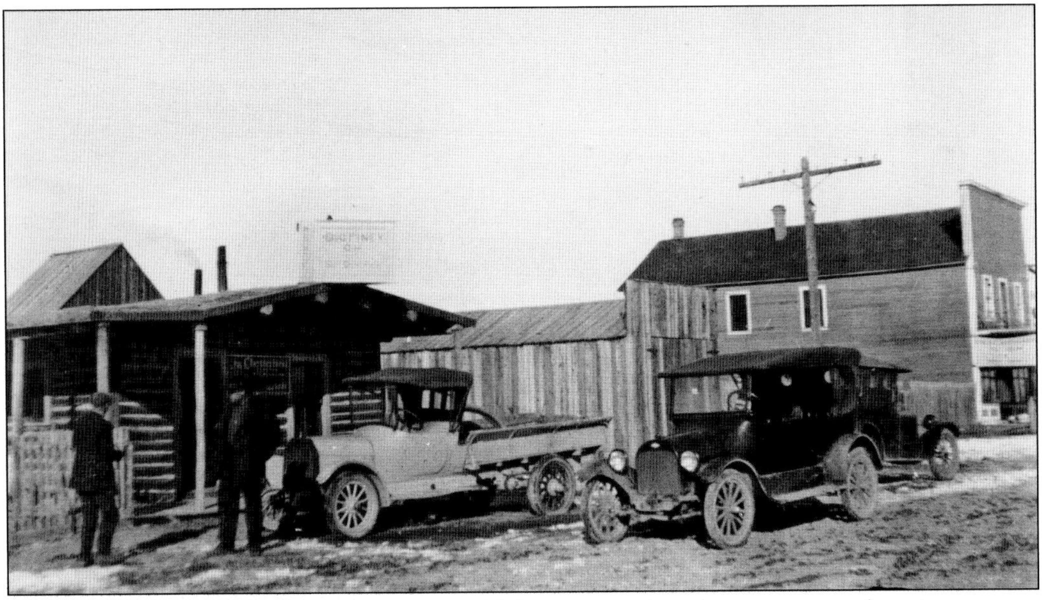

The introduction of vehicles to Big Piney and Marbleton induced the opening of service stations and repair shops. It would be years, however, before paved roads made vehicle travel easy in the area. (Courtesy of Bill Cox.)

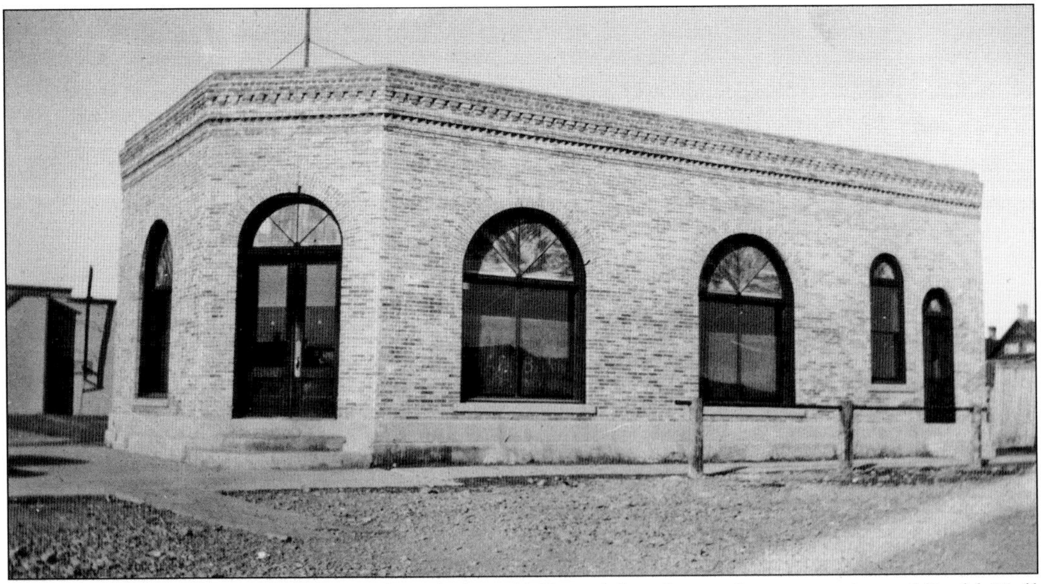

The State Bank of Big Piney was founded in 1912 and first housed in a portion of Budd Hall and had a cement vault. In 1914, several local residents joined the corporation and a new brick building was constructed from locally kilned bricks. Albert Larson was chief executive officer, serving the bank from 1915 until his death in 1947. The structure would later serve as the town hall. (Courtesy of Jonita Sommers.)

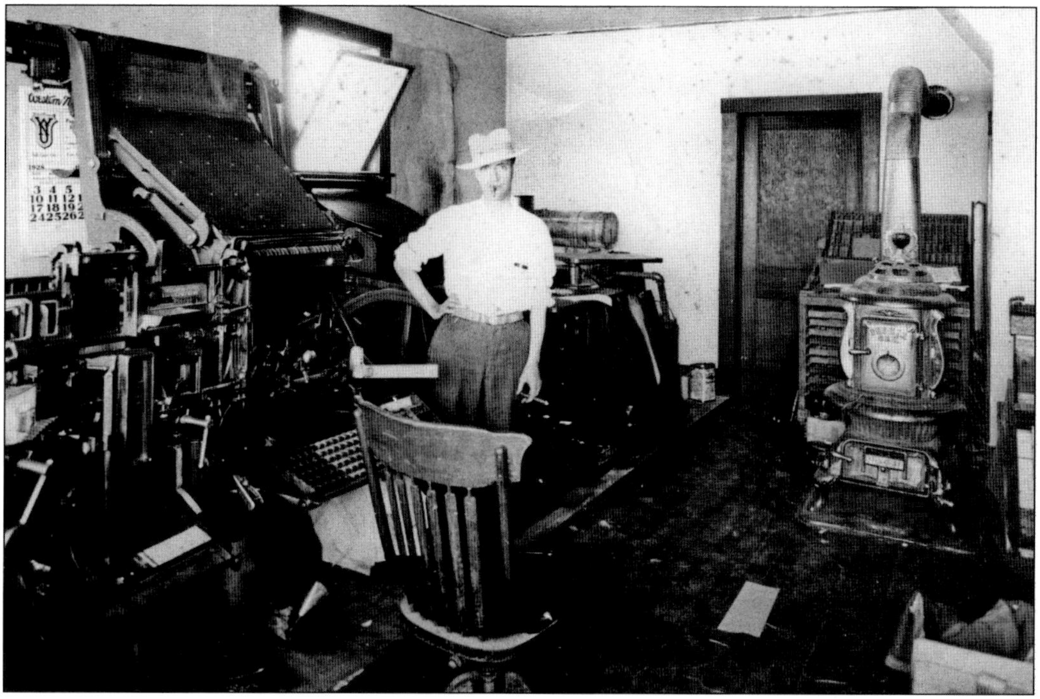

In 1918, George Washington Hopkins bought the Big Piney newspaper, which had been started in 1911 by the Big Piney Printing and Publishing Company. Hopkins published the newspaper for decades. The newspaper's flag read, "Big Piney Examiner, The Green River Valley Newspaper, Big Piney, Wyoming." Hopkins was an active community member, serving as a councilman, mayor, and health officer for Big Piney. (Courtesy of Green River Valley Museum.)

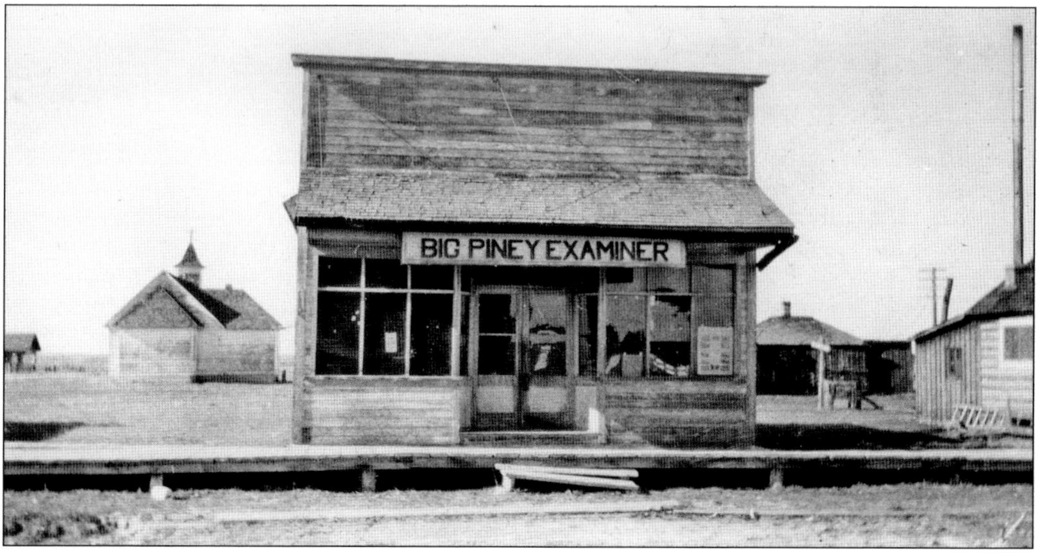

In 1926, George W. Hopkins built an office for his newspaper, *Big Piney Examiner*, on Budd Avenue next to the bank. The two-story structure housed the office and his home. The back of the building contained a dining room, living room, kitchen and bath, and three bedrooms were upstairs. The front part of the building was just one room, where the paper was published until the end of February 1968. (Courtesy of Jonita Sommers.)

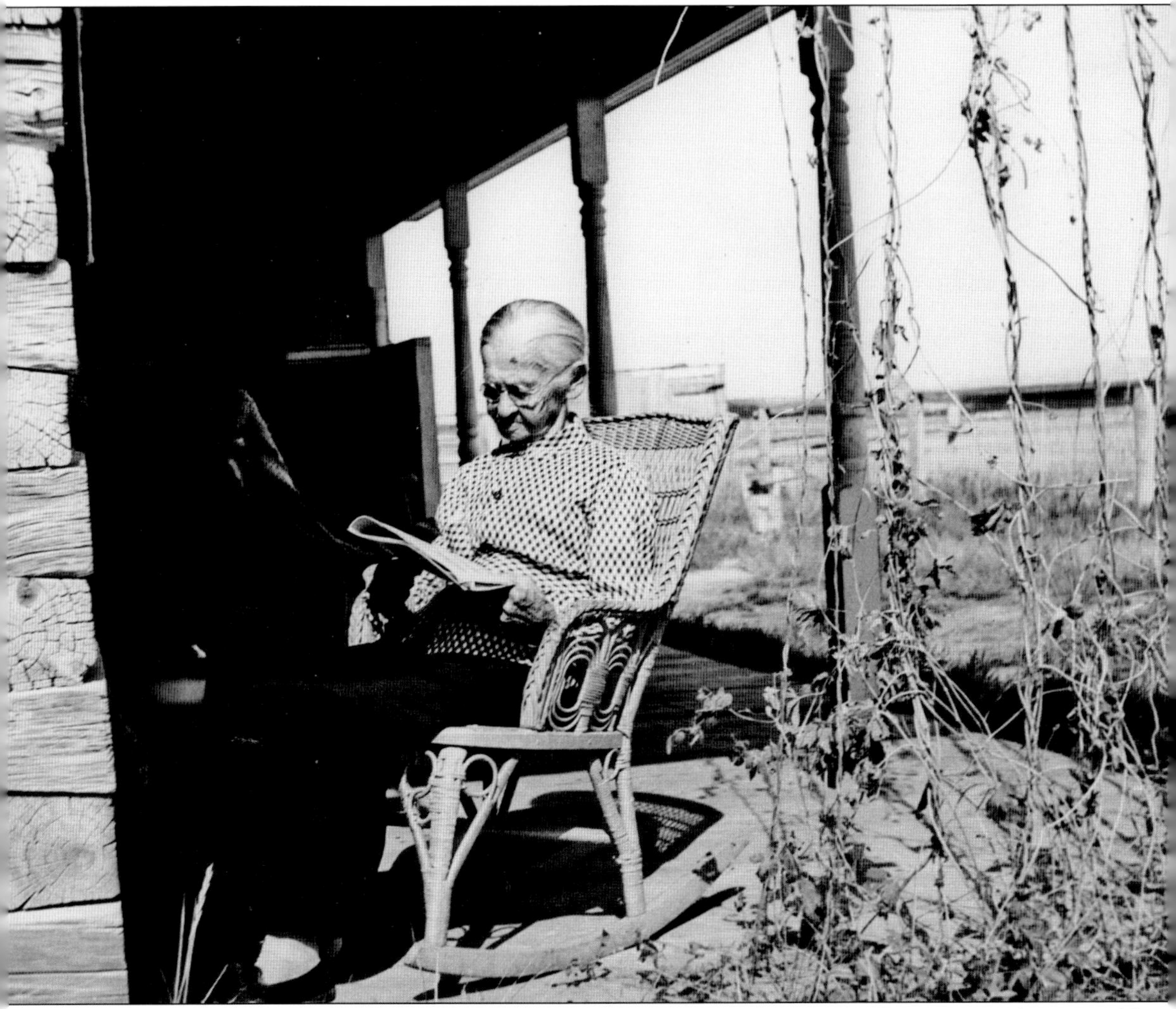

Big Piney pioneer Josephine A. Budd is seen here at her home in 1933 at age 91. Josephine would live to be 102 years old. Her granddaughter Dorothea Budd Newcomb wrote of Josephine, this "tiny hardy woman loved and spoiled us to the day she died." Note the hops growing on her porch. Hops were commonly used to acquire the yeast to make bread by early pioneer women. (Photograph by Pearl Budd Spencer; courtesy of Bill and Carrie Budd.)

Two

Growing Communities

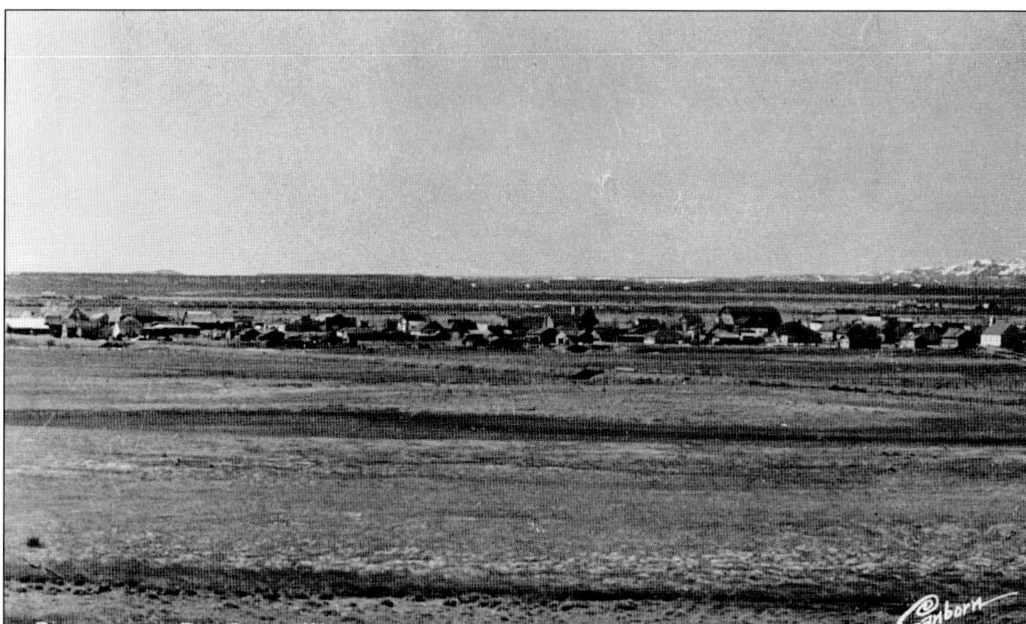

This Harold Sanborn photograph was taken in the late 1930s and captures the panorama of Big Piney on US Highway 189. The photographer is standing northeast of town, looking southwest. The Wyoming Range is visible on the horizon. Sanborn visited the West during the 1930s and photographed many small towns similar to Big Piney. (Courtesy of Green River Valley Museum.)

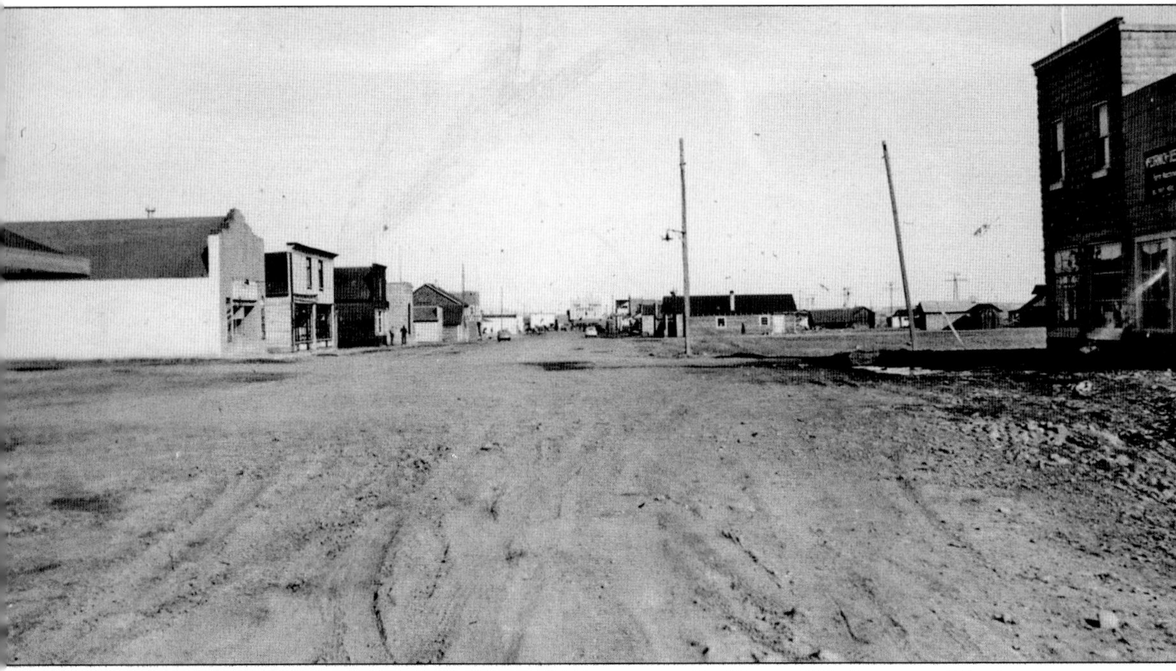

This photograph is looking east down Budd Avenue in Big Piney. While most of the businesses are located on this street, at the end and on the crossroad is the Piney Hotel. This picture, taken in the 1930s, shows dirt streets but a modern streetlight in the center. (Courtesy of Jonita Sommers.)

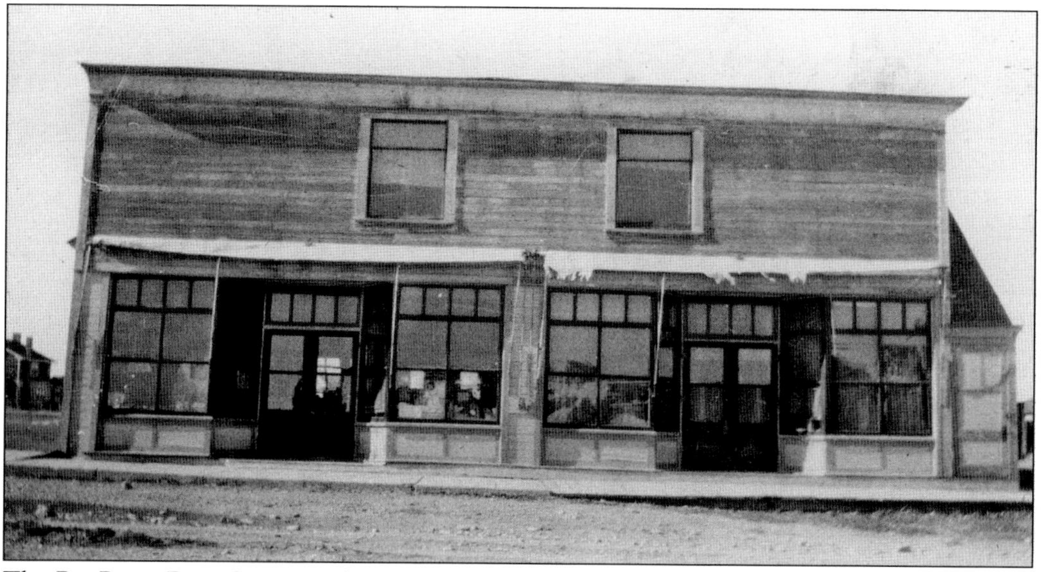

The Big Piney Drug Store was located in the left side of this building on Budd Avenue. It had a soda fountain, sundries, gifts, and a glass case with penny candy. It also had slot machines—a favorite for the young people on lunch break from school. The right side of the building housed various businesses, including a law office, an office for the Uinta County Irrigation Company, and a bar. (Courtesy of Jonita Sommers.)

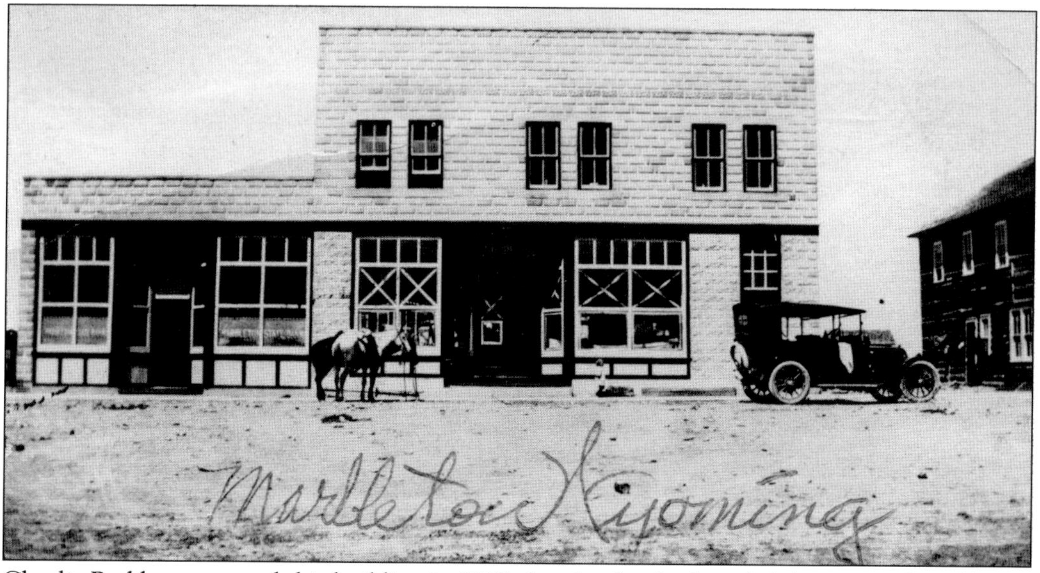

Charlie Budd constructed this building in 1915, shortly after he founded the town of Marbleton. The left side of the first floor housed the Bank of Marbleton, and the right side had a grocery store operated by Joe and Rose Ollivere. The second floor was a basketball gym, roller skating rink, boxing and wrestling ring, and dance hall. In the late 1940s, the building—minus the bank part—transitioned to a Masonic hall. (Courtesy of Mary Moffat Alexander.)

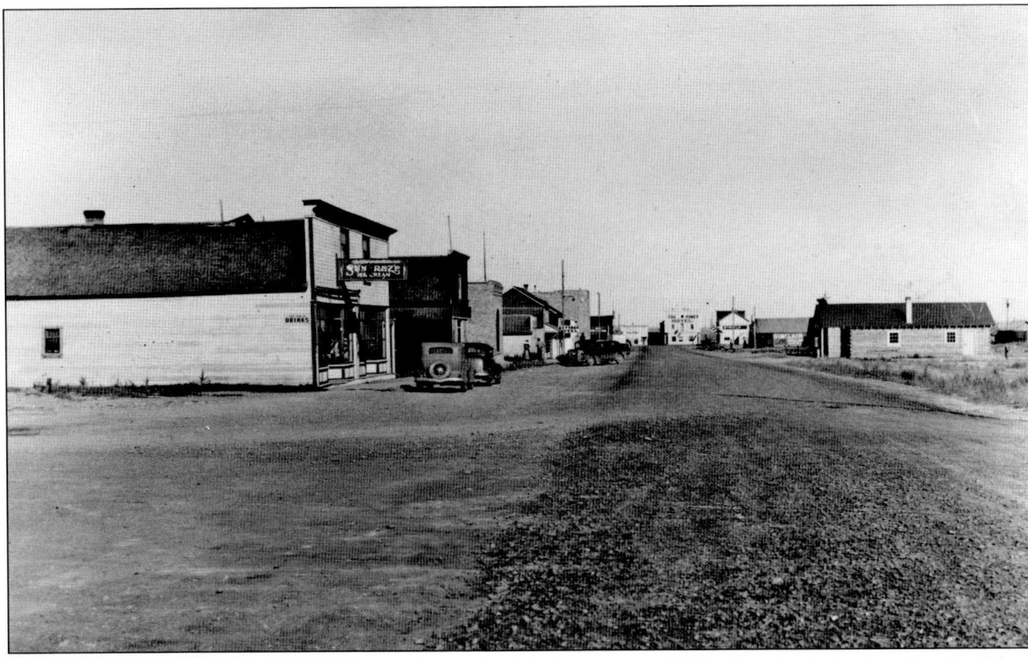

This view of Big Piney is looking east down Budd Avenue in 1938. On the left, the first building is the drugstore, and on the right is the post office. The road has been graveled, making vehicle travel easier, especially during rainy mud season. It appears that there are not yet rules for parking vehicles by the way the two cars on the left have parked. (Courtesy of Bill and Carrie Budd.)

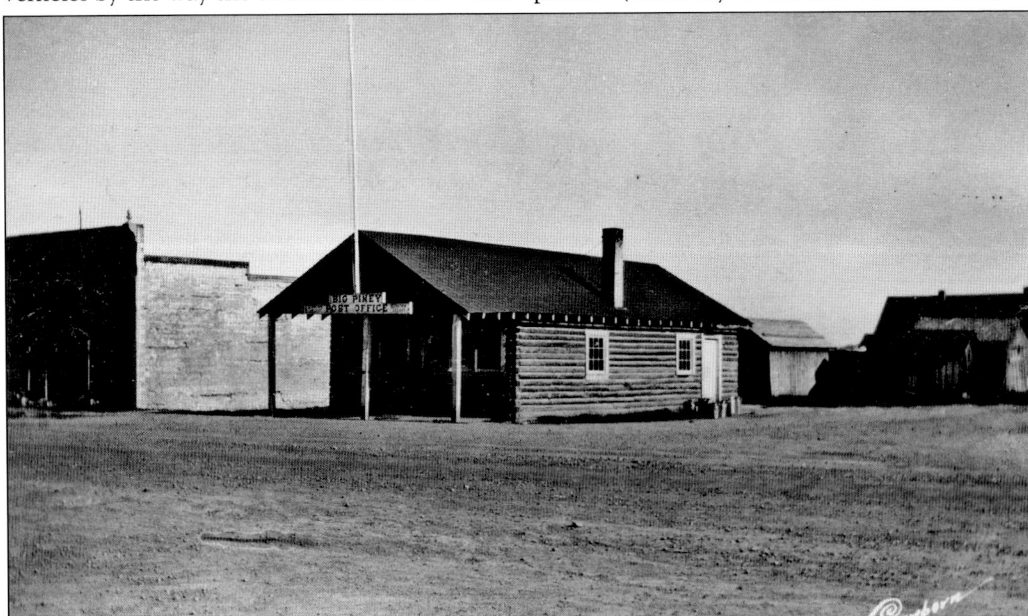

The original Big Piney post offices were located in the two Budd stores. The post office was removed from the stores when the government constructed this building on Budd Avenue. The Budds tried to have the name of the local post office changed to Big Pine, but the request was rejected because of Big Tree, Montana, and Lone Tree, Wyoming, being in the same general area of the West. (Photograph by Harold Sanborn; courtesy of Clint Gilchrist.)

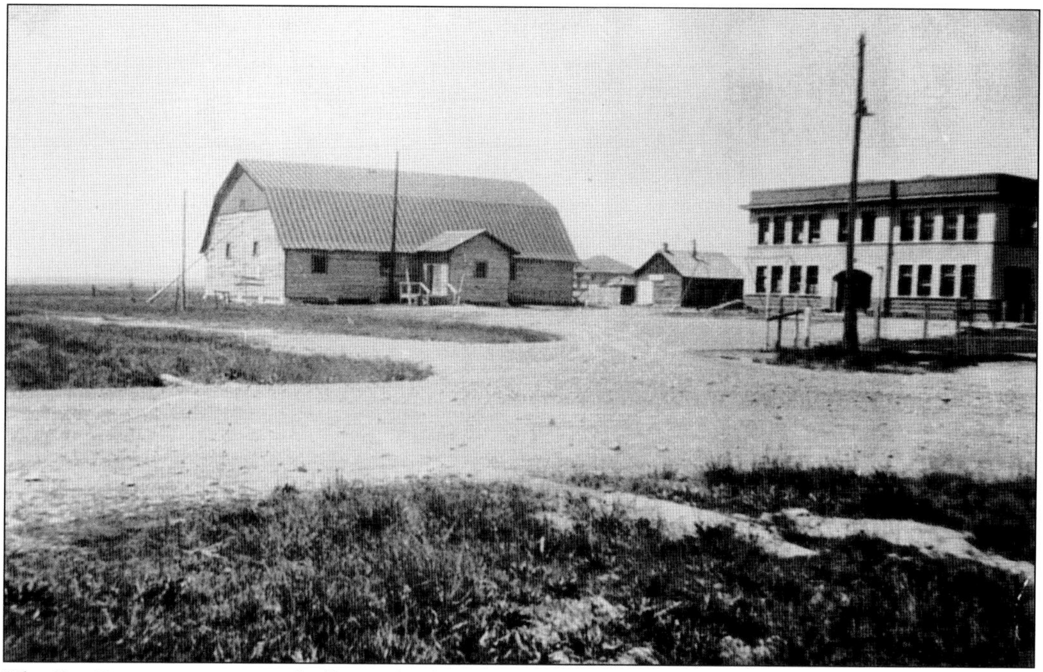

The Big Piney community hall, on the left, was built during the 1930s with financial assistance from the Works Progress Administration under the New Deal and erected by volunteer labor. The logs were brought down from Middle Piney by team and sled and transferred to trucks for the rest of the trip. After considerable discussion, it was decided that the ideal location would be close to the school, at the right. (Courtesy of Green River Valley Museum.)

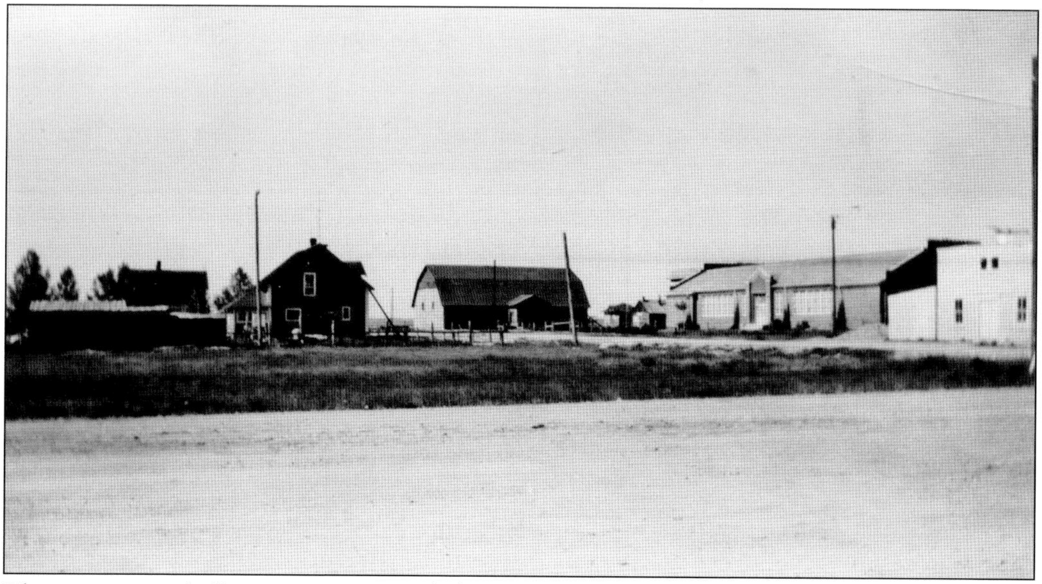

The community hall was soon surrounded with other buildings, as seen here, and continued to be the center of community gatherings. The big building, with rough logs inside and out, was complete with stage and dressing rooms, adequately lit by a string of lights, and heated by two oversized potbellied stoves. Many dances were held at the hall, as well as political rallies, school and community plays, and amateur hours. (Courtesy of Helen Atwood.)

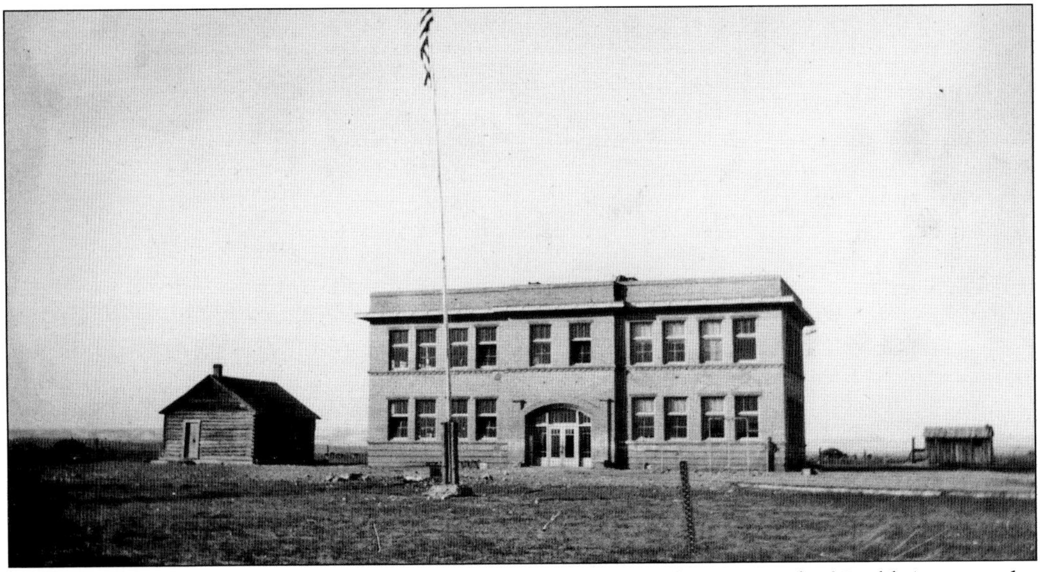

The cinder-block school opened in the fall of 1914. Built on the west end of Budd Avenue, the cost of construction was $11,000. The first high school graduating class from this school consisted of three young ladies, Cornelia O'Neil, Ursula Tanner, and Ellen Swanstrom. (Courtesy of Jonita Sommers.)

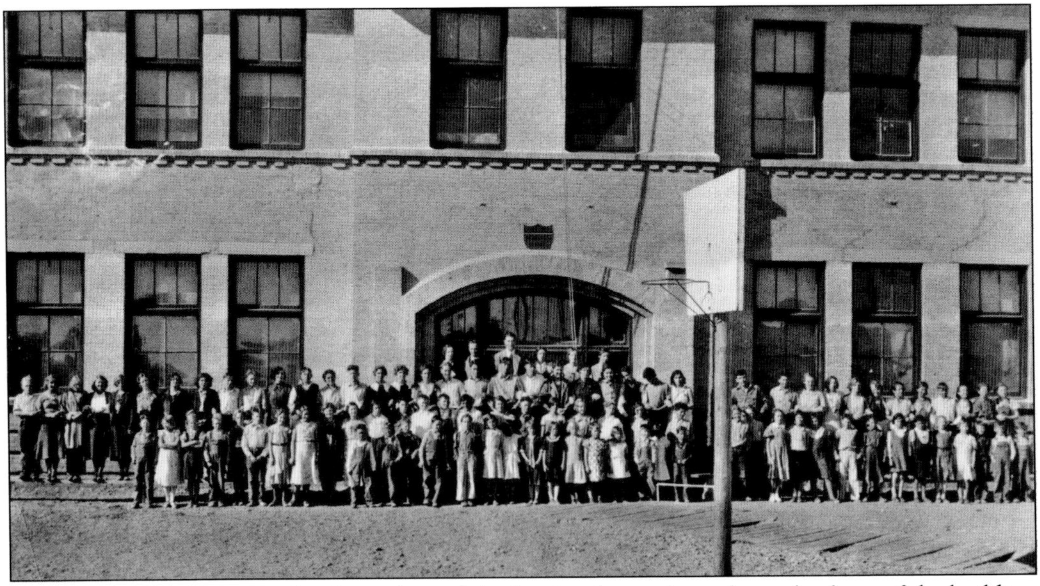

All the schoolchildren, grades three through high school, were brought to the front of the building for this picture in 1933. The junior and senior high school students were on the second floor, while the elementary grades were on the first floor. There was a small log building next to the big school, called the annex, which was used for the first and second grades when more room was needed. (Courtesy of Mardell Fear and Ava Davis.)

The Gaiety Theatre was built by Frank A. Fear in 1938 or 1939. It was immediately popular, with its luxury plush-covered seats instead of the common folding chairs, a carpet, and a sloping floor. It also featured a popcorn machine. The theater offered welcome entertainment in the isolated community, especially during the long winters. (Courtesy of Helen Atwood.)

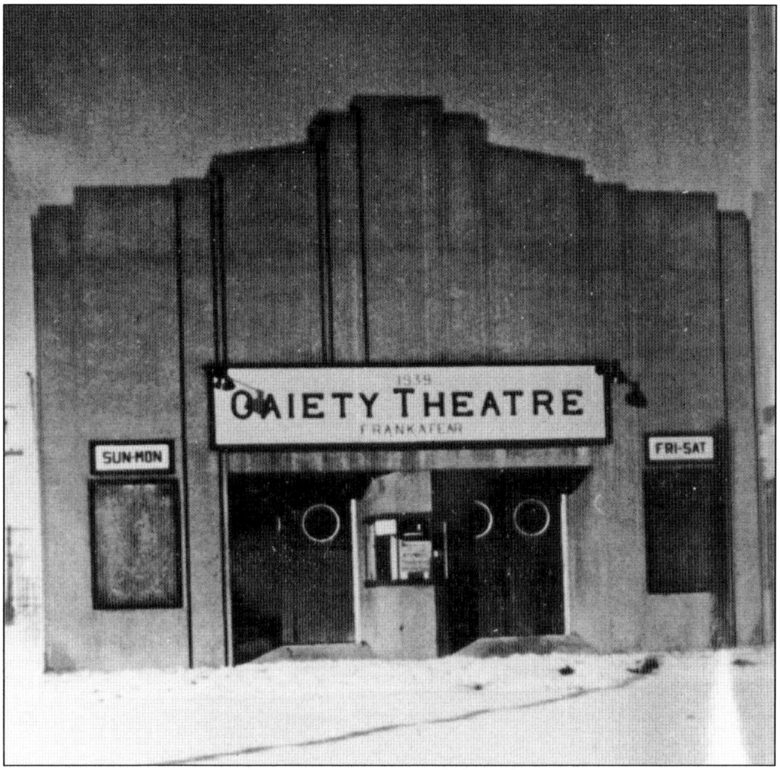

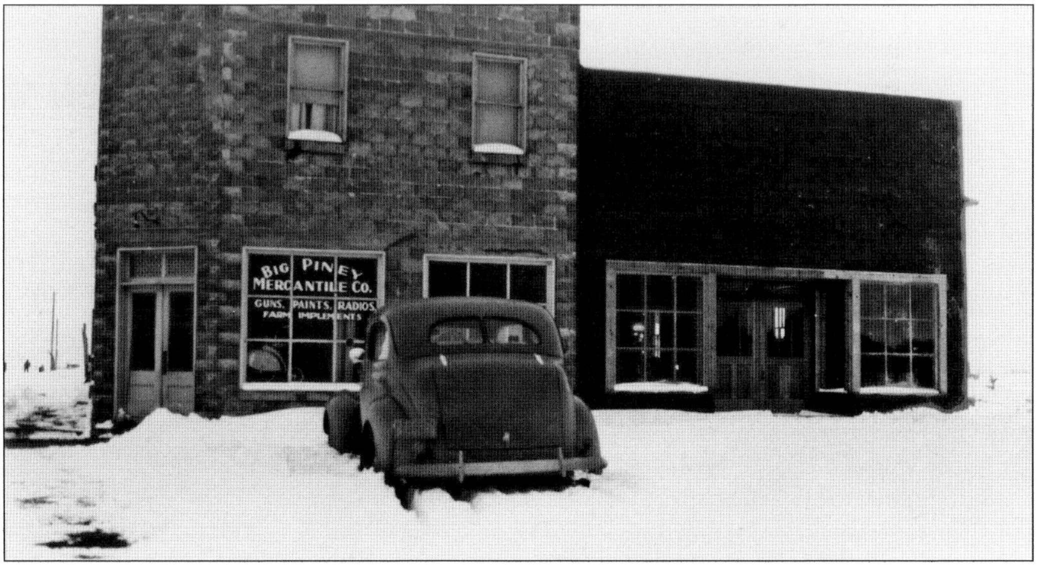

Typical of all towns, many businesses came and went in Big Piney. For a time, this brick building on Budd Avenue was the Big Piney Mercantile Company, which advertised guns, paints, radios, and farm implements in its windows. The shopper in this photograph forded a significant amount of snow to get to the store. (Courtesy of Bill Cox.)

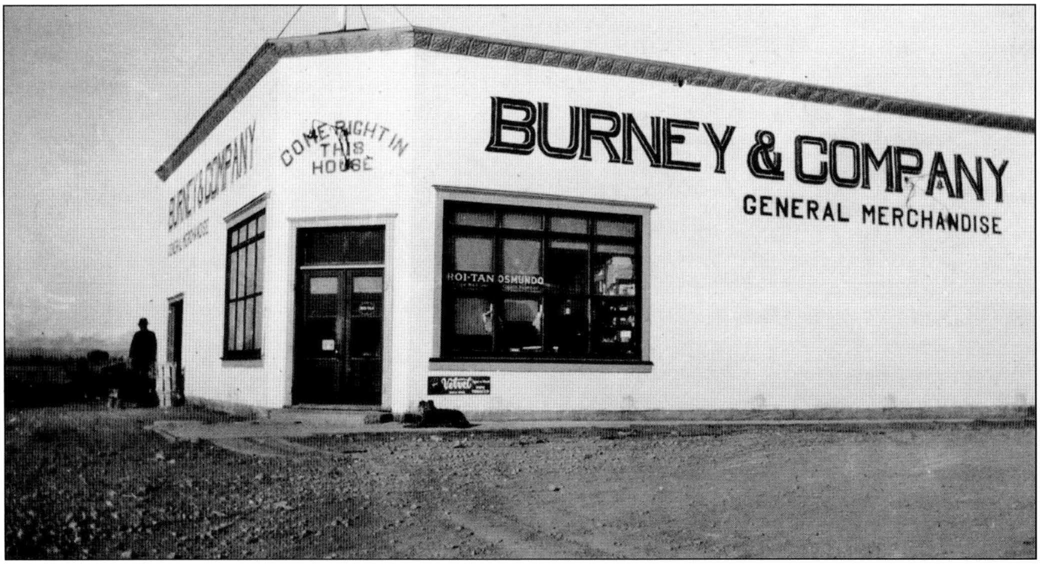

Burney and Company General Merchandise has always been located on the corner of Budd Avenue and Nichols Street. Frank Burney was remembered for greeting his customers by saying, "Come right in this house," which was also painted onto his building. Above is Burney's first building, with a second replacement store pictured below in a Harold Sanborn photograph. Sanborn was a well-known photographer in the West during the 1920s and 1930s. Burney and Company would be the main grocery store in the two towns for decades, while remaining in the family for four generations. (Above, courtesy of Jonita Sommers; below, courtesy of Nancy Budd Espenscheid.)

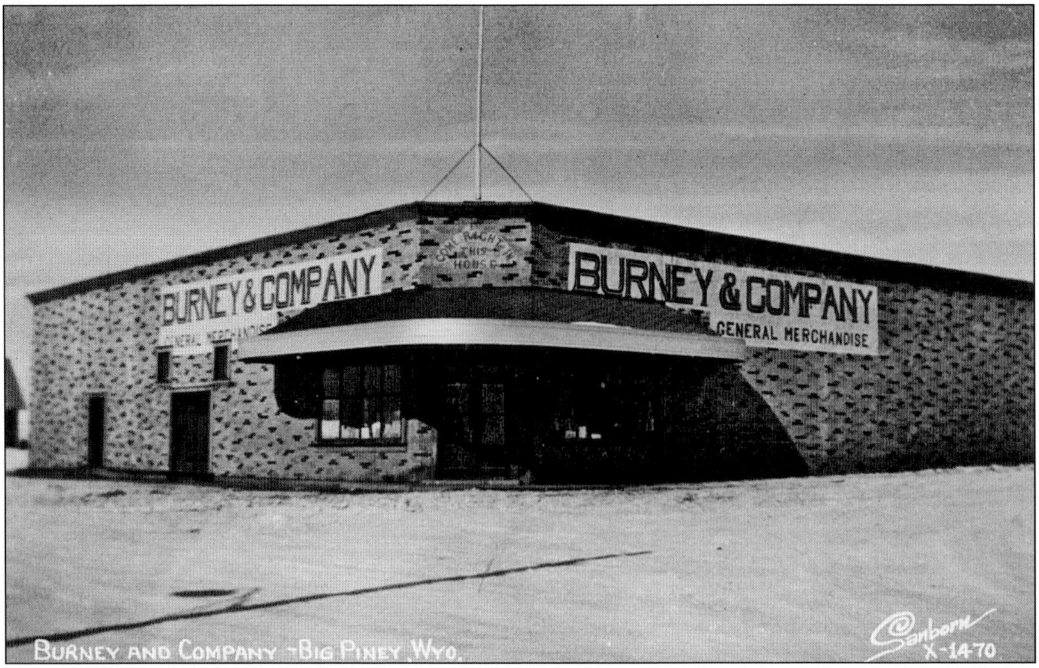

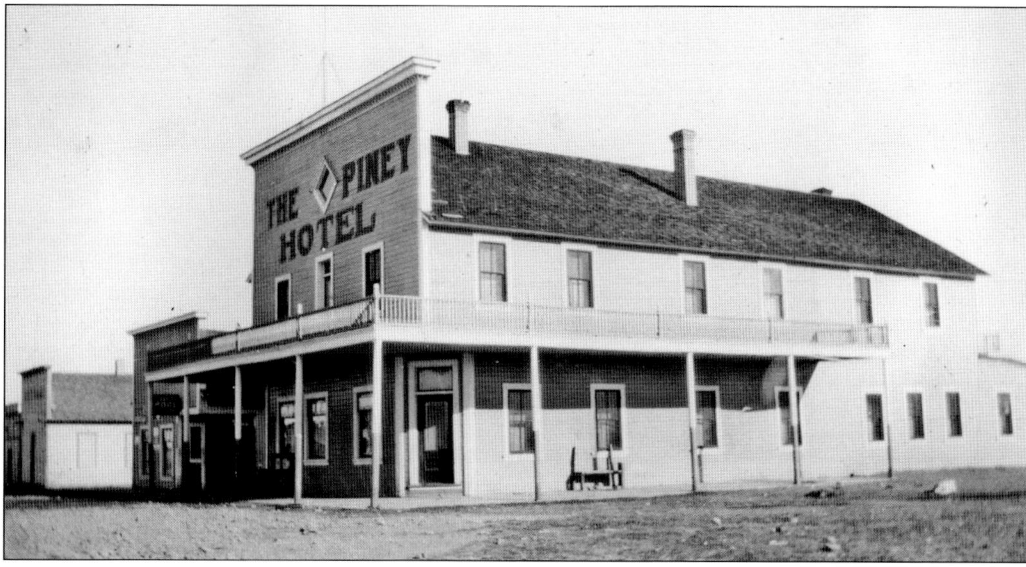

The Big Piney Hotel was sometimes called "The Piney" and had a bar next door. Built by Frank and Elizabeth Chapel in 1912, the two-story structure had a dining room and barbershop. The hotel was lost to a fire in 1948 that also destroyed the town hall, jail, two bars, and three homes. (Courtesy of Jonita Sommers.)

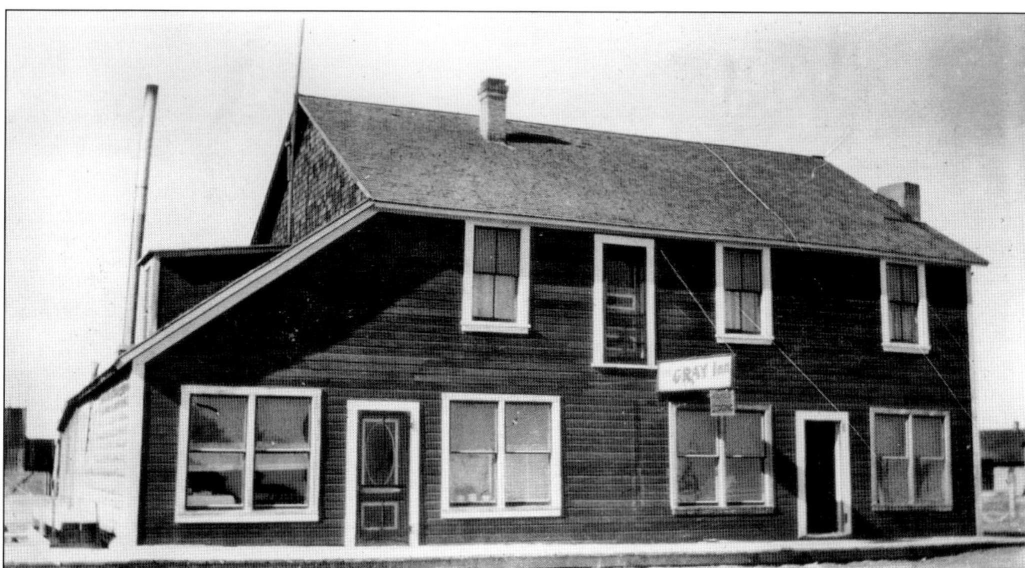

The Gray Inn or Hotel was operated by Lena Gray starting in 1917. When she sold it to Mrs. Henry McDonald in the early 1920s, the name was changed to the Cottage Hotel. The hotel also offered a café and bakery, patronized by the hotel guests and local residents. (Courtesy of Jonita Sommers.)

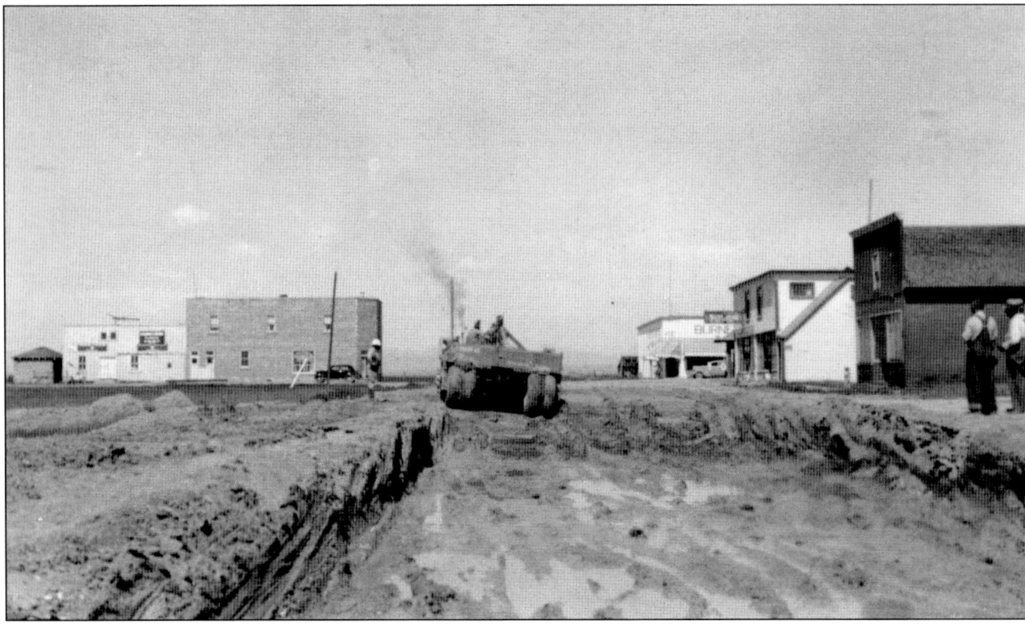

Big Piney was constructed in a bog hole, making the streets difficult to travel on, especially in the springtime and after summer rainstorms. The town finally installed drainpipes and reconstructed Budd Avenue in 1945, when construction supplies became available after the end of World War II. Seen here is the equipment used in the street reconstruction. The photograph above has a view looking east down Budd Avenue at the construction work. In the photograph below, construction is taking place in front of the town's businesses right, "Doc Morgan's" Drug Store (left) and the *Big Piney Examiner* printing office. (Courtesy of Bill Cox.)

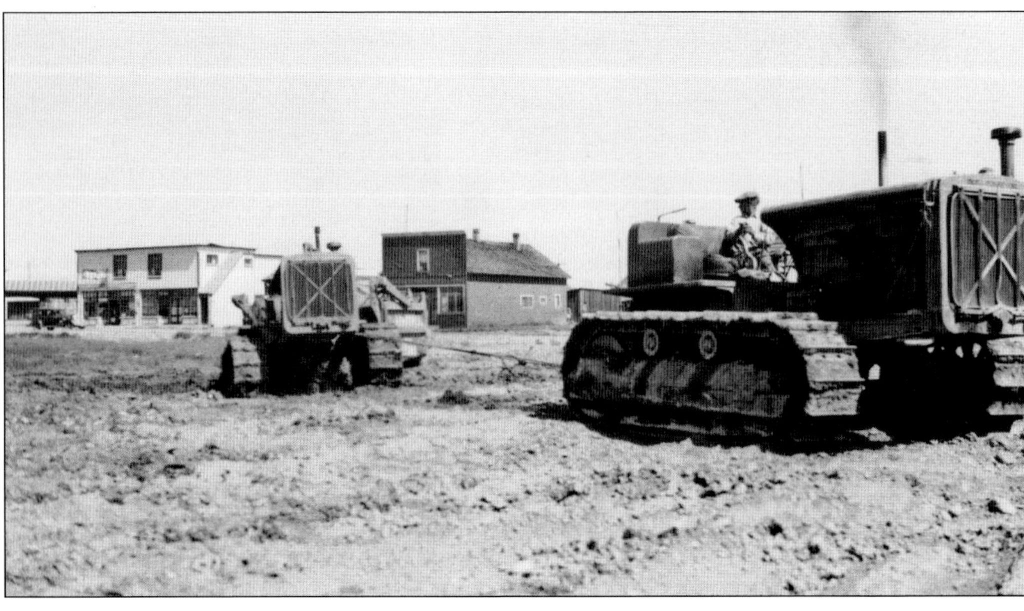

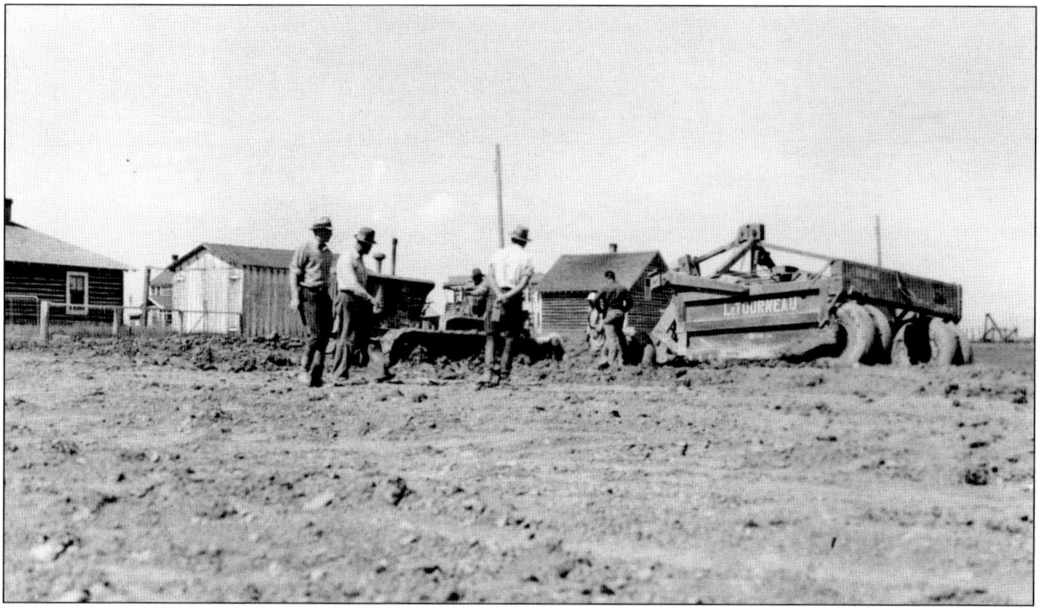

The Big Piney street reconstruction work on Budd Avenue is taking place in front of private residents. The streets were impossible to travel on several months of the year due to the boggy ground the town was built upon. Following this construction and drainage pipe installation, travel was much improved. (Courtesy of Bill Cox.)

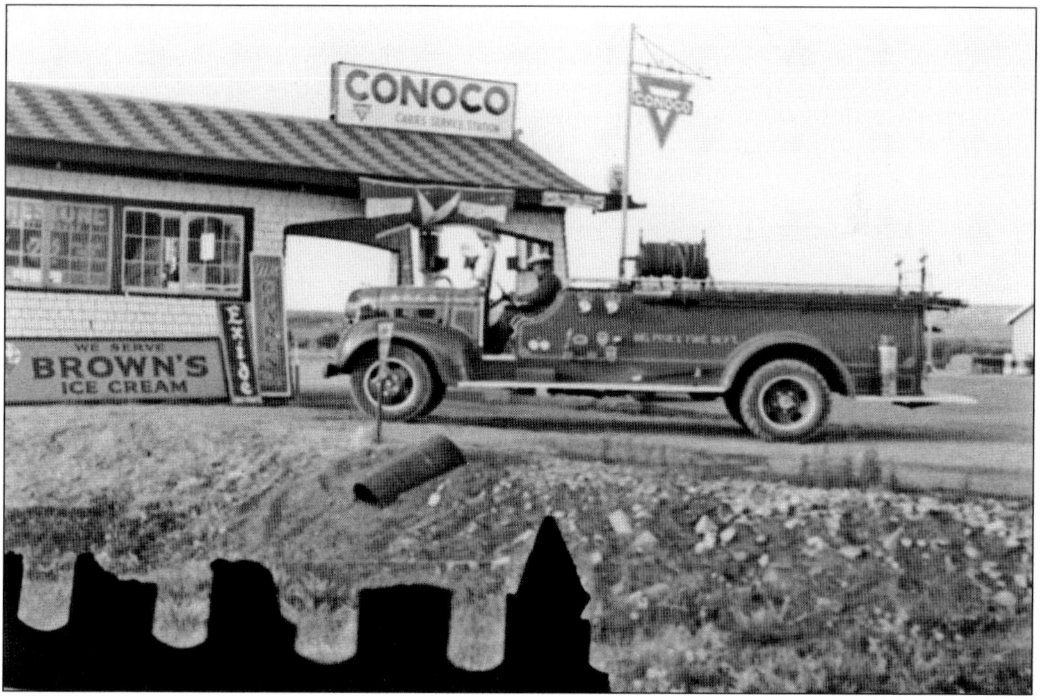

The Big Piney Fire Department truck sits in front of the Conoco Station on the south end of Big Piney in the late 1930s. Built by Butch Norris, the station was across the street from a restaurant and a common stopping place for travelers, especially after the road it was on became a Wyoming highway. (Courtesy of Marjorie Guio.)

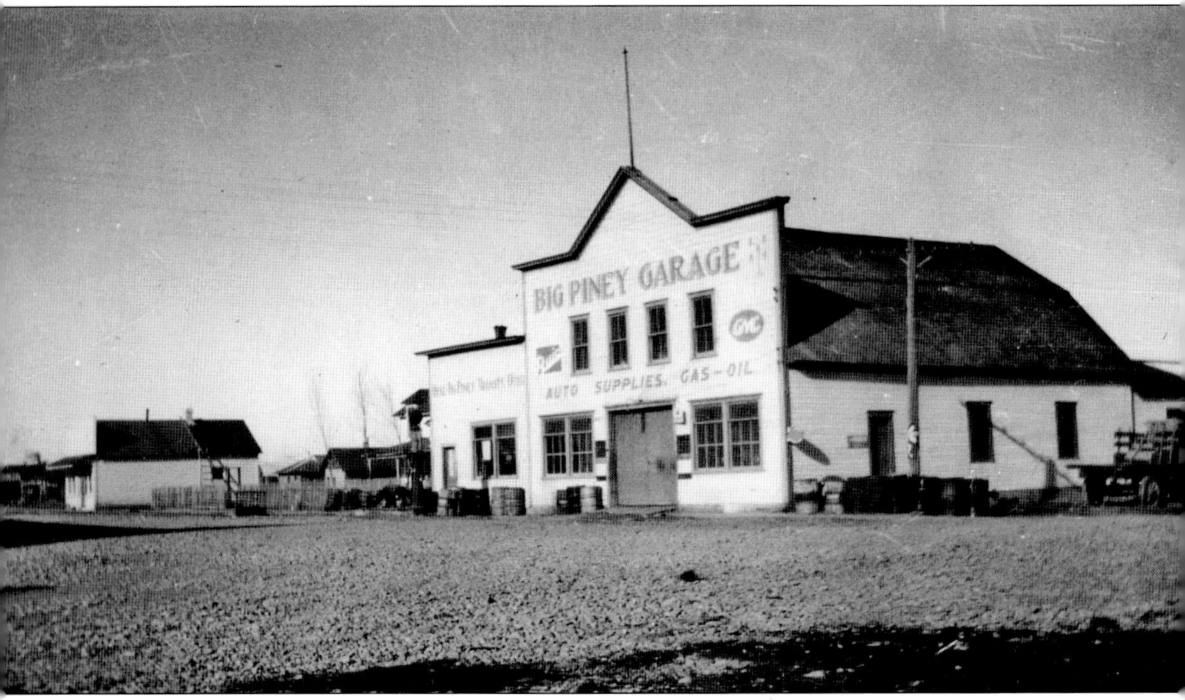

The Big Piney Garage was the first garage to open in Big Piney, about 1912. It was owned and operated by Lawrence Bess and Gull Whitman. It remained in business for decades under various owners. Located on the corner of Budd Avenue and US Highway 189, the corner was later cut out of the building. (Courtesy of Jonita Sommers.)

Three

Home on the Range

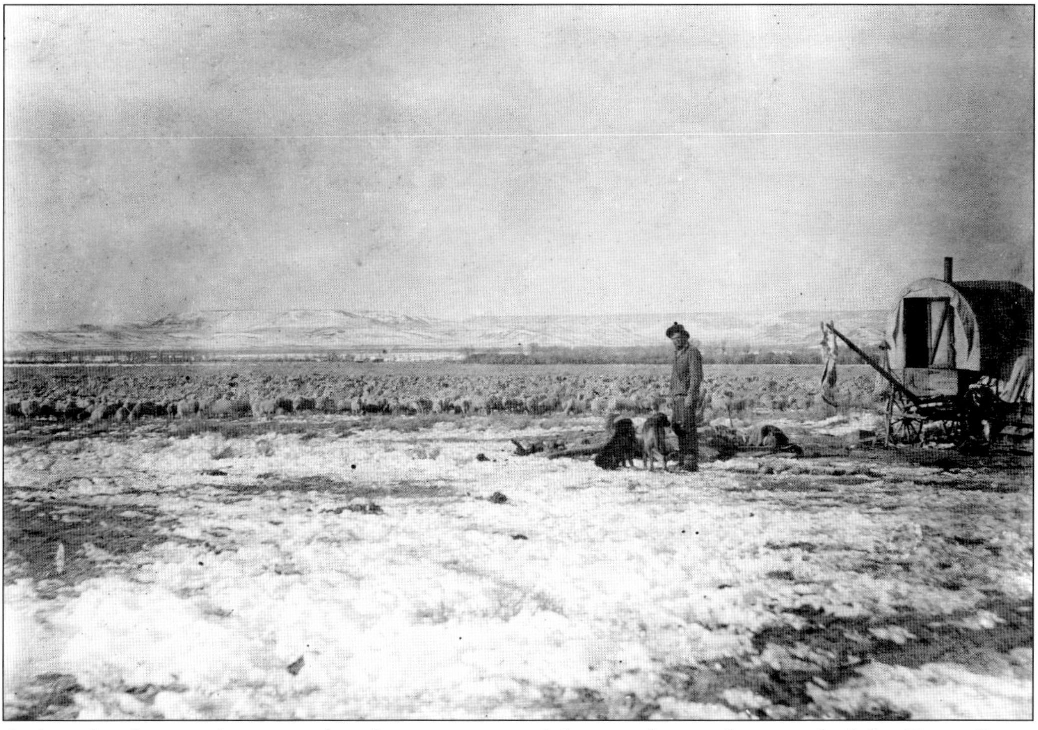

A sheepherder stands next to his sheep wagon and dogs in the southern end of the Green River Valley. In the background are the sheep under his care. The grasses that were good for cattle grazing were good for sheep, too, resulting in out-of-area ranchers bringing sheep to the area starting in the late 19th century. The out-of-area sheep, however, were unwelcome by the local cattlemen. (Courtesy of Bill and Carrie Budd.)

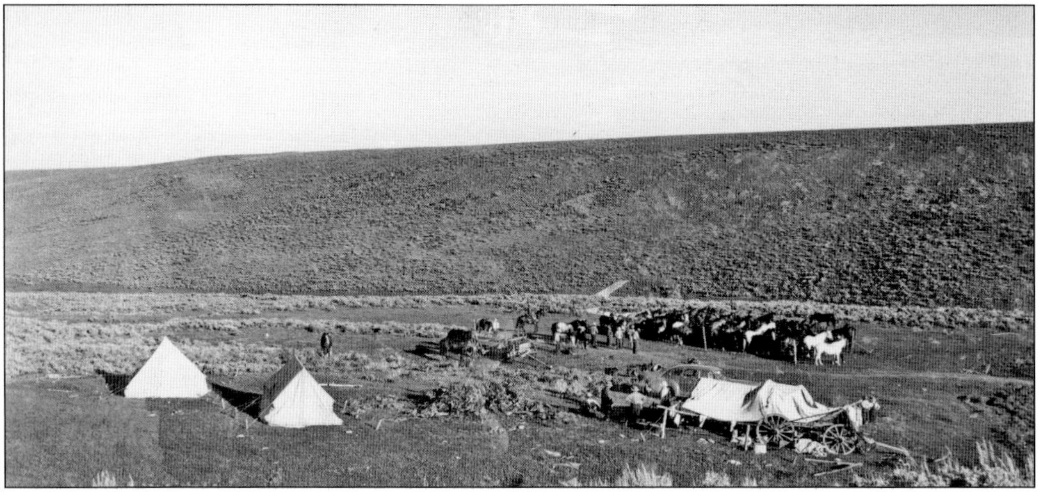

Cattlemen began to cultivate their land for hay and to fence it, ending the free-roaming cattle-grazing practices of the early days. This was a result of the "Equalizer Winter" of 1889–1890, when blizzards killed most of the area's cattle. The Big Piney Roundup Association was established in 1890 to work together for cattle roundups and movement. Pictured here is a roundup camp in 1944. (Courtesy of Mardell Fear.)

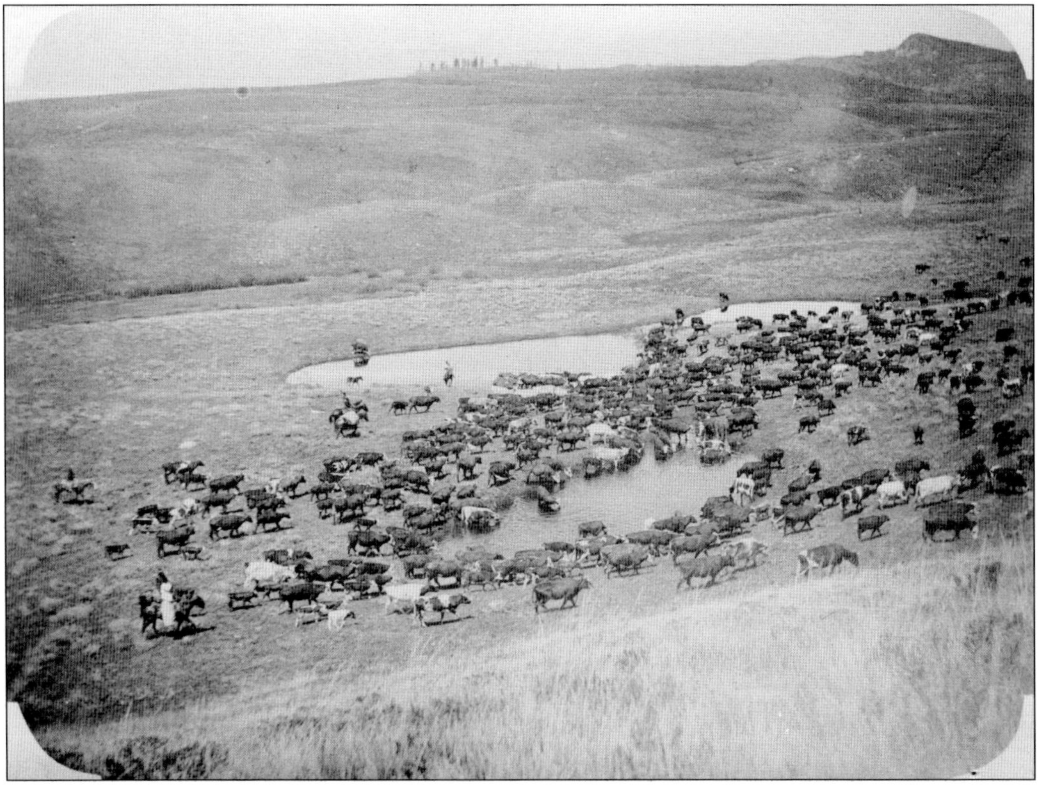

In 1896, members of the Big Piney Roundup Association started using the Green River Drift Trail. A group of cattle using the drift are going to the mountains while using water holes near Black Butte. May McAlister Sommers, on horseback in the white dress at the bottom left-hand corner of the picture, is helping move her family's cattle. (Courtesy of Sommers family.)

It would take several weeks to move cattle up and down, to and from summer range. To feed the cowboys, a "mess wagon" was provided, driven by the cook. The wagon carried all the cooking equipment and foodstuffs. The end of the mess wagon folded down and formed a table for the cook to work on. Roundup cook Steve Baldwin is seen here working on the Big Piney roundup in 1930. (Photograph by Pearl Budd Spencer; courtesy of Bill and Carrie Budd.)

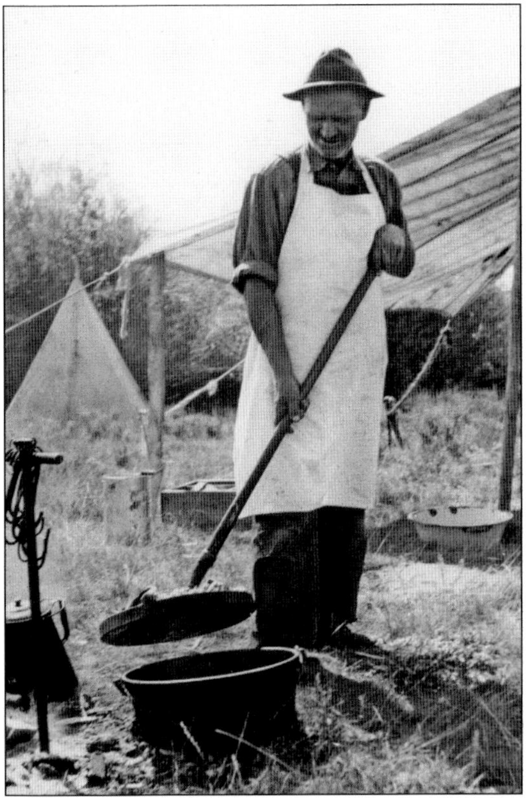

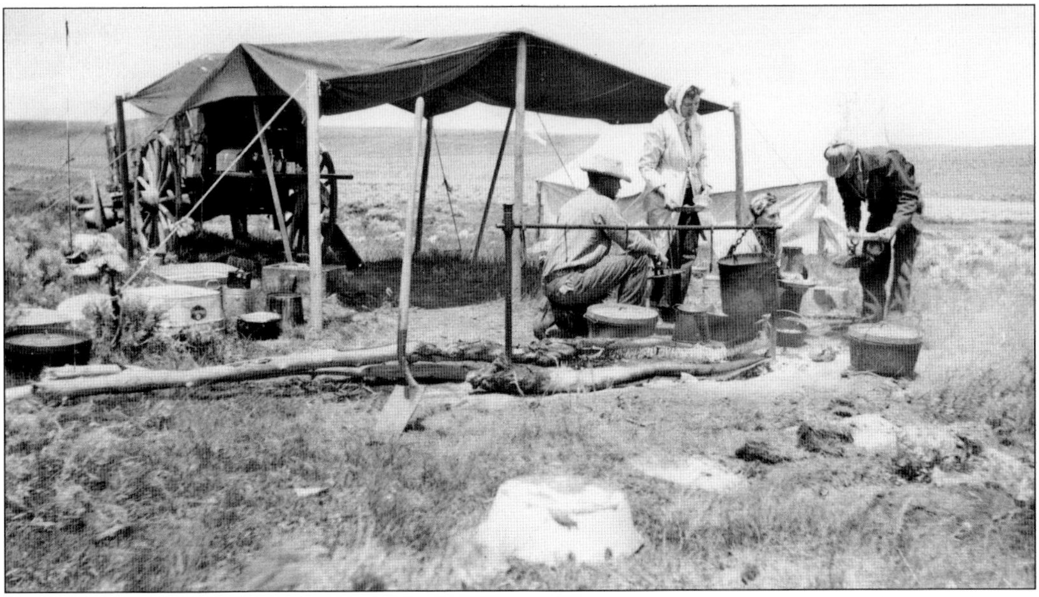

The mess (or grub) wagon for the Big Piney Roundup Association is set up, and the cooks are preparing another meal for the cowboys moving the cattle. Extended from the back of the wagon is the fly, a cover to protect from sun, rain, and sometimes snow. Ira Williams, the cook, is kneeling while preparing the meal. (Photograph by Pearl Budd Spencer; courtesy of Bill and Carrie Budd.)

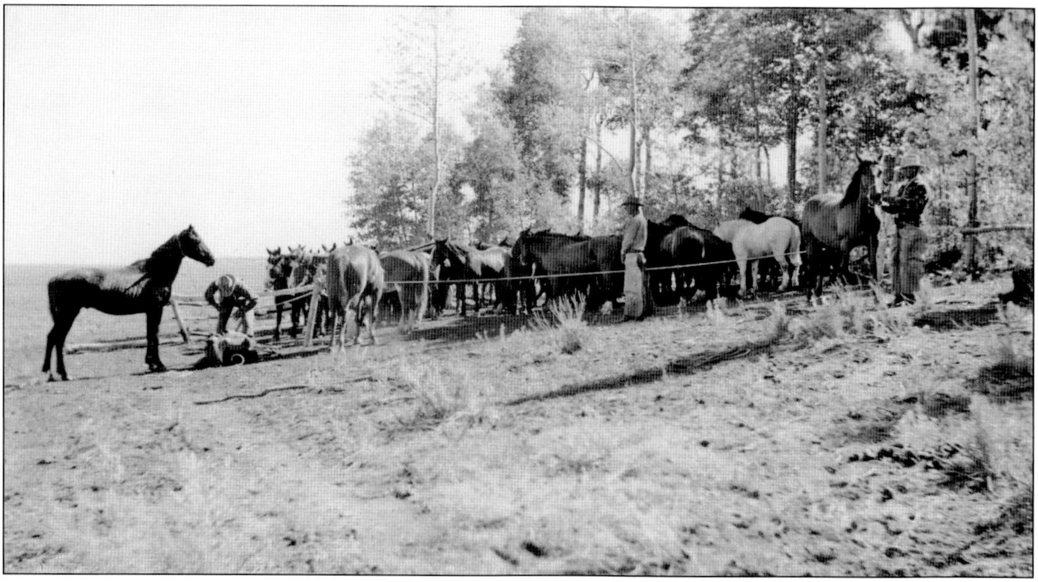

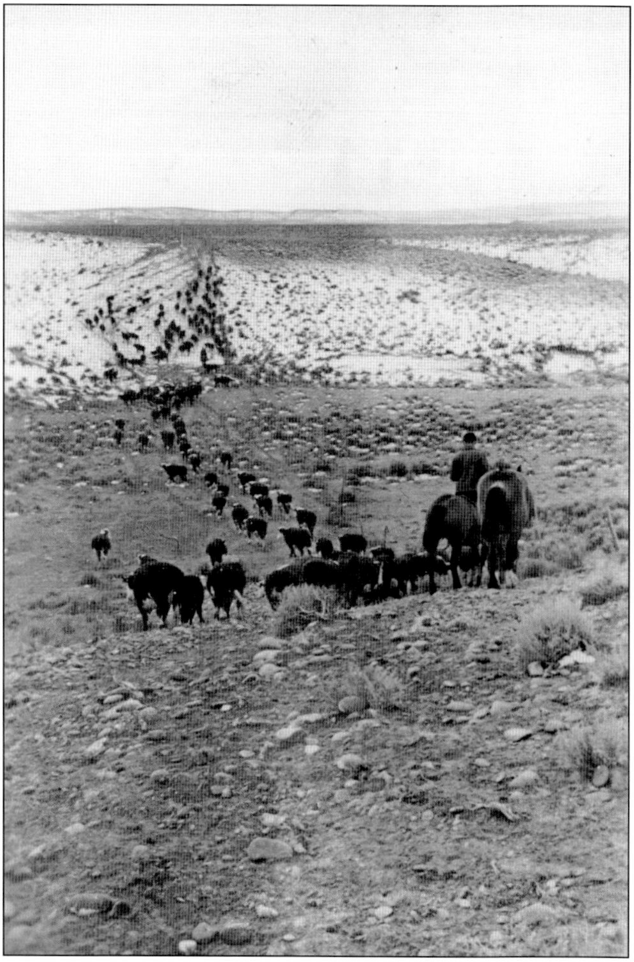

While working on a cattle drive, each cowboy had from eight to 12 horses. The day wrangler drove the horses that were not in use when he moved camp and kept a general lookout for them during the day. The night wrangler's job was to keep track of the cavvy until morning. A rope corral is used here to corral the horses on a Big Piney Roundup Association cattle drive. (Photograph by Pearl Budd Spencer; courtesy of Bill and Carrie Budd.)

A cowboy is trailing cattle as they moved along the Green River Drift Trail in the fall of 1939. They are along Price's "School Section" (land belonging to the state with proceeds from the lease going to the state schools) at the south end of the Sommers Ranch. The full length of the Drift is nearly 68 miles, with an additional 32 miles of spurs covering from the New Fork River to Wagon Creek. (Courtesy of Sommers family.)

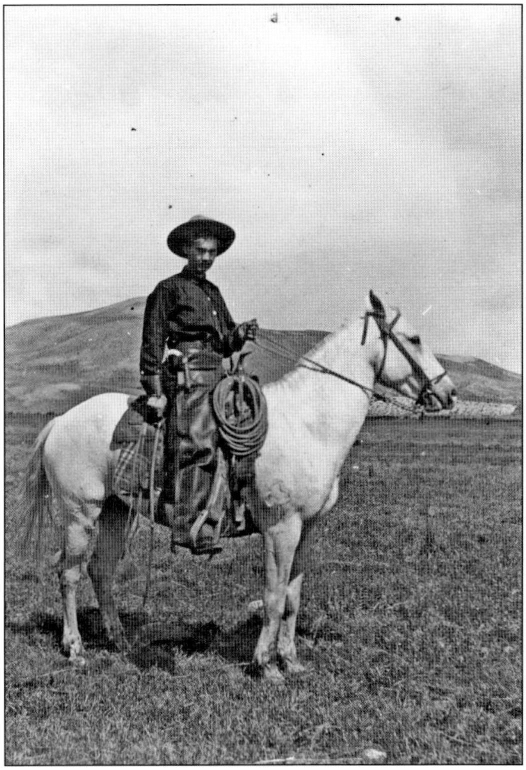

Several cowboys were required to assist with cattle moving up and down the Green River Drift Trail. Members of the Big Piney Roundup Association, and later the Upper Green River Cattle Association, were required to provide a certain number of riders to assist with the cattle movement. It was common for various family members and hired men to work the drives. Helen Beck (right) is riding Old Brady in the 1910s. Her attire is typical of what a man would wear, though a few women wore dresses while riding during that time. Paul Knott (below) rode for the Sommers Ranch while his wife did the cooking for the ranch crew. (Courtesy of Sommers family.)

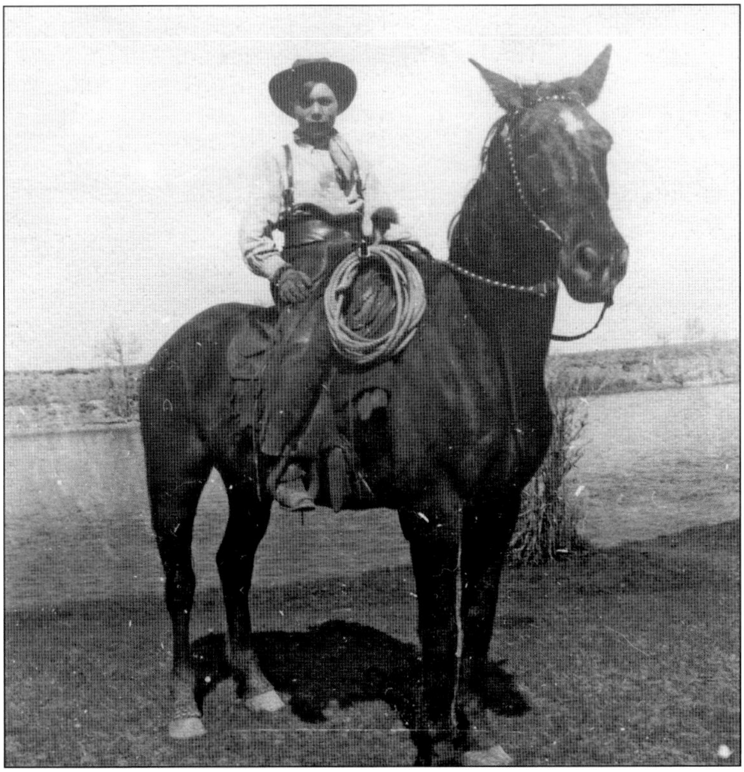

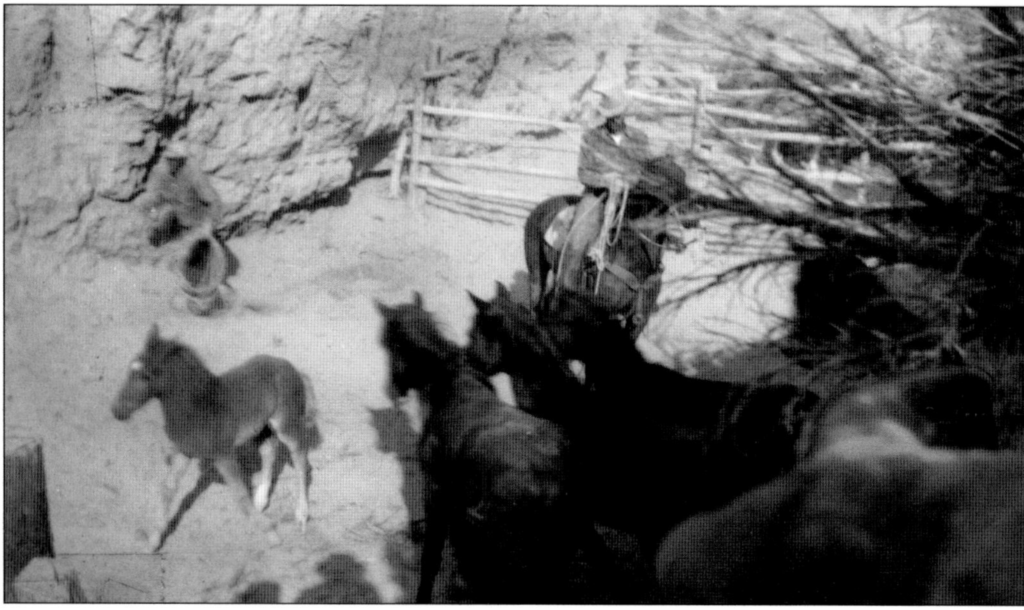

Several horses were needed by the ranchers to conduct their work. Horses were used on their ranches and while moving cattle across the range to different pastures or to railroad stops to get the animals to market. It was common for ranchers in the Green River Valley to capture wild horses from the desert or mesa south of the valley, where they lived. Wild horses are run into a fenced-in canyon by the cowboys in the photograph above. In the picture below, cowboys are capturing a horse, which they will take home and hopefully train for ranch use. (Courtesy of Mardell Fear.)

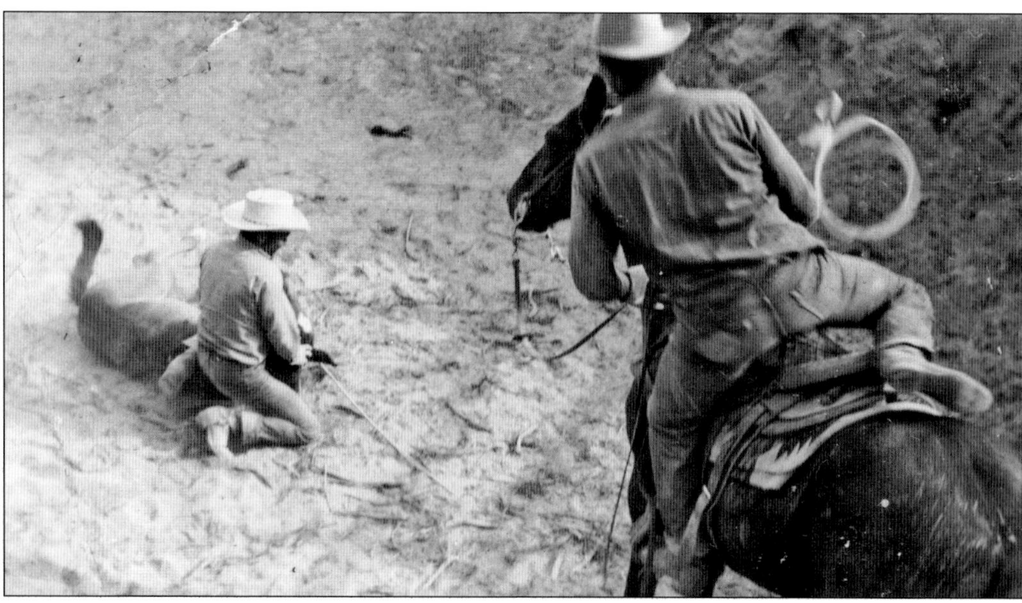

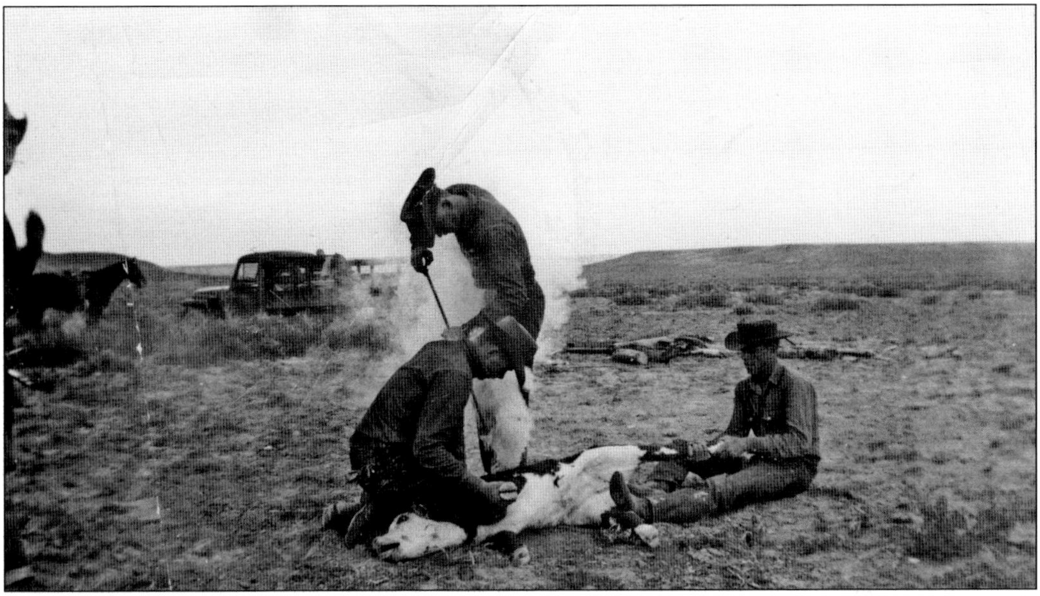

With cattle scattered throughout miles of the Green River Valley, ranchers branded their cattle on the open range as late as 1974. In 1949, Sprout Wardell is branding a calf on the desert. Eddie Luman is holding the calf's head, and Sonny Hittle has the hind legs. Branding irons would have been heated by a big fire, often made from burning sagebrush. (Courtesy of Sprout and Jane Wardell.)

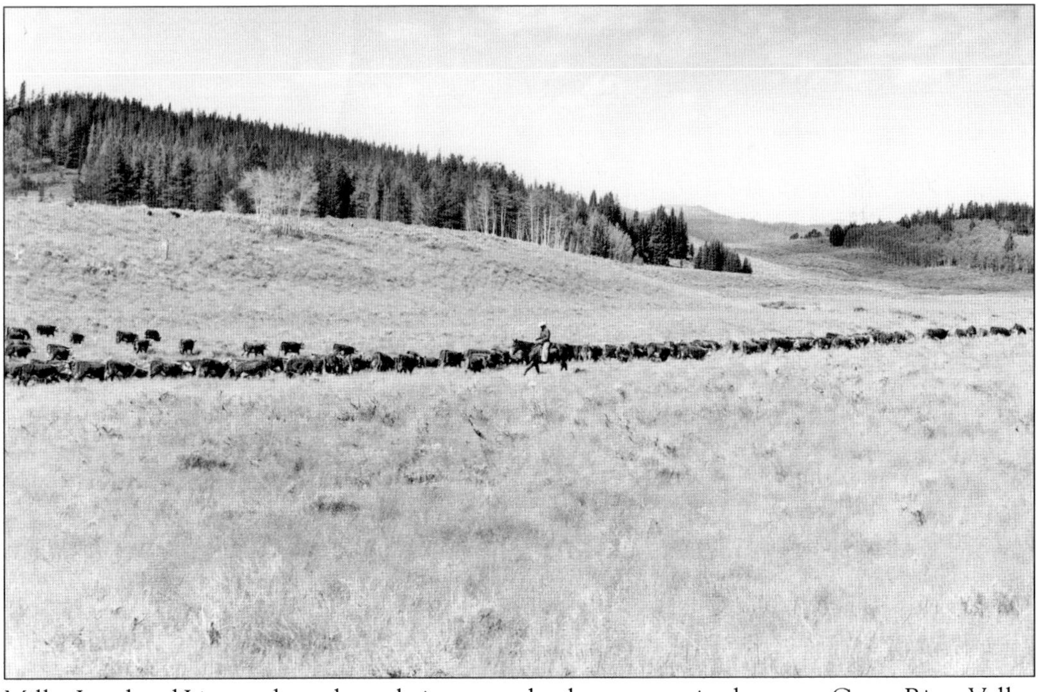

Miller Land and Livestock cattle are being moved to better grass in the upper Green River Valley on Beaver Creek. The ranch is one of the oldest in Big Piney and uses the 67 brand. It is one of the oldest brands in the area, having been started by A.W. Smith, who came with Budd and McKay as their foreman in 1879. (Courtesy of Mike and Tara Miller.)

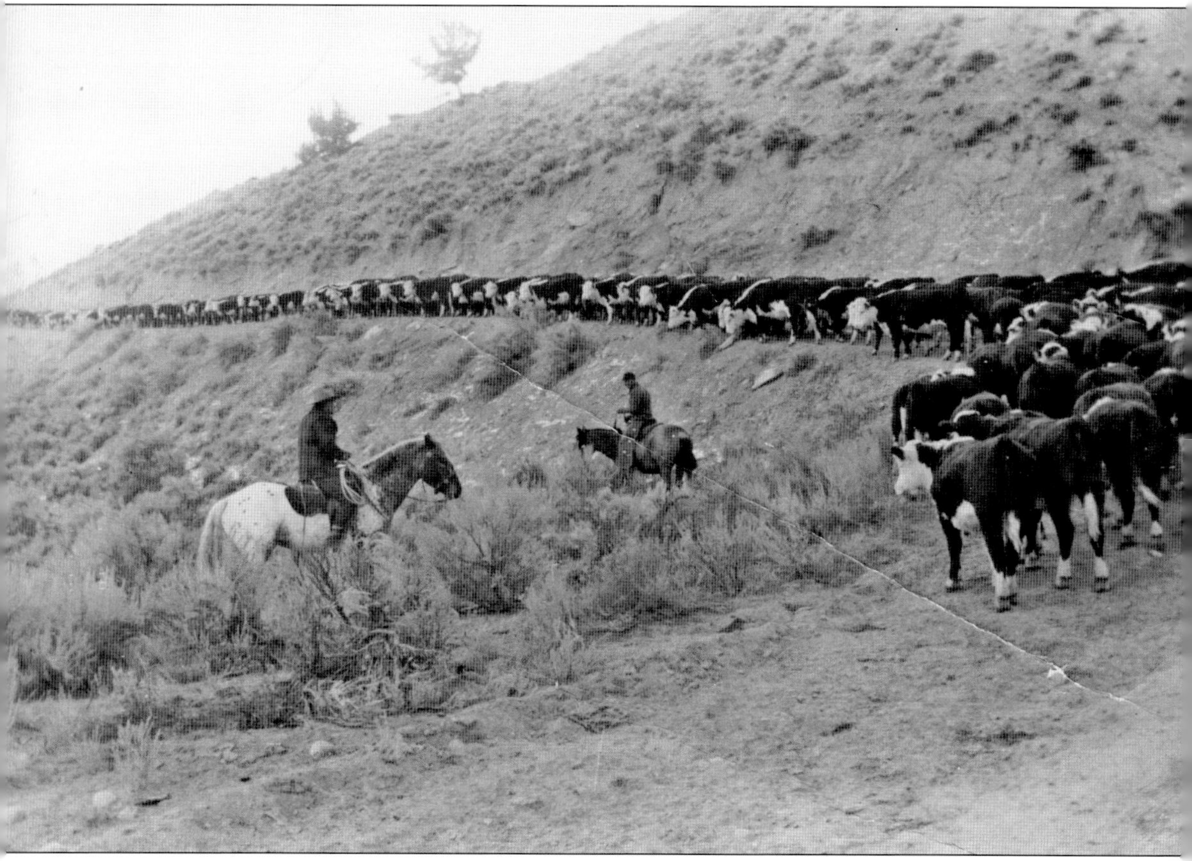

The last beef cattle drive from the Sommers Ranch is shown here in 1939. Assisting on horseback is Joe Murdock, left, and Bud Sommers. Cattle were trailed on horseback to market from the earliest cattle years until the early 1940s. Cattle were then hauled by trucks. Most of the cattle from the Big Piney area were taken to Opal, Wyoming, a stopping point for the Oregon Shortline Railroad. (Courtesy of Sommers family.)

Four

Home on the Ranch

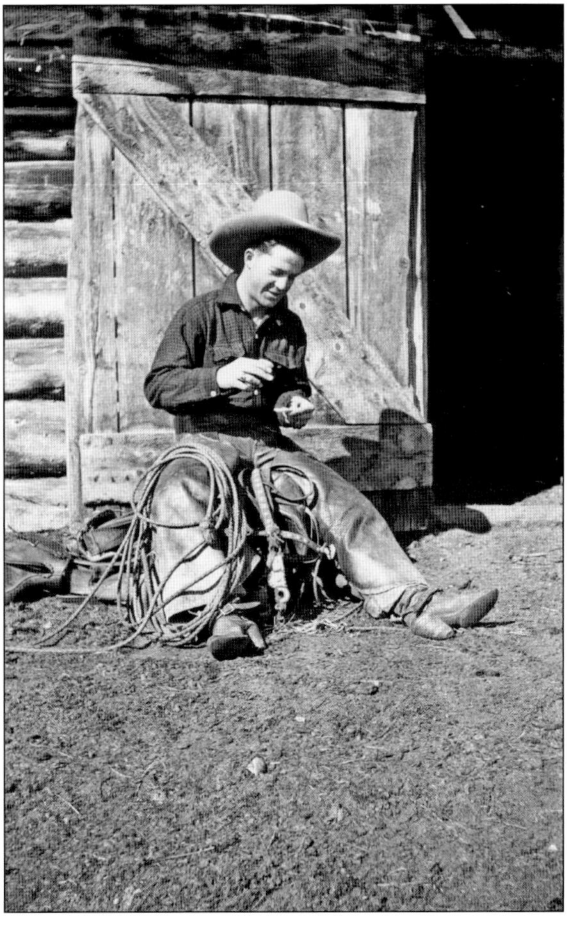

Pearl Budd photographed her brother William "Bill" H. Budd in the ranch corral about 1928. Bill's rope and lariat lie in his lap and he sits on his saddle, rolling a cigarette. Packaged cigarettes were not yet available, so rolling one's own was required for smokers. (Photograph by Pearl Budd Spencer; courtesy of Bill and Carrie Budd.)

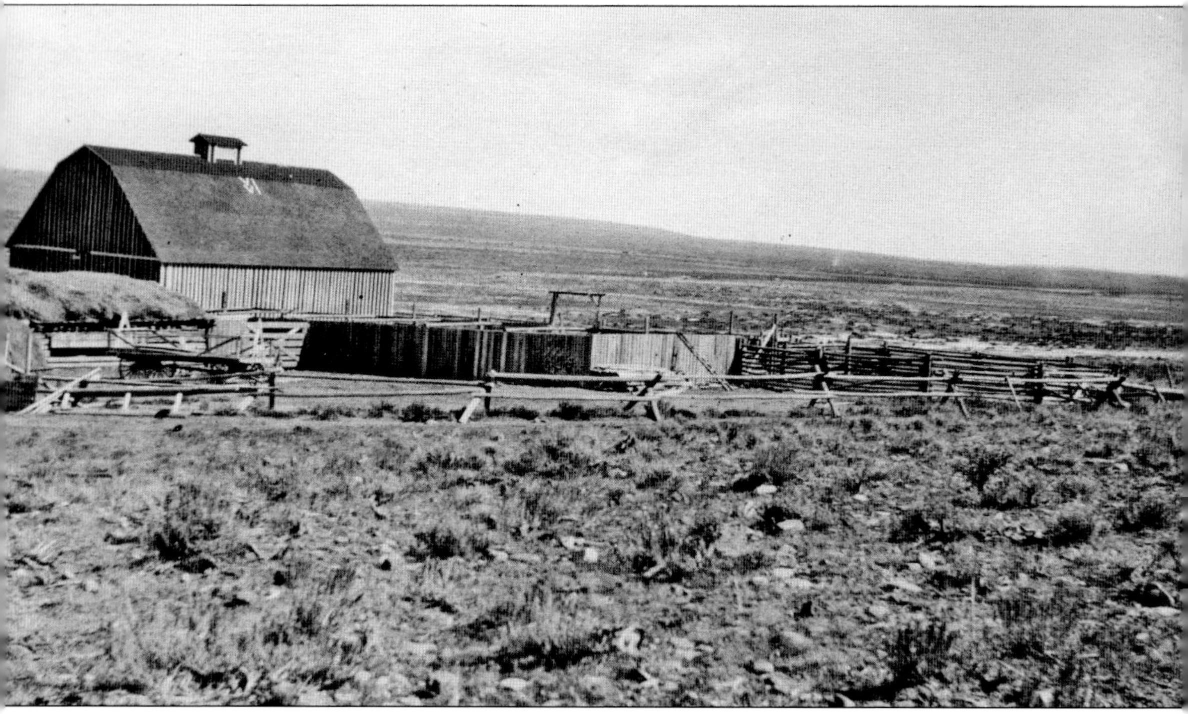

The John C. Budd homestead is pictured here in its early years. The barn and corrals became the Budd Ranch headquarters. Note the ranch brand on the roof, the Vee Vee Bar. A buck fence surrounds the ranch yard. During the early years, that was all the fencing the ranches had, with most of the animals roaming freely. (Courtesy of Nancy Budd Espenscheid.)

Henry Budd stands in the door of his barn at his ranch in the 1920s. His ranch, called the North Piney Place, was the headquarters for the original Budd Cattle Company. (Courtesy of Nancy Budd Espenscheid.)

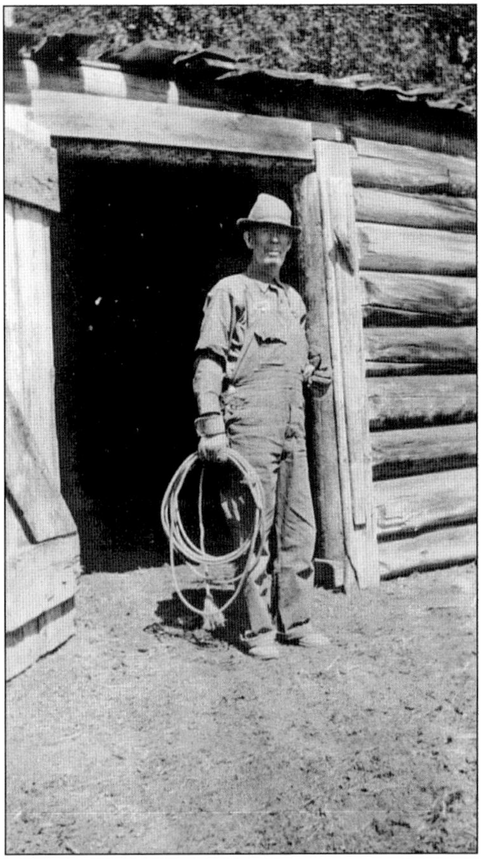

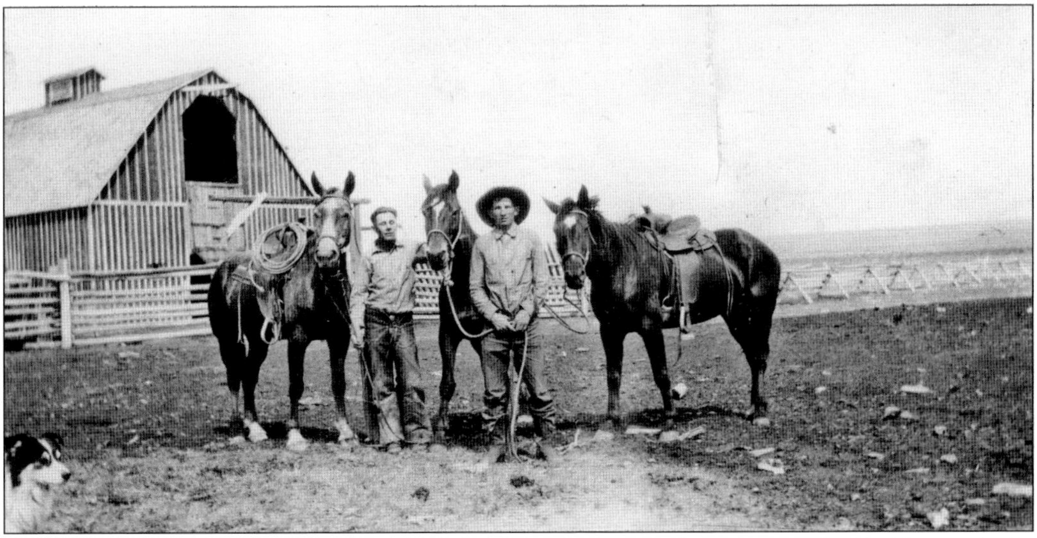

Joe Budd stands on the left with his horse and an unidentified cowboy in the Budd corrals. At left is the original Budd barn at John C. Budd's homestead in Meadow Canyon. Note the cow dog in the bottom left-hand corner. Dogs were very helpful on ranches, especially in moving cattle. It was often said that a good cow dog was better than two cowboys. (Courtesy of Nancy Budd Espenscheid.)

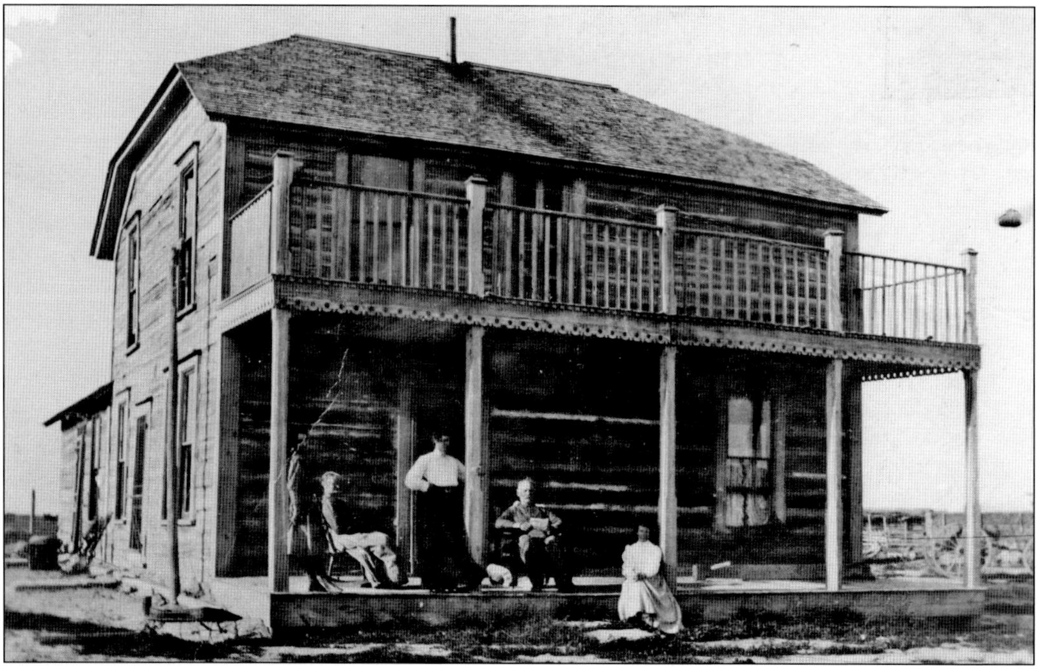

Cora McGinnis, who married John Budd, stands with her family in front of her home at Midway, south of Big Piney. The two-story home was built in the early 1890s, and it was larger than most homes in the area. Building supplies were difficult to come by because everything had to come by train, which was several miles away, and then hauled by wagon. (Courtesy of Nancy Budd Espenscheid.)

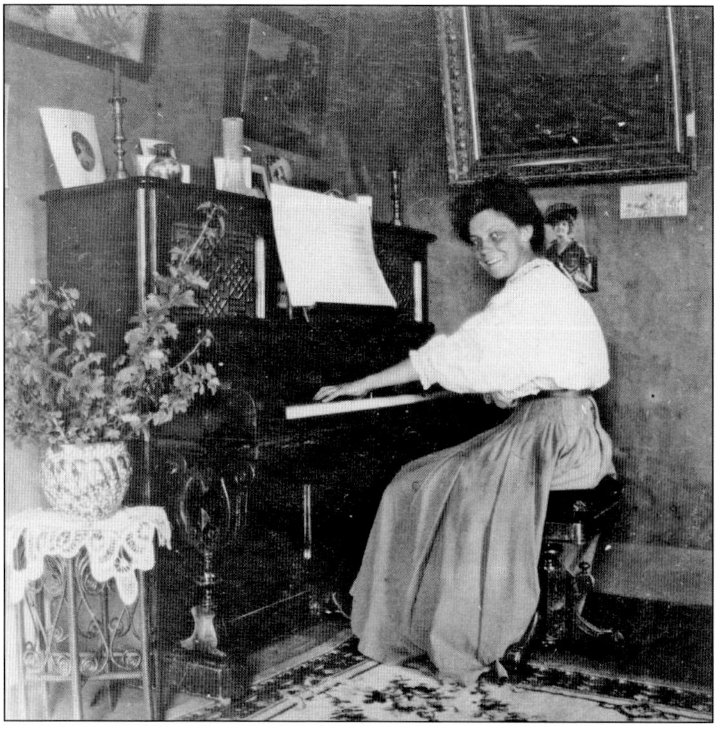

Mrs. Paul Knott plays her piano at her home south of Big Piney. The piano would have had to travel by train across the country to Opal, Wyoming, the nearest railroad stop. From there, the piano would have traveled by wagon to the Big Piney area, a distance of nearly 70 miles. Despite the shipping challenges, a surprising number of ranch homes had pianos in the Big Piney and Marbleton area. (Courtesy of Sommers family.)

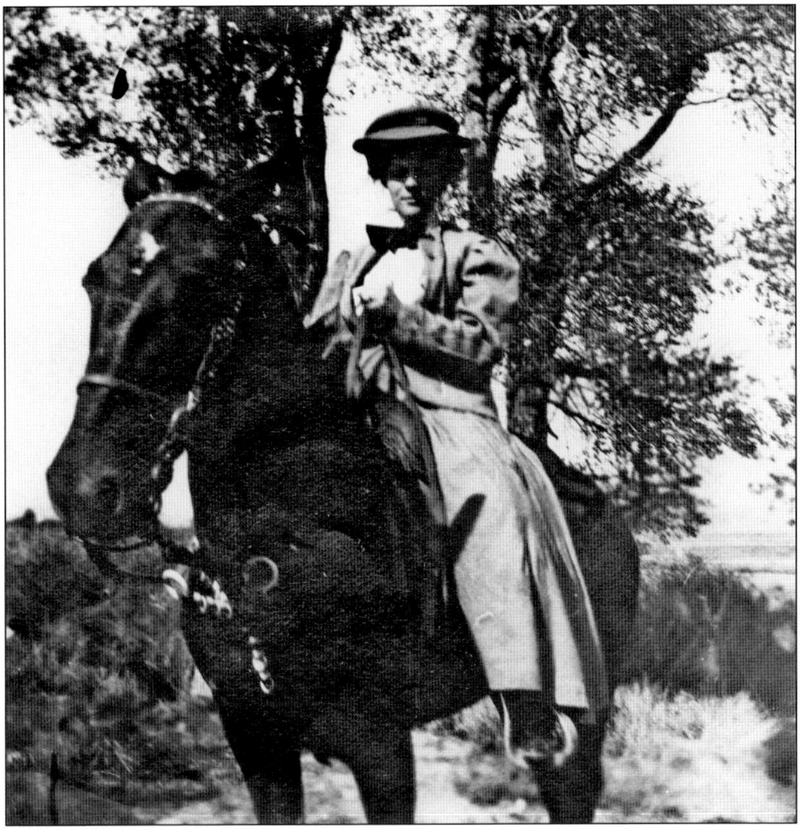

May McAlister Sommers is well dressed as she sits on her horse. Ranch women often rode horseback while in their fine clothes because horseback or horse-drawn buggies were the only modes of transportation available. May rode horses to teach school, get the mail, visit neighbors, and attend community functions, such as meetings of the Sublette County Artists' Guild, started in 1928. (Courtesy of Sommers family.)

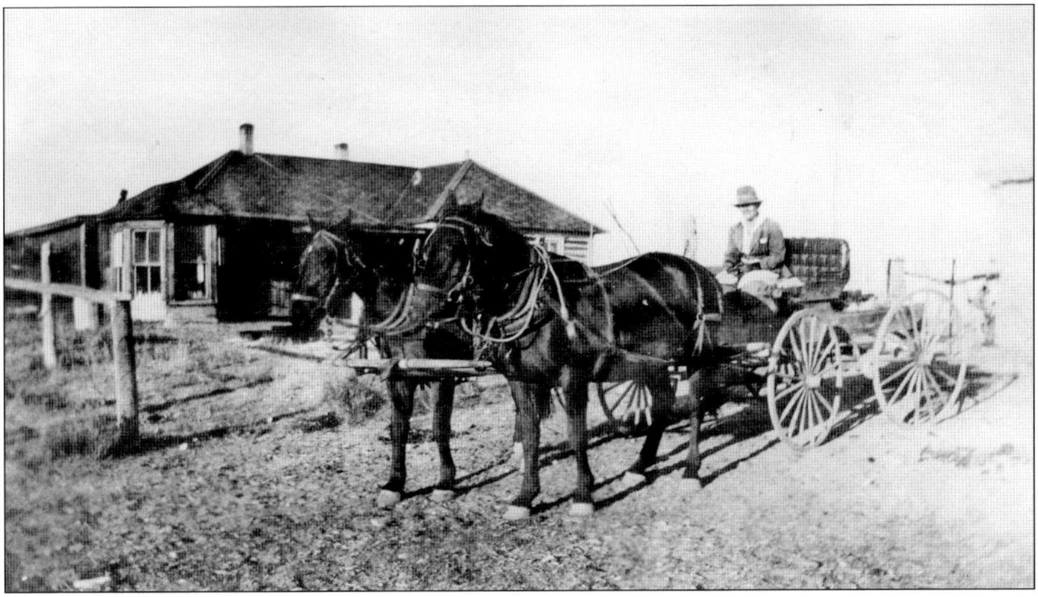

Mary Murdock is driving her team in an open buggy by the Wardell ranch home in the early 1920s. It was common for women to travel by themselves in the area. Mary became a widow in 1916, with four small children to raise and a ranch to manage. She had to travel for ranch and family business. (Courtesy of Sprout and Jane Wardell.)

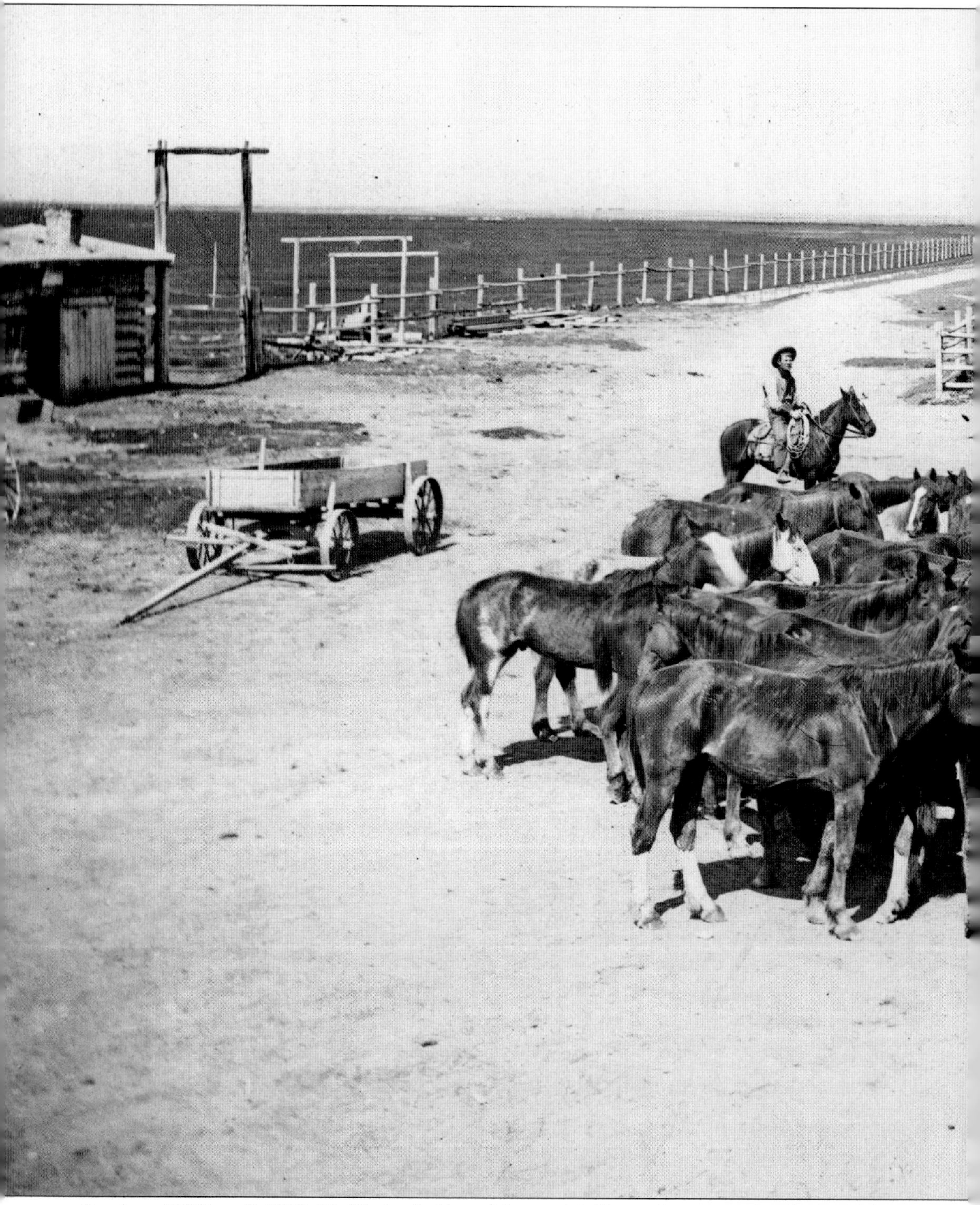

Cowboys William E. "Billy" Mills Jr. (left) and Buster McIllvain bring in a herd of wild horses for breaking, or taming, and hopefully to use. They have brought the herd into the Budd ranch yard in 1893. On the left are the post office and blacksmith shop, and to the right is the Budd

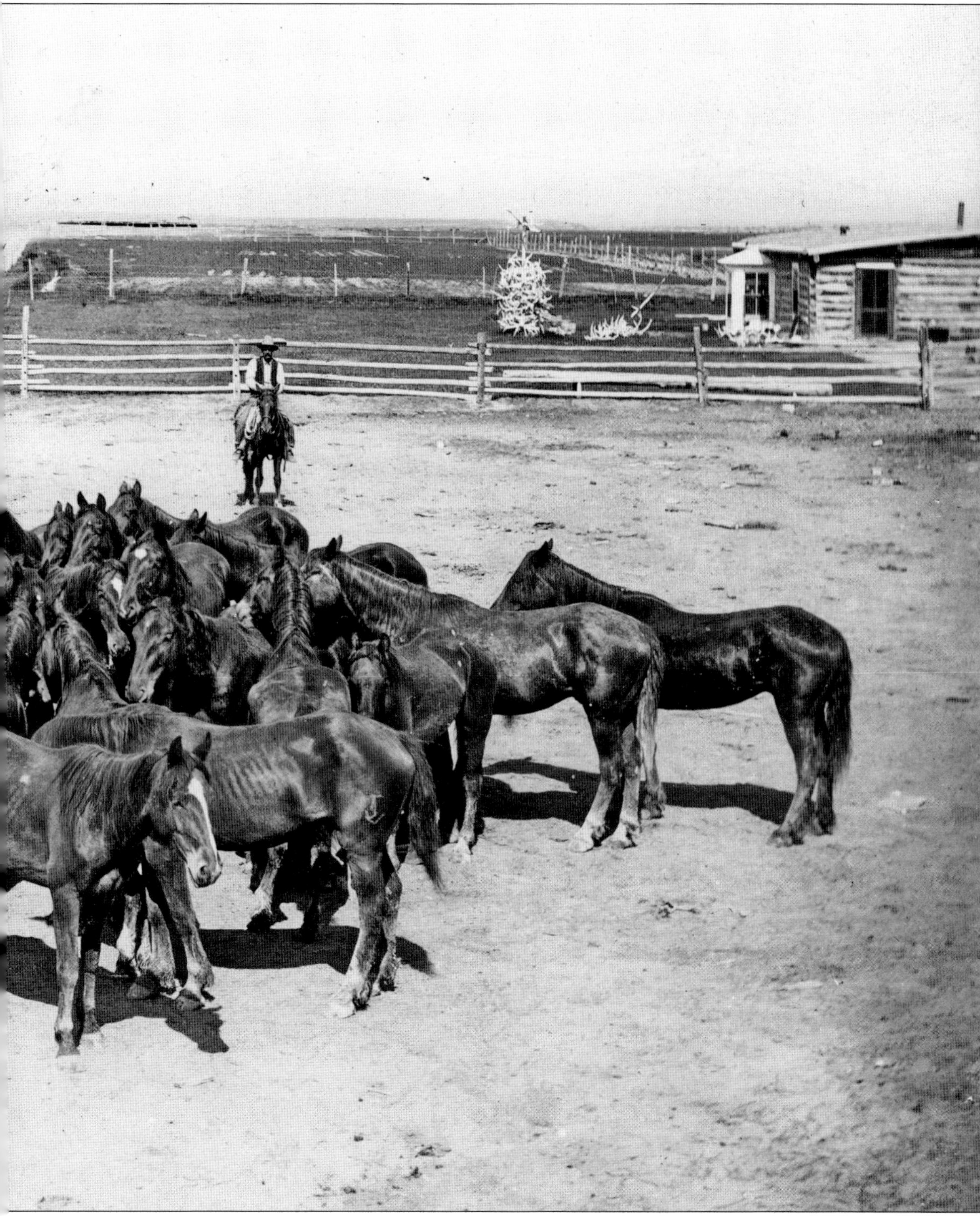

home and yard. The road leading out of the yard would later become Wyoming Highway 350. (Courtesy of Bill and Carrie Budd.)

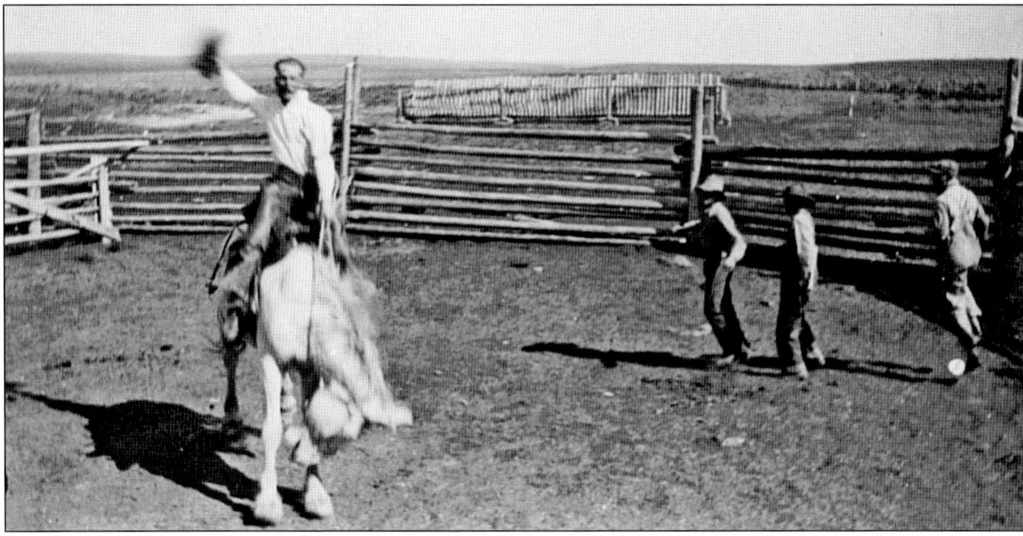

Cowboys at the Budd ranch are trying to break a wild horse. Breaking a horse means teaching it to follow commands. Naturally the horse would want to buck off its rider. It was a cowboy's mark of skill on how well he could ride a rank bronc. The dog in the photograph below may not be helping the rider if he is irritating the horse. (Courtesy of Nancy Budd Espenscheid.)

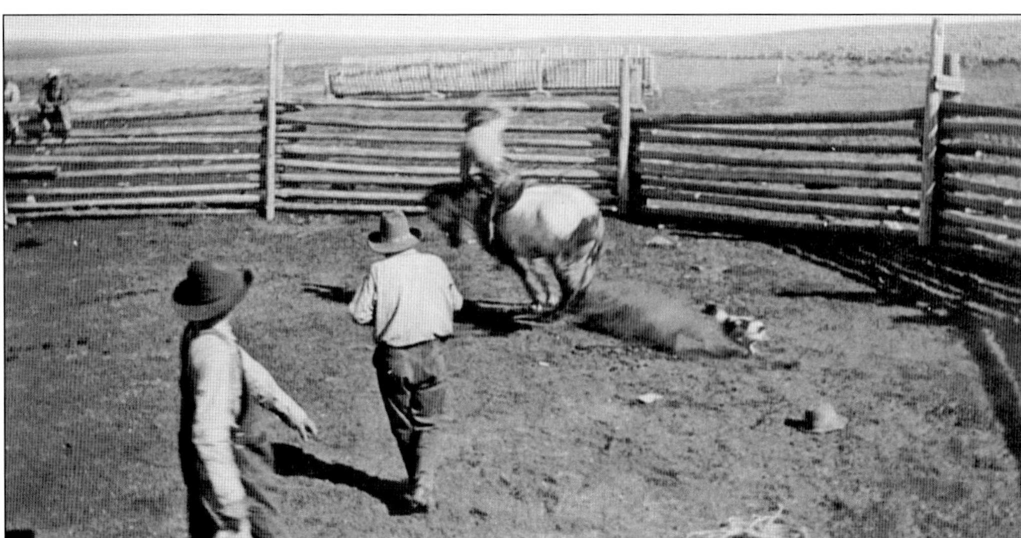

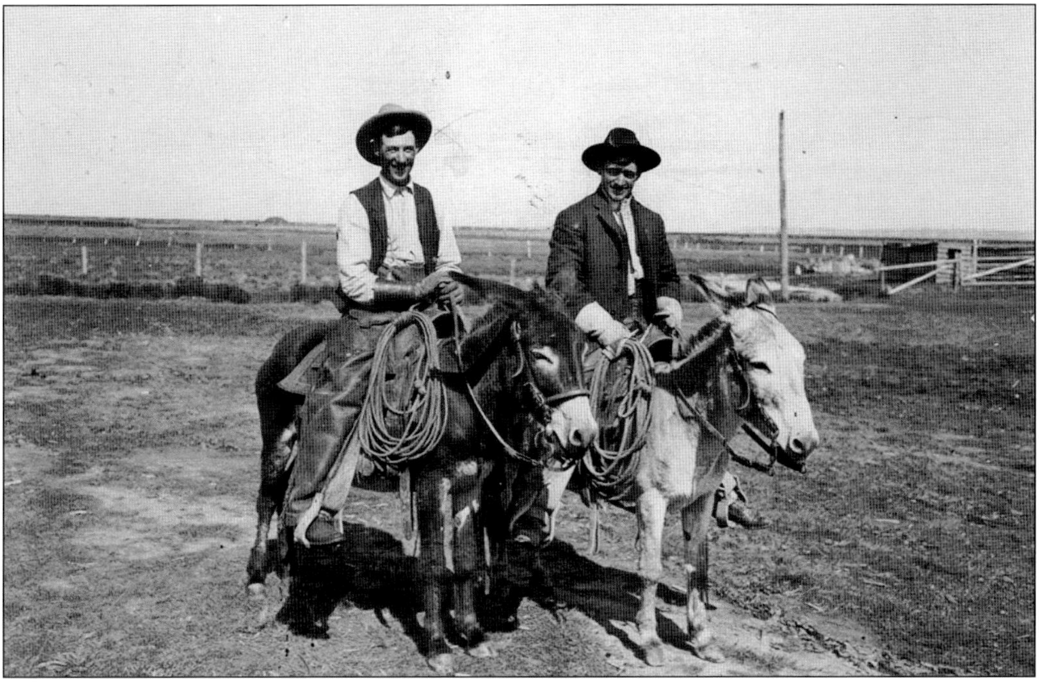

These two young cowboys are riding mules, though this was not common. Perhaps they have saddled the steeds for show. Cowboys took great pride in their horses, saddles, and equipment. Note the rawhide braided ropes attached to the saddles. In downtime, cowboys often made their own ropes and bridles. (Courtesy of Green River Valley Museum, Lorena Carr Collection.)

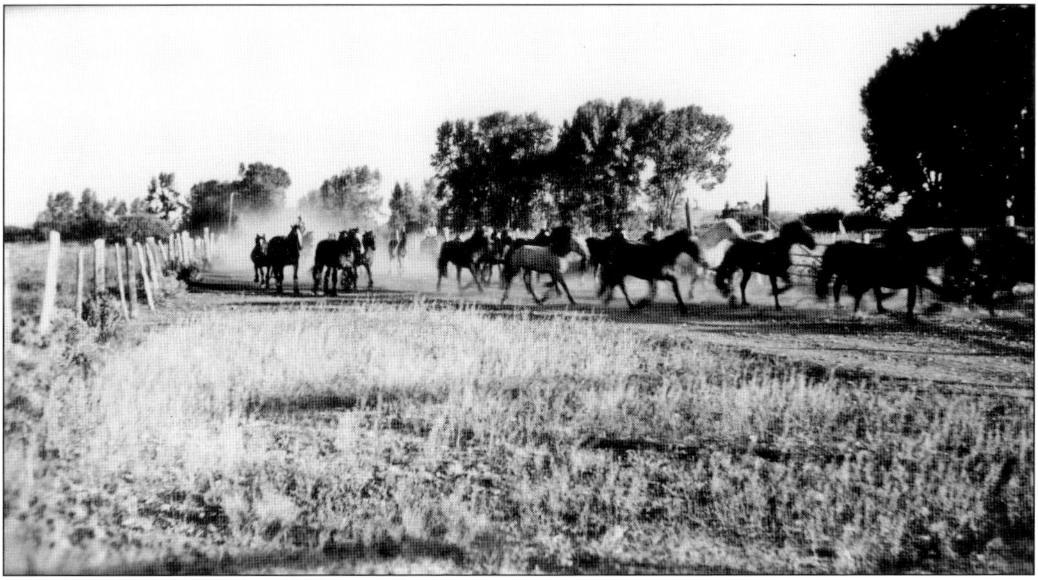

The rider in the background, Bill Budd Sr., is bringing in the haying horses one morning about 1920. Many horses were needed to get the hay crop mowed, raked, and stacked. One set of horses were used in the morning while a different fresh, or rested, set of horses worked in the afternoon. It took several hours a day just to attend to the horses. (Photograph by Pearl Budd Spencer; courtesy of Bill and Carrie Budd.)

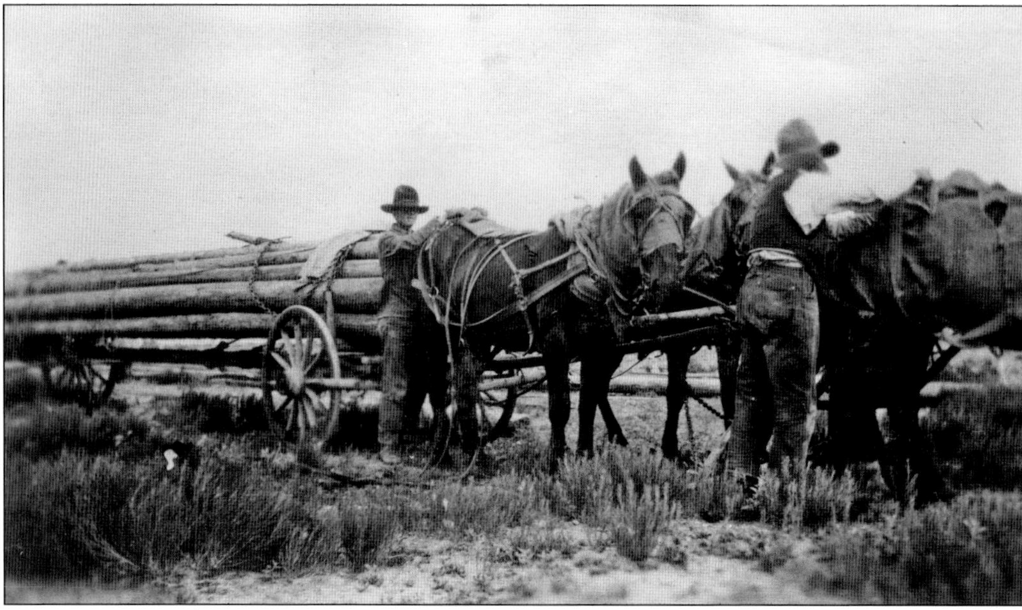

Martin Wardell (left) and John Wardell Sr. are preparing their four-horse team to bring a load of timber home to the ranch. Lumber from the local mountains was used to construct all the buildings and fences in the towns and on the area ranches during the early settlement years. Note the burlap sacks wrapped around the horses' heads. This is to protect them from flies and other biting insects. (Courtesy of Sprout and Jane Wardell.)

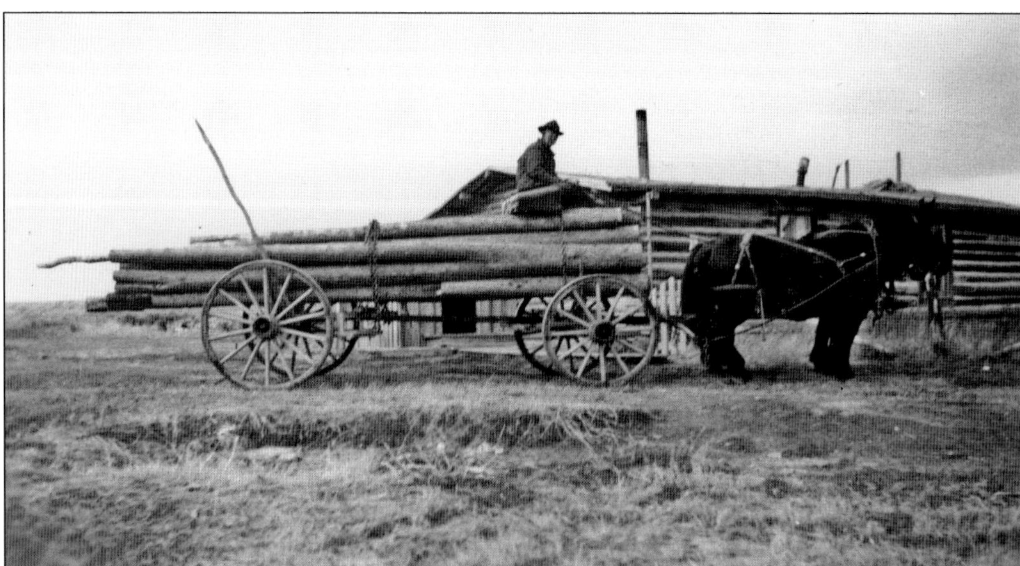

Henry Budd brings in a load of lumber to his ranch on North Piney around 1946. He is passing the Muir Place, visible behind the wagon load. The wood would be used with coal from local "wagon mines" to provide heat and a cooking source throughout the long winter. Wagon mines were nearby coal sources that were gathered and brought back in wagons. (Courtesy of Bill and Carrie Budd.)

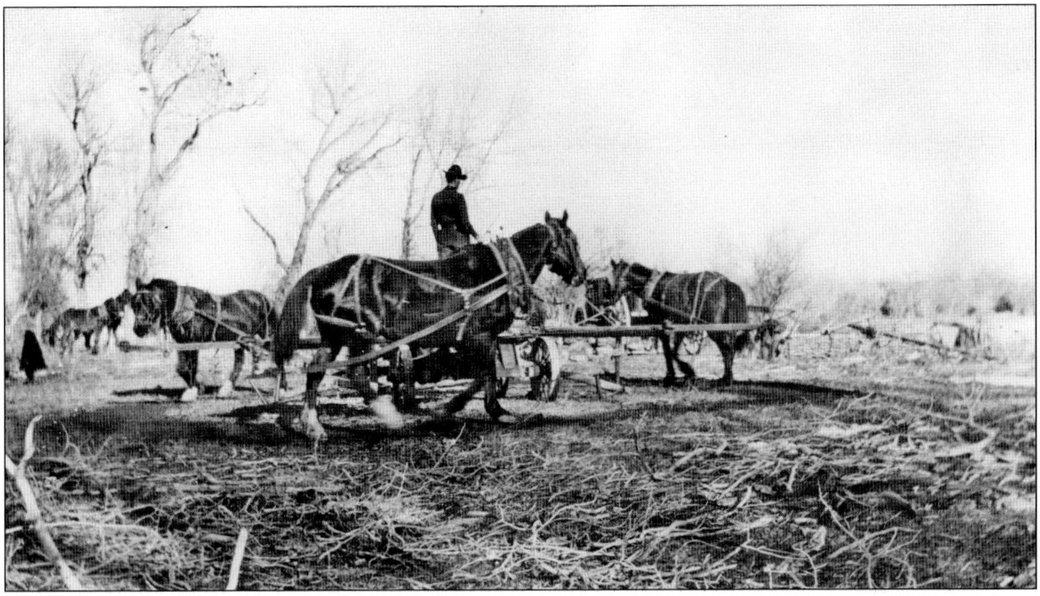

The horses are generating the power for a saw to cut wood on the Wardell ranch in 1920. Ranchers were highly self-sufficient during the early settlement years in the Big Piney and Marbleton areas. Obtaining their own wood was common. (Courtesy of Sprout and Jane Wardell.)

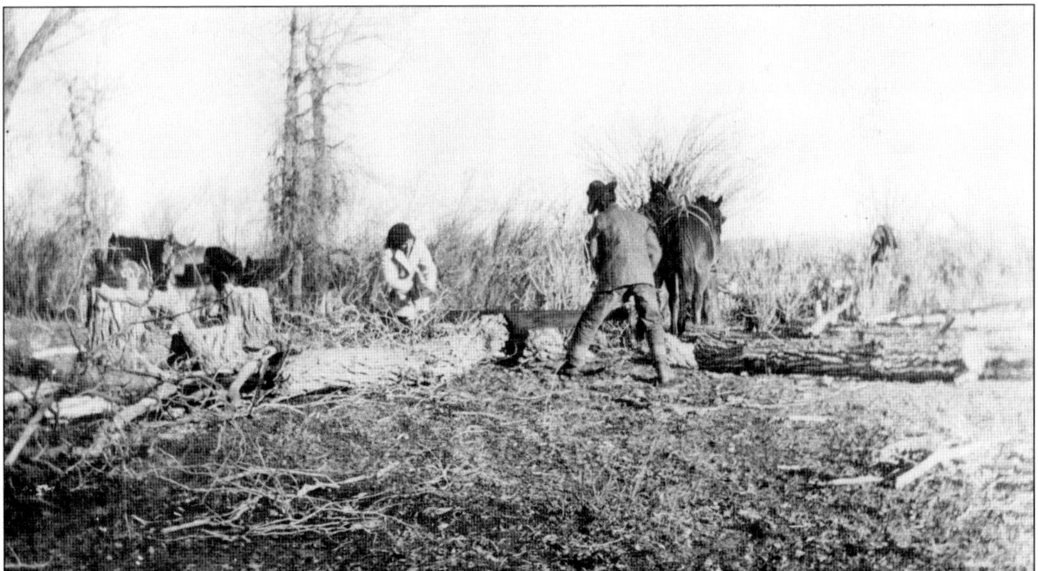

Una Thomas, in the white dress, was the schoolteacher at the Riverside School near the Wardell ranch. She is assisting the Wardells with cutting wood in 1920. Wood was needed for heating, cooking, and building everything from the houses, barns, fences, corrals, and, of course, the schools. (Courtesy of Sprout and Jane Wardell.)

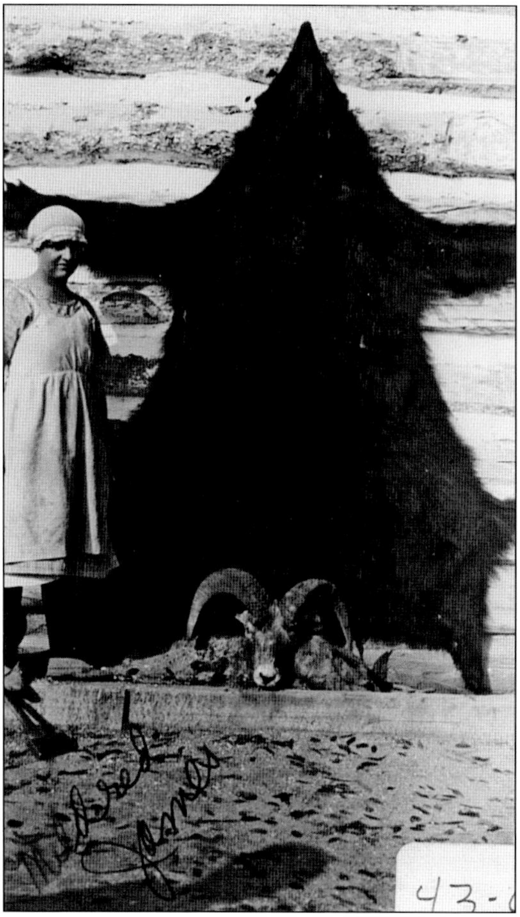

Mildred James stands next to a black bear hide mounted against a cabin wall for this photograph. Also pictured are the head and horns of a bighorn mountain sheep. The 1912 or 1913 hunting trophies are on display at the James Ranch. The animals were likely caught not far from the ranch. (Courtesy of the Green River Valley Museum, Helen Atwood Collection.)

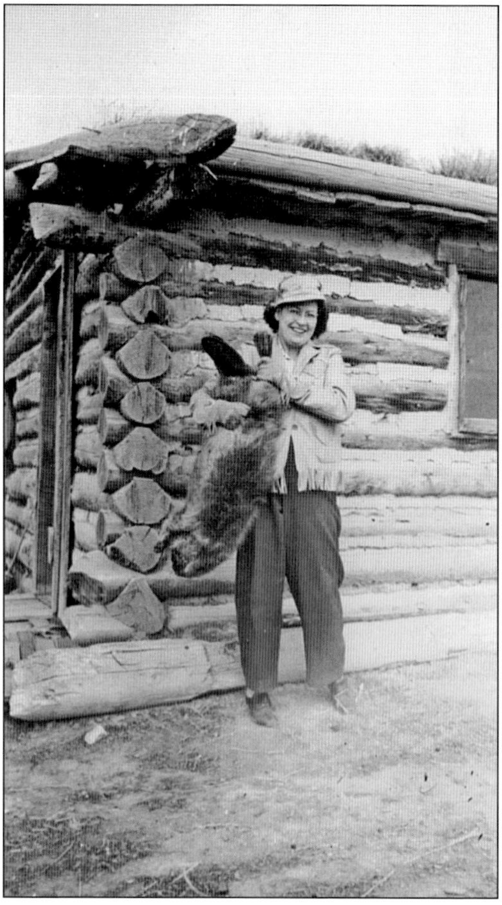

Beavers could be a nuisance for ranchers when the animals' dams prevented irrigation water from getting to the hay fields. Perhaps that is why Pearl Budd captured the one she is holding. The animals could get quite large and hard to trap because they lived underwater much of the time. (Courtesy of Nancy Budd Espenscheid.)

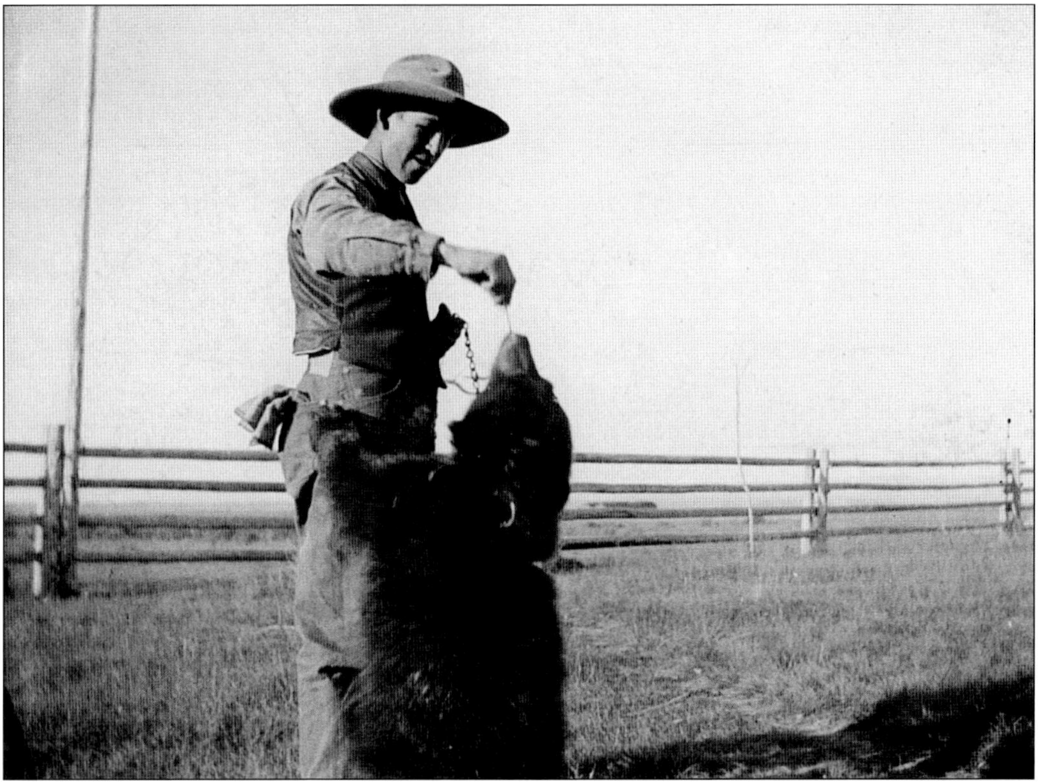

Charles P. Budd, the founder of Marbleton, is with his pet bear at the Budd ranch in Big Piney. The bear was caught as a cub and learned to be friendly with Charles, especially when he fed him, as pictured here. When bears grew big, however, they never remained pets. They returned to the wild when they became dangerously big. (Courtesy of Green River Valley Museum.)

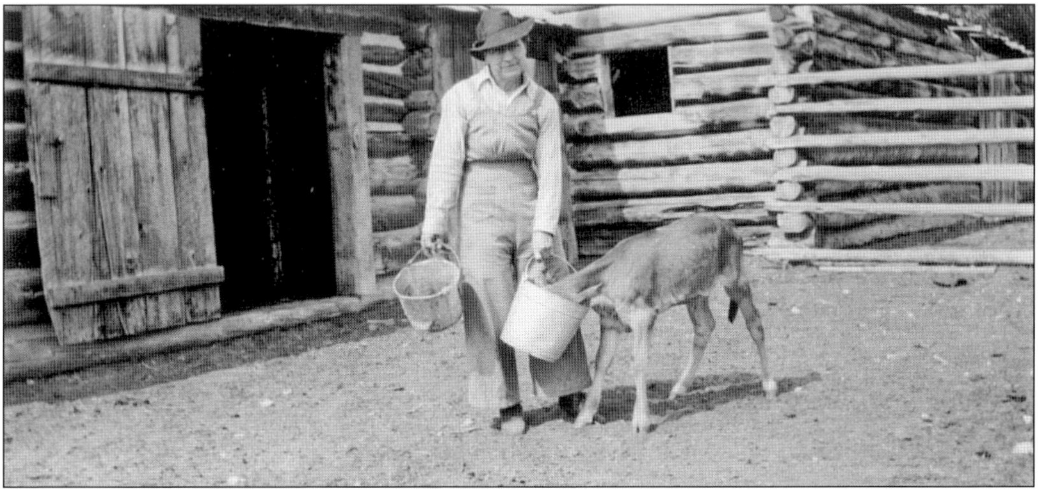

Leta Budd feeds a "bum" calf, an expression used to refer to a calf without a mother, either through abandonment or death of the cow. In some instances, the calf may be a twin and the mother cow only able to provide enough milk for one. Leta is dressed for ranch work in attire many city women would not have been comfortable wearing in the early 20th century. (Courtesy of Nancy Budd Espenscheid.)

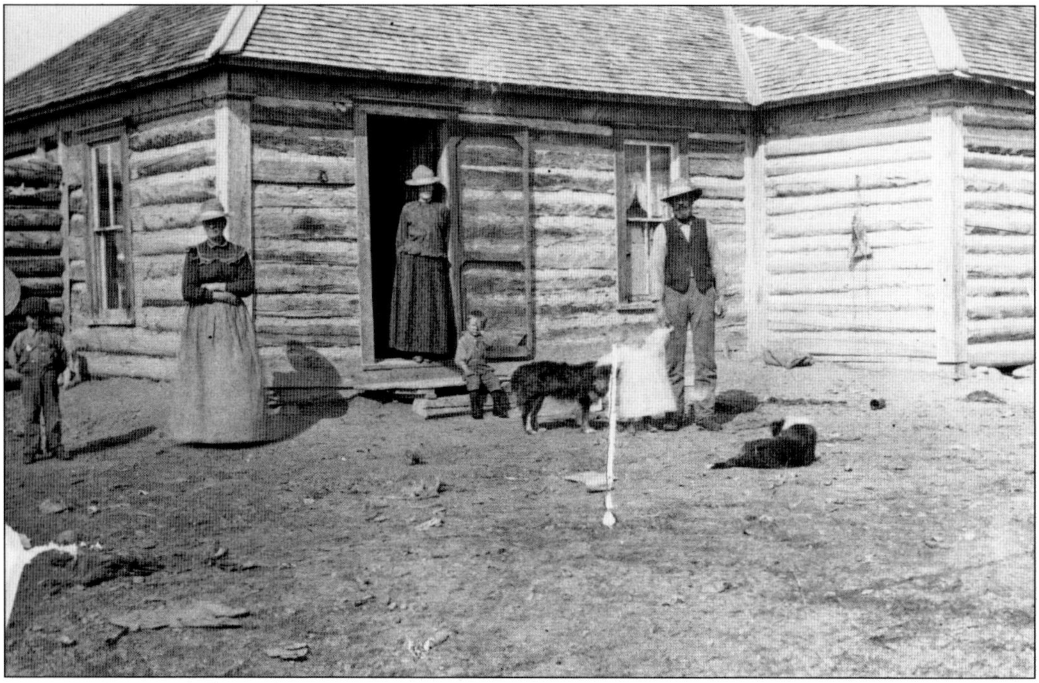

In 1905, the Wardell family stands in front of their home. From left to right are Rex, Jane, Maggie, Martin (seated), baby Bell in the white dress, and John Wardell. It was pioneering families like this one who settled the Big Piney and Marbleton area despite a dry, cold climate where it was not easy to make a living from the land. (Courtesy of Sprout and Jane Wardell.)

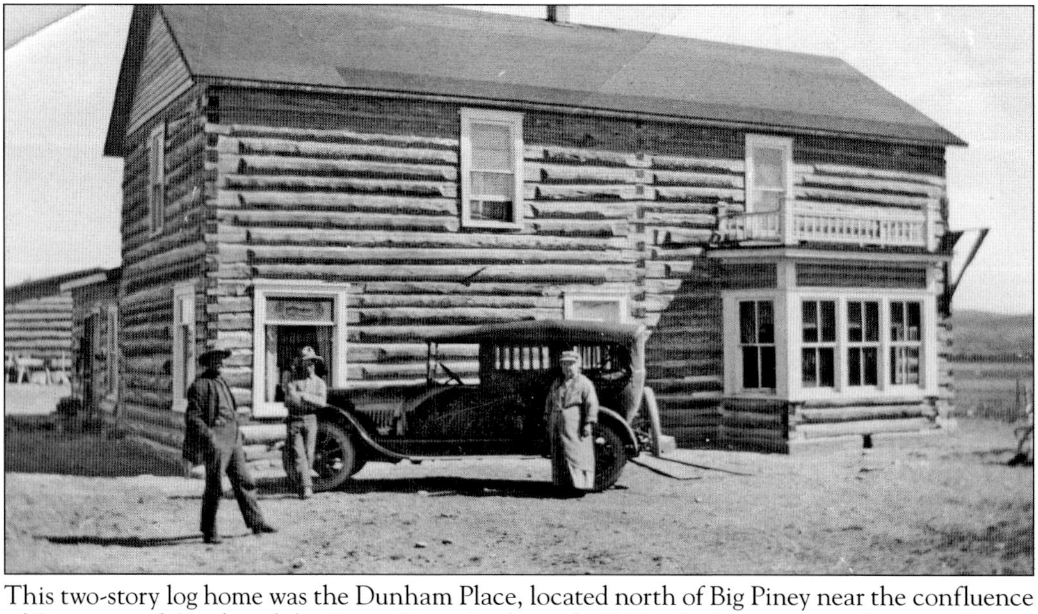

This two-story log home was the Dunham Place, located north of Big Piney near the confluence of Cottonwood Creek and the Green River. In the early 1900s, the home was used as a roadhouse for travelers coming through the area. (Courtesy of Sommers family.)

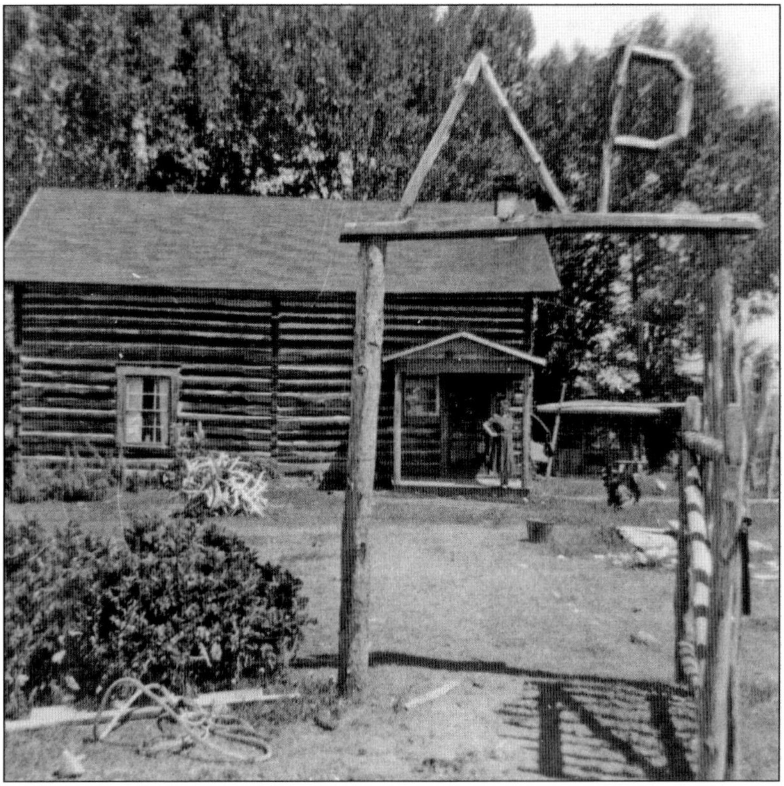

Carolyn Johnson, May Sommers's niece, stands on the porch at the Sommers homestead. Logs for the home were floated down the Green River from the mountains in 1908. The ranch brand, open AP, is posted above the ranch gate. Because the house was located on the Ada Ditch, large cottonwood trees were in the yard, unusual for many ranch yards in the dry climate. (Courtesy of Sommers family.)

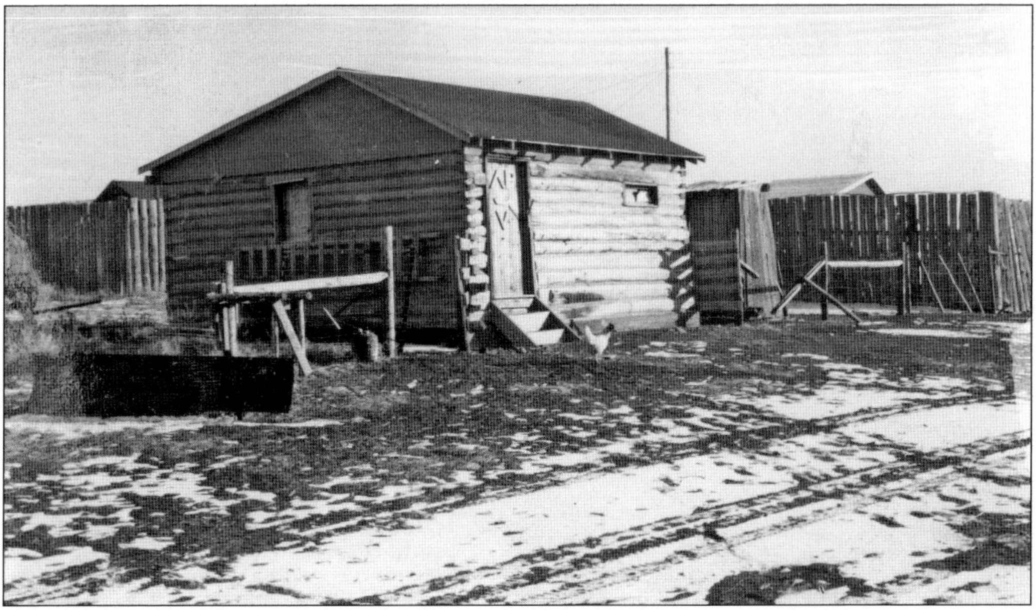

The Sommers Ranch bunkhouse was built around 1910. Note the brands marked on the door—the open AP was Albert P. "Prof" Sommers's brand and the Quarter Circle V was Albert's brother Pearl V. Sommers's brand. A brand was synonymous with ranch or family name, akin to the coat of arms of a rancher. The bunkhouse was later transitioned into a granary. It was common to change the use of buildings as the needs of a ranch changed. (Courtesy of Sommers family.)

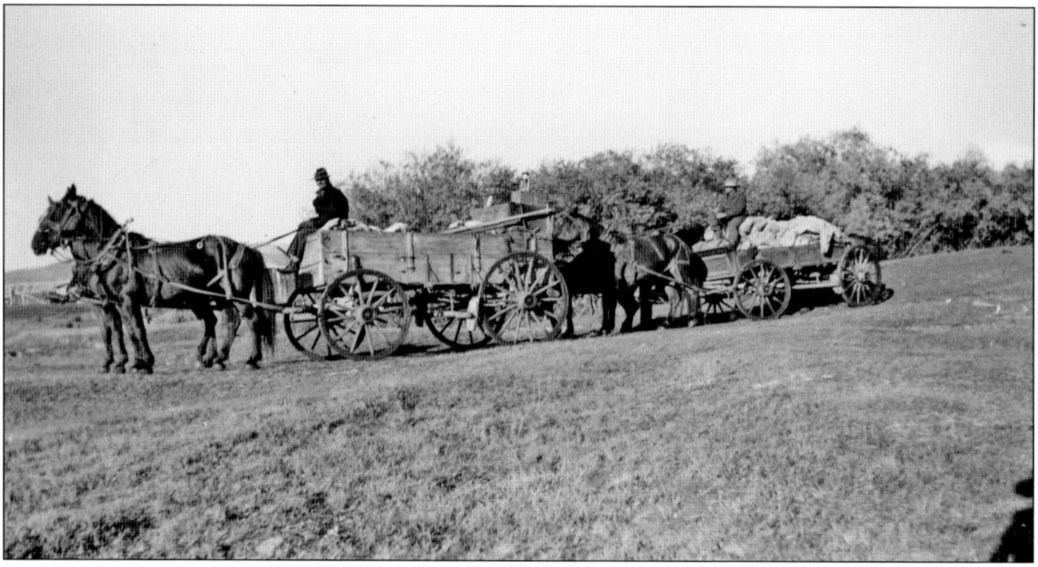

Supply wagons are leaving the Budd ranch in the early 20th century. Ranchers were dependent on their horses for all their ranch work and transportation. A trip away from the ranch usually took several days, with travel slow and distances far. (Courtesy of Bill and Carrie Budd.)

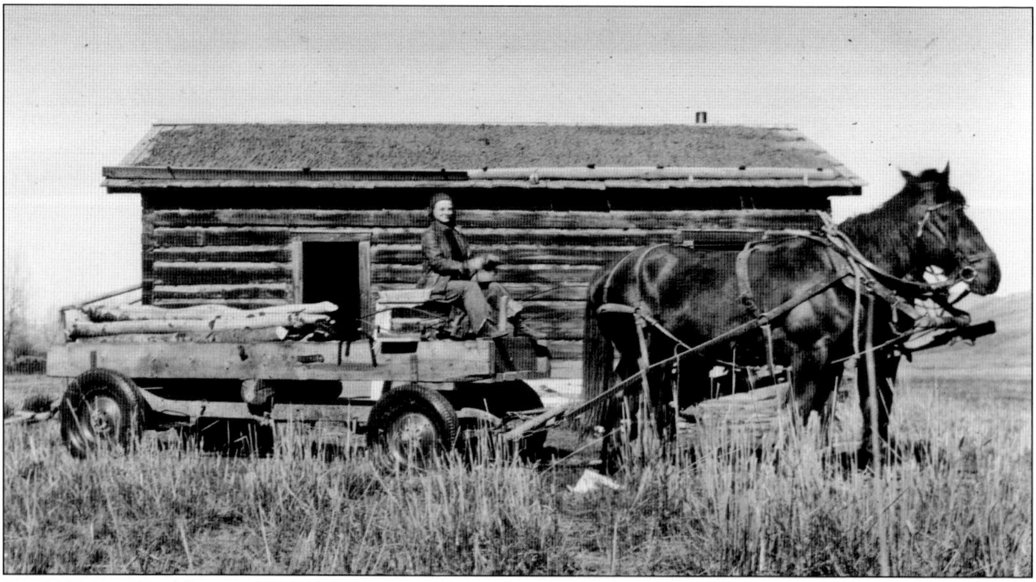

Ruth Tanner smiles as she holds the team of horses for this photograph. Ruth is bringing a load of logs for fence posts. It was common to see women in these parts wearing pants and doing what might have been considered men's work. The labor supply was short and work was plentiful, so women did what needed to be done, both inside the house and outside. (Courtesy of Nancy Budd Espenscheid.)

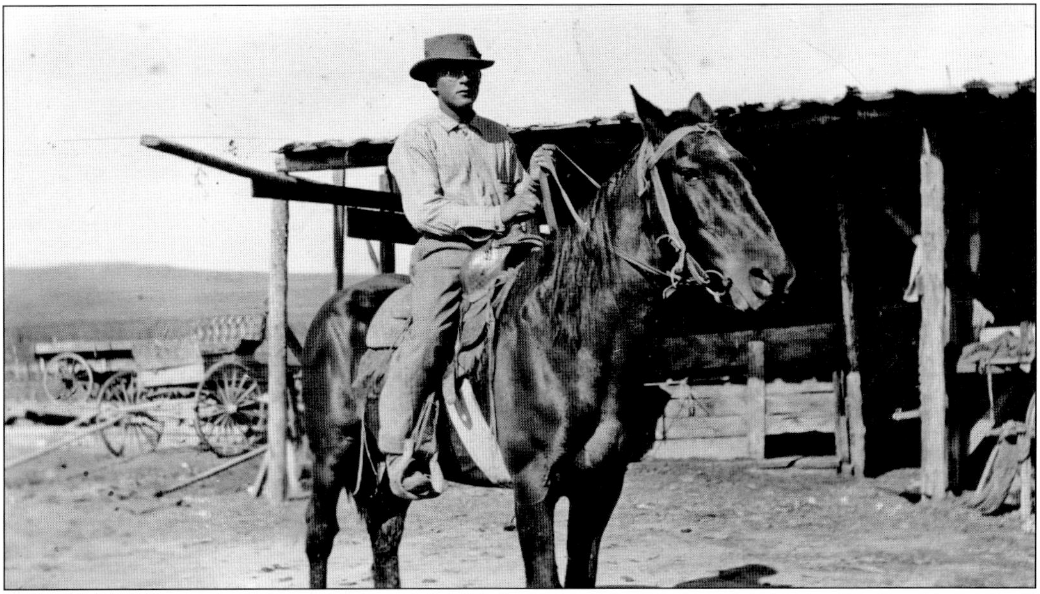

Roy Tyler mounts his horse in front of the Sommers Ranch barn. Tyler had a ranch north of the Sommers place. It was common for ranchers to visit one another and help each other when several people were needed for a job. Note the open buggy and wagon at the left of the photograph. (Courtesy of Sommers family.)

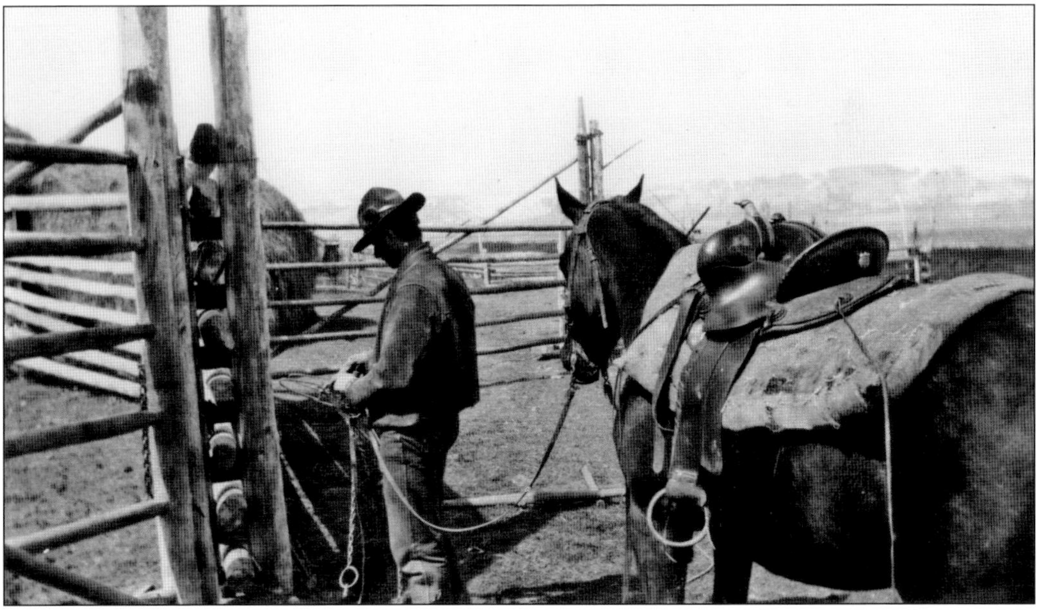

Jim Wardell stands at the ranch corral gate in the late 1910s. His saddle was a Hamley, a saddle maker in Pendleton, Oregon, well known and respected throughout the West. Note that the stirrup on the saddle is only a metal ring, which was called a bull ring. (Courtesy of Sprout and Jane Wardell.)

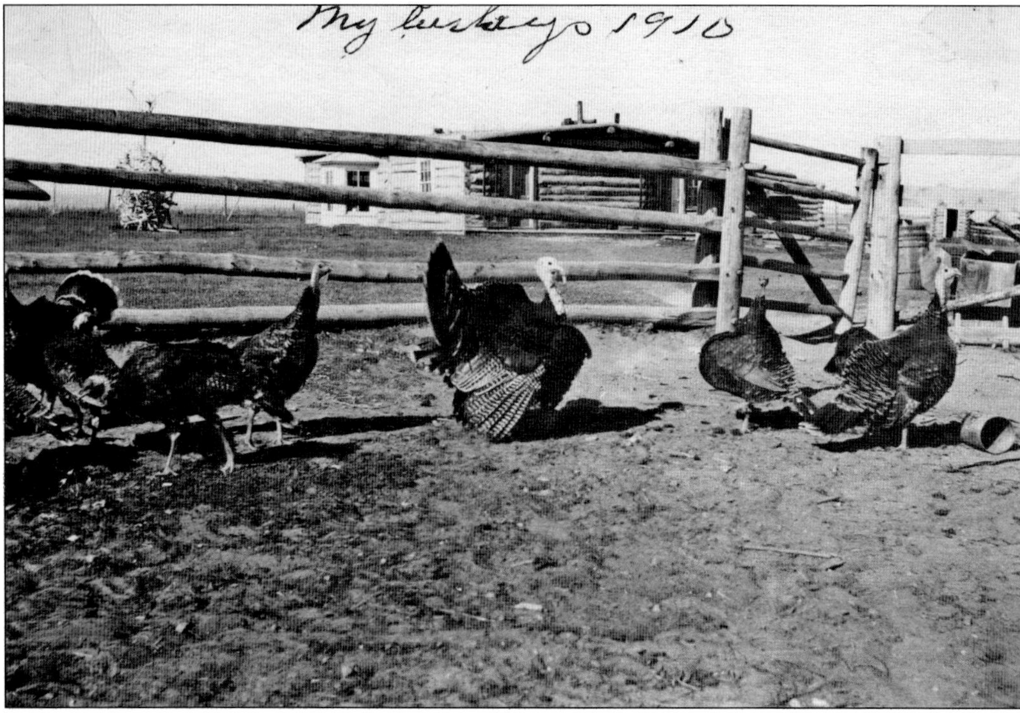

Local ranchers mostly raised beef cattle for their cash crop, but for home consumption they typically raised poultry. Turkeys are seen here at the Budd ranch in 1910. Chickens were also commonly raised on the ranches for eggs and meat. Turkeys and chickens were often eaten in the summer, when a beef cow, with its large quantity of meat, would have spoiled in the era prior to refrigeration. (Courtesy of Nancy Budd Espenscheid.)

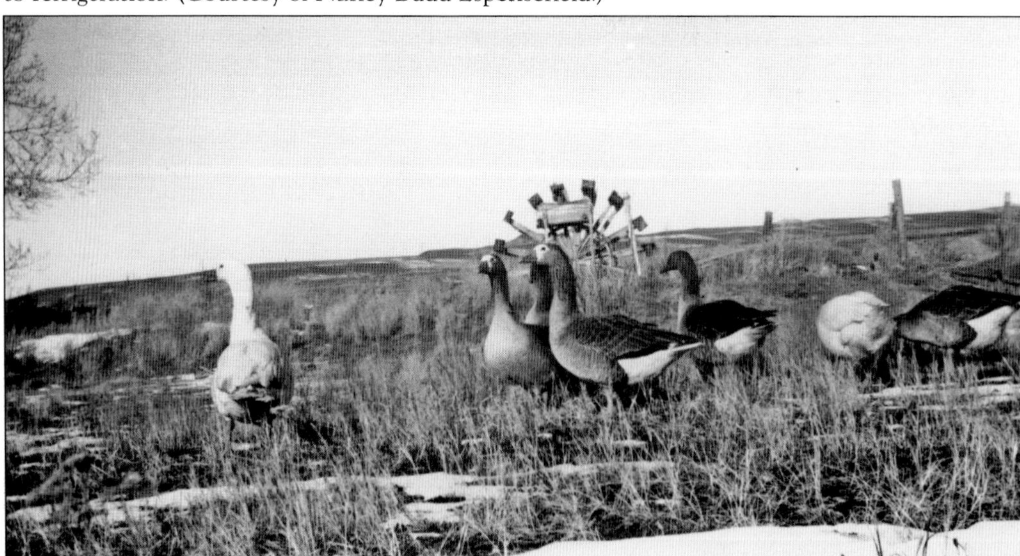

Domestic geese are seen here in the late 1940s on the Sommers Ranch. They were raised here, though wild geese were known to have stayed in the yard. Eggs from the geese were gathered and used by the family, as well as consuming the geese for some dinners. In the background is a water wheel used to water the garden. (Courtesy of Sommers family.)

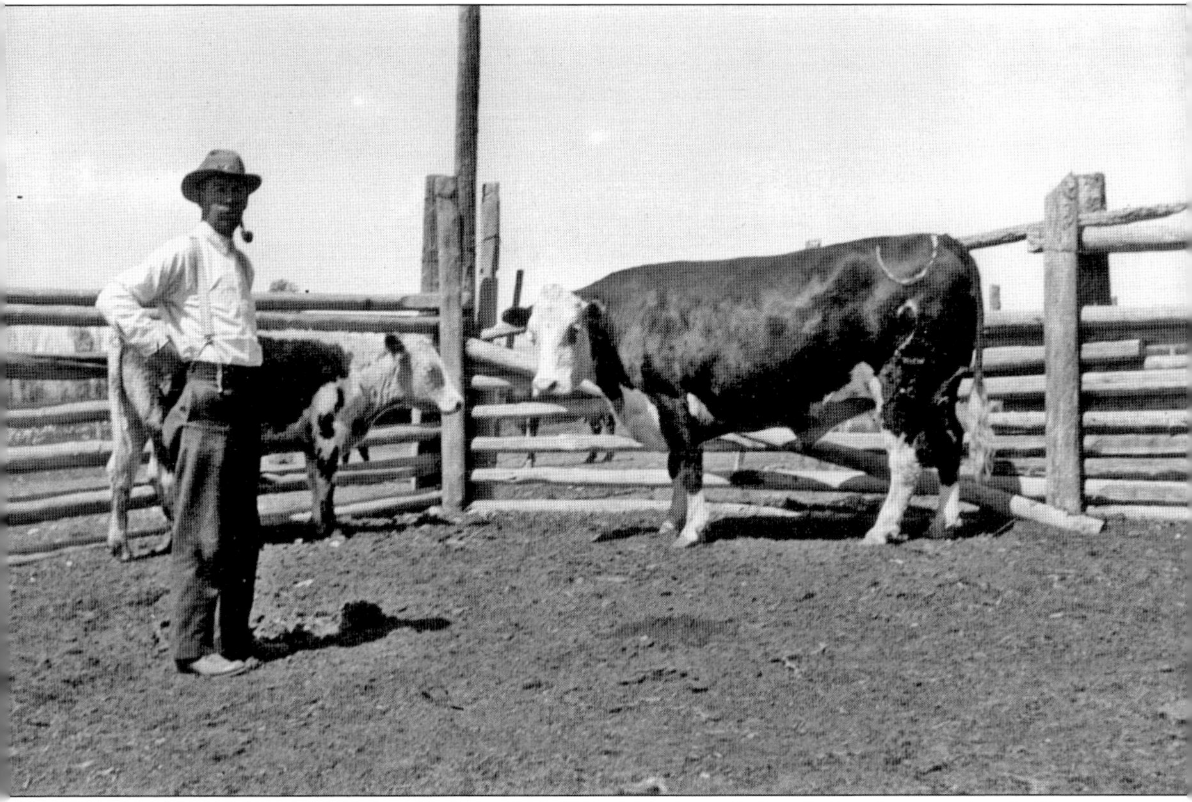

Henry Budd stands with his Hereford cattle. The steer is branded with his Quarter Circle Two brand in the left hip. The Budds would become well known for their Hereford cattle. Their annual bull sales drew customers to Big Piney for decades. (Photograph by Pearl Budd Spencer; courtesy of Green River Valley Museum.)

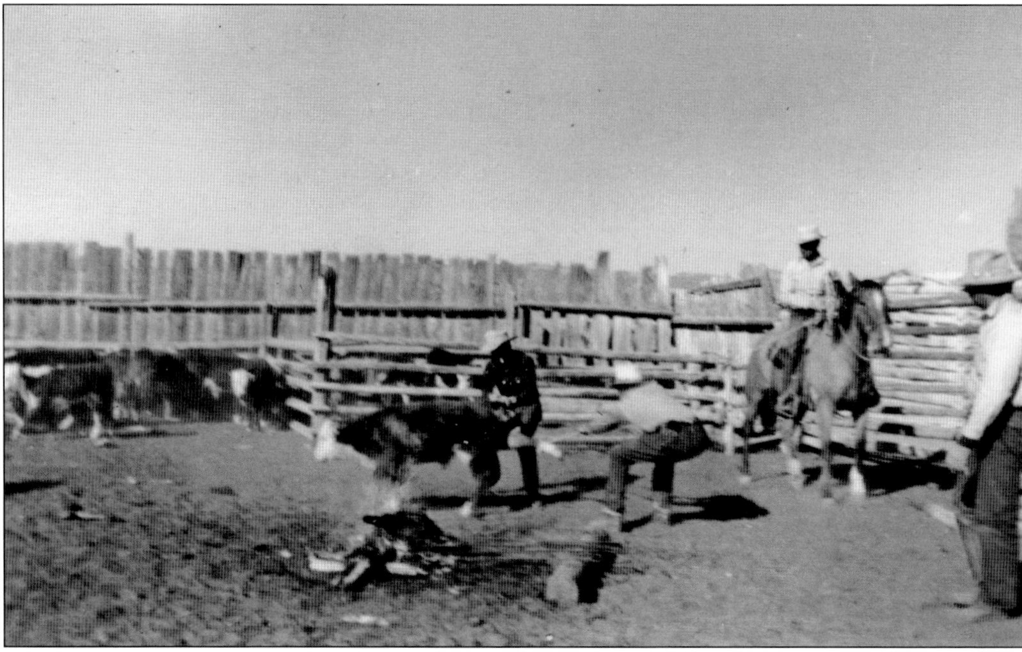

Cowboys are trying to bring a calf down for branding in the 1952 photograph at the Sommers Ranch. Most of the branding took place in the spring, when the calves were smaller. But those missed would be branded in the fall. This was usually more work because the calves were bigger and harder to hold, such as the one pictured here. Note the branding fire heating the irons. (Courtesy of Sommers family.)

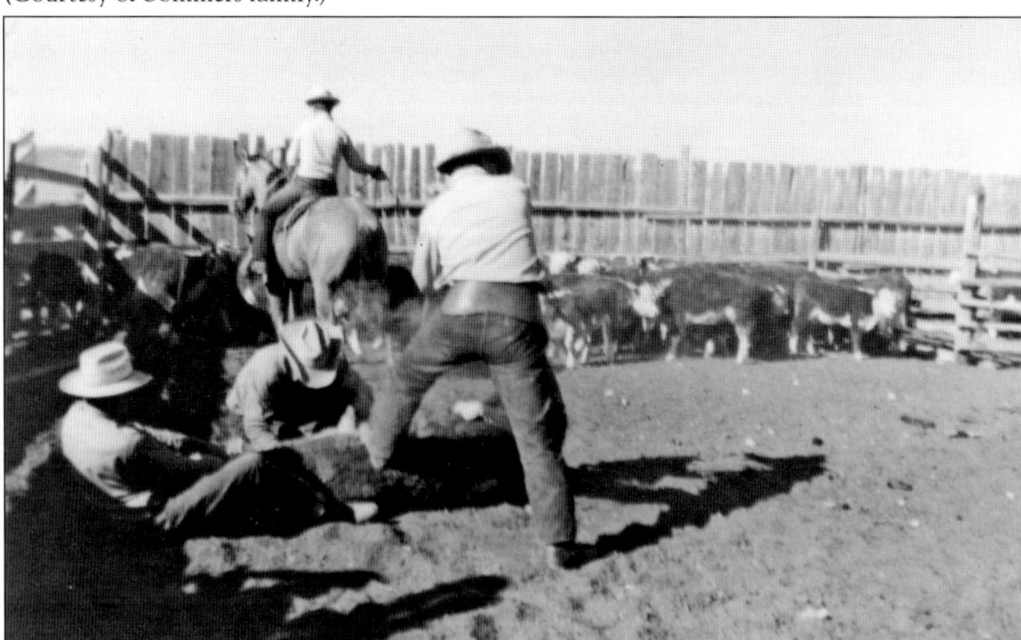

Louis Wardell is roping while Ed Murphy and Hugh Huff wrestle the calf and Bud Sommers castrates it. This is during the fall 1953 branding of Price's cattle in the Sommers Ranch corral. Branding is strenuous work, requiring strength and skill by the ranchers. (Courtesy of Sommers family.)

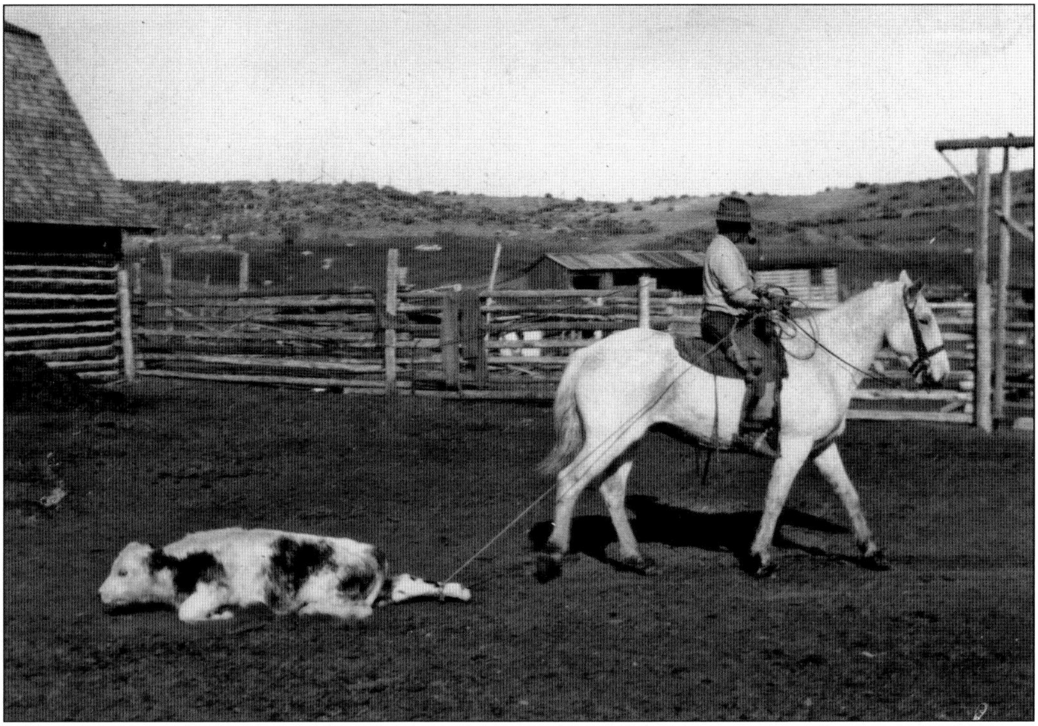

Henry Budd has roped a calf and is dragging it to the wrestlers for branding. The work does not inhibit his pipe smoking. (Courtesy of Bill and Carrie Budd.)

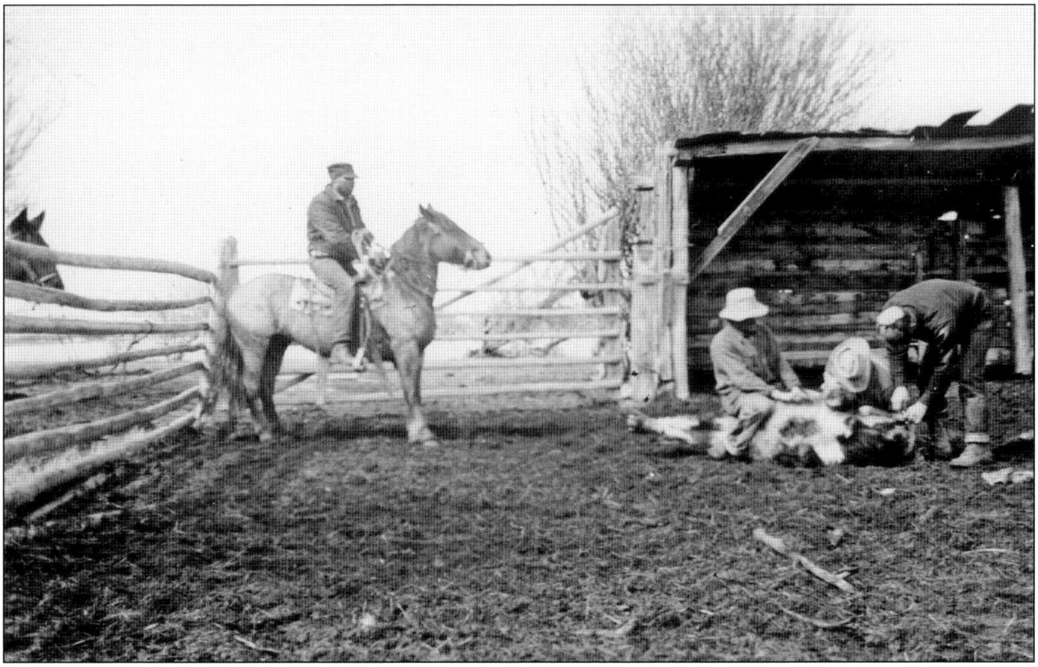

Doug Price is on horseback roping the calves for branding, ear marking, and castrating in the late 1940s at the Sommers Ranch. These jobs are being performed by, from left to right, an unidentified cowboy, Eddie Murphy, and Bud Sommers. (Courtesy of Sommers family.)

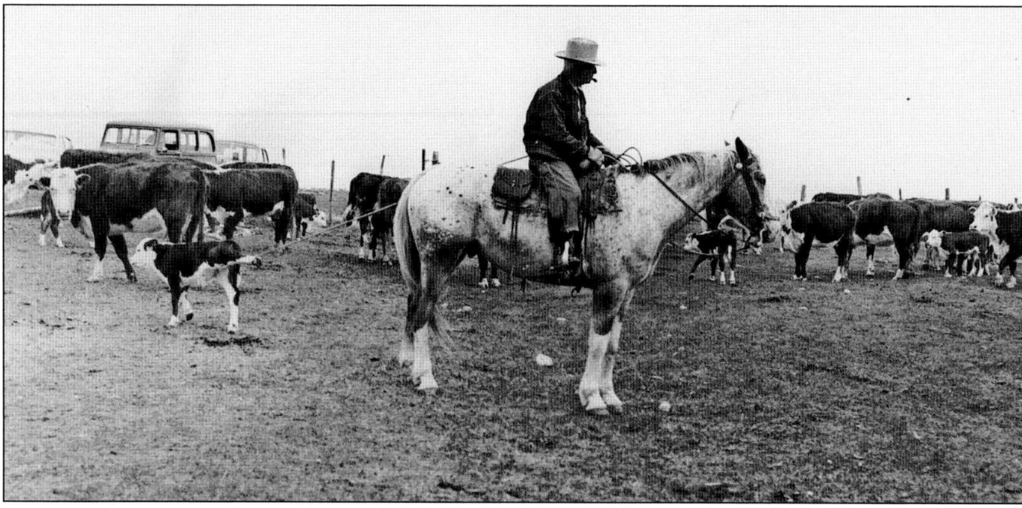

John C. Budd smokes his pipe and sits on his horse Frosty while roping and catching calves for branding about 1950. Branding calves has always been an important ranch chore. Cattle ownership was solely determined by the animal's brand, particularly important when they roamed on the open range. (Courtesy of Nancy Budd Espenscheid.)

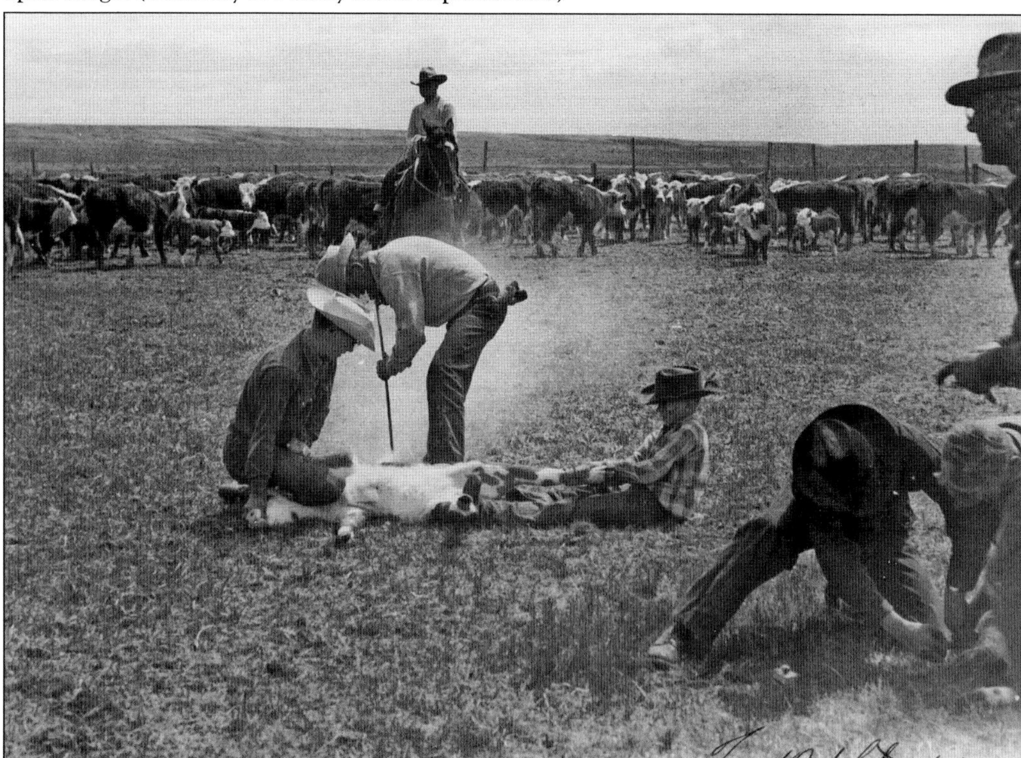

Branding calves in the Big Piney and Marbleton area in 1950 included wrestlers John Tanner, left, and Dick Nelson, brander Bill Budd, and roper Jack Centers. The men on the right are castrating and dehorning the calf. Branding has always been hard, dirty work, requiring much strength and skill by the ranchers and cowboys. It was also an important gathering and social time for families and neighbors. (Courtesy of Nancy Budd Espenscheid.)

Five

Harvest Time

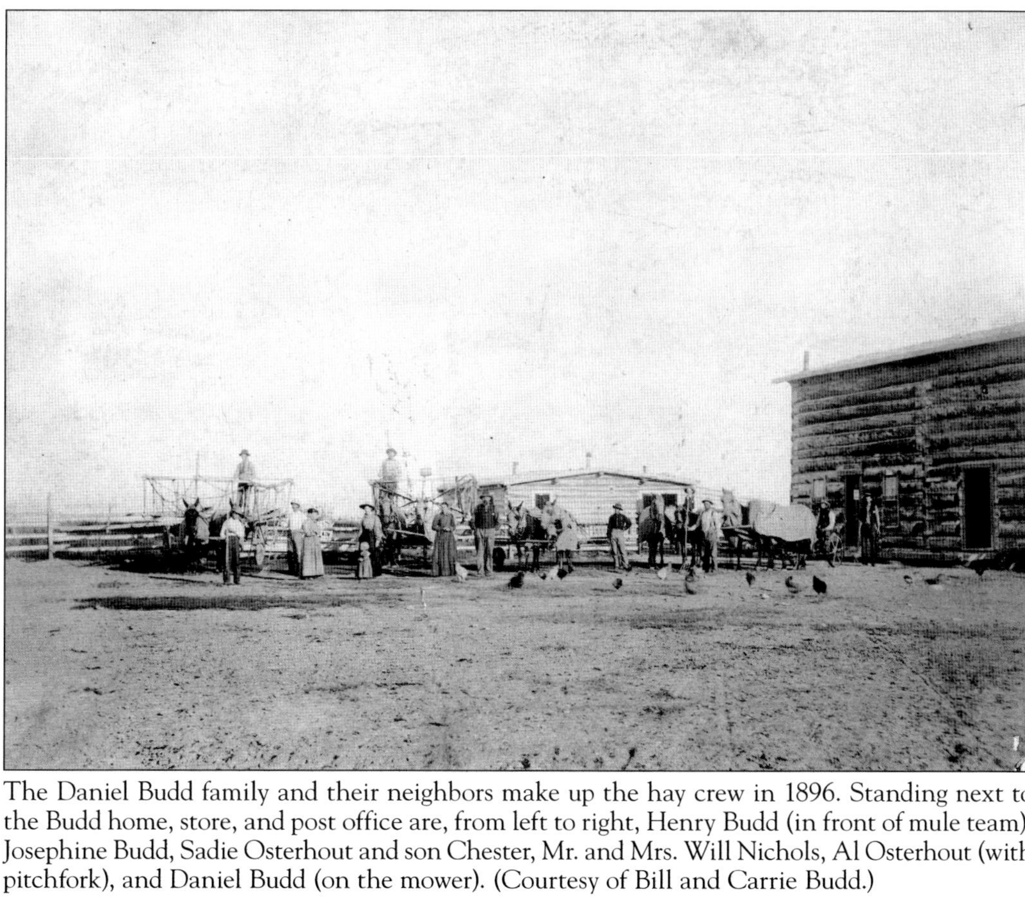

The Daniel Budd family and their neighbors make up the hay crew in 1896. Standing next to the Budd home, store, and post office are, from left to right, Henry Budd (in front of mule team), Josephine Budd, Sadie Osterhout and son Chester, Mr. and Mrs. Will Nichols, Al Osterhout (with pitchfork), and Daniel Budd (on the mower). (Courtesy of Bill and Carrie Budd.)

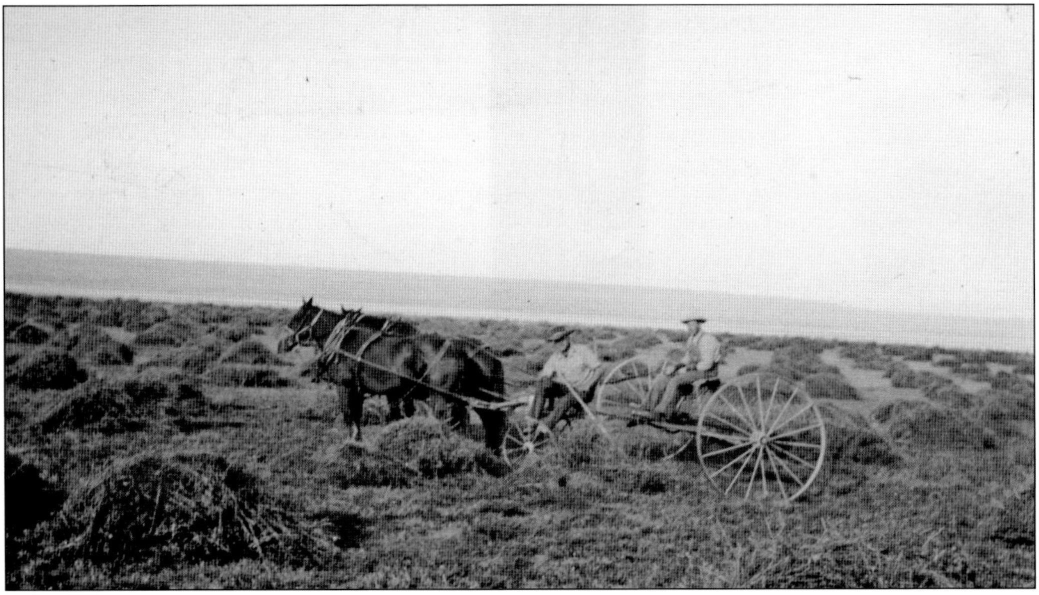

Two men sit on a dump rake in an alfalfa field on the Budd ranch in 1913. After the hay was mowed and dried, it was raked into windrows. Wagons followed these rows up and down. Boys walked beside the wagons and pitched forks full of hay into the nets spread in the wagons. The loads were then taken to where the hay would be stacked. (Courtesy of Nancy Budd Espenscheid.)

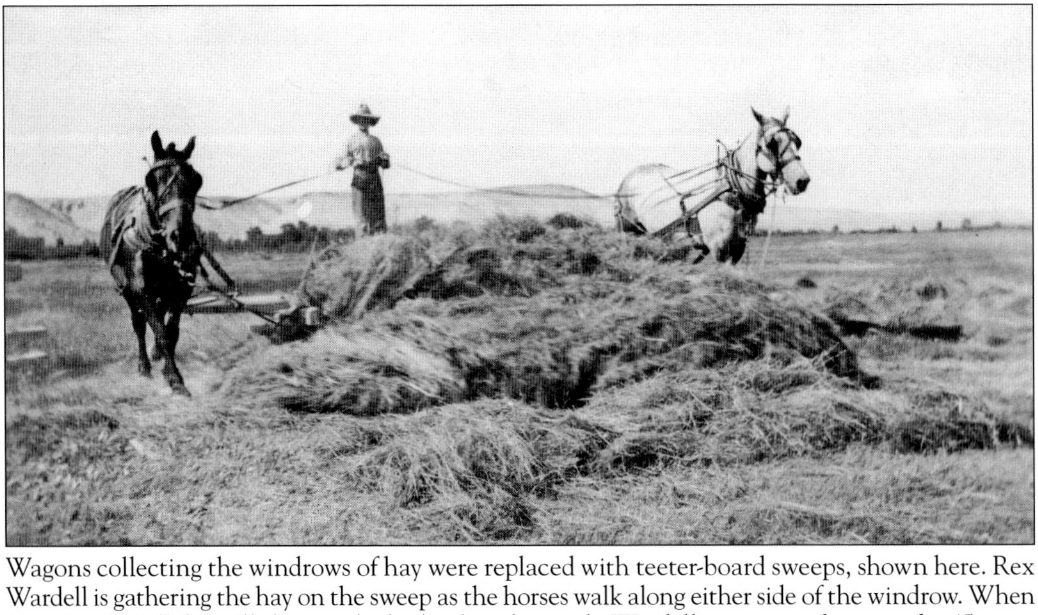

Wagons collecting the windrows of hay were replaced with teeter-board sweeps, shown here. Rex Wardell is gathering the hay on the sweep as the horses walk along either side of the windrow. When his sweep is full, he will then push the load to the stack. Wardell was range foreman for 45 years with the Upper Green River Cattlemen's Association. (Courtesy of Sprout and Jane Wardell.)

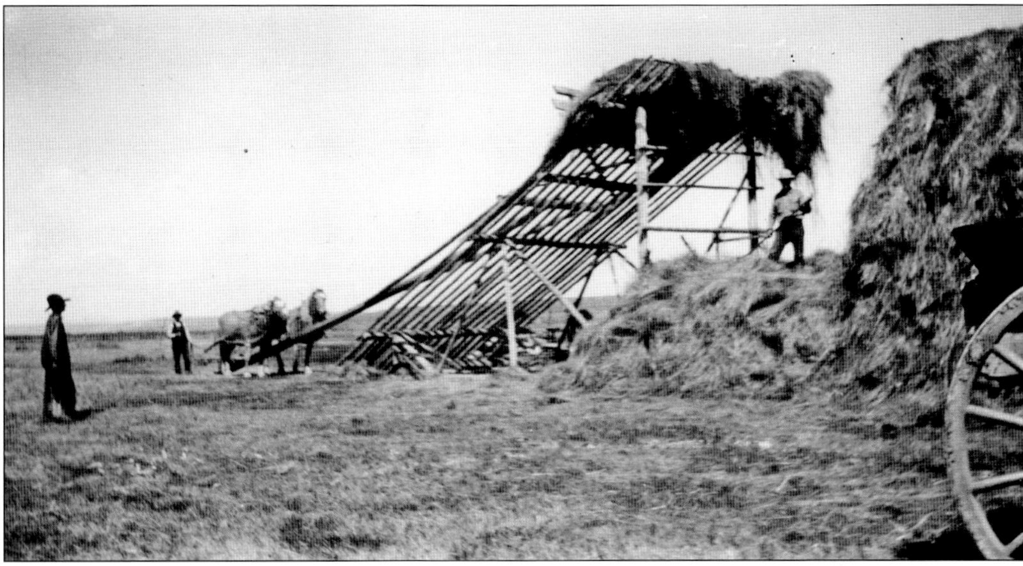

One way the hay was stacked was by using a beaver slide stacker. The loose hay was placed at the bottom of the slide then pushed up with a long pole. Several secure boards and two rollers were attached to the end and often called a plunger. The haystack was built with continuous loads, followed by hands "topping out" or leveling the hay to build a sturdy, large pile. (Courtesy of Nancy Budd Espenscheid.)

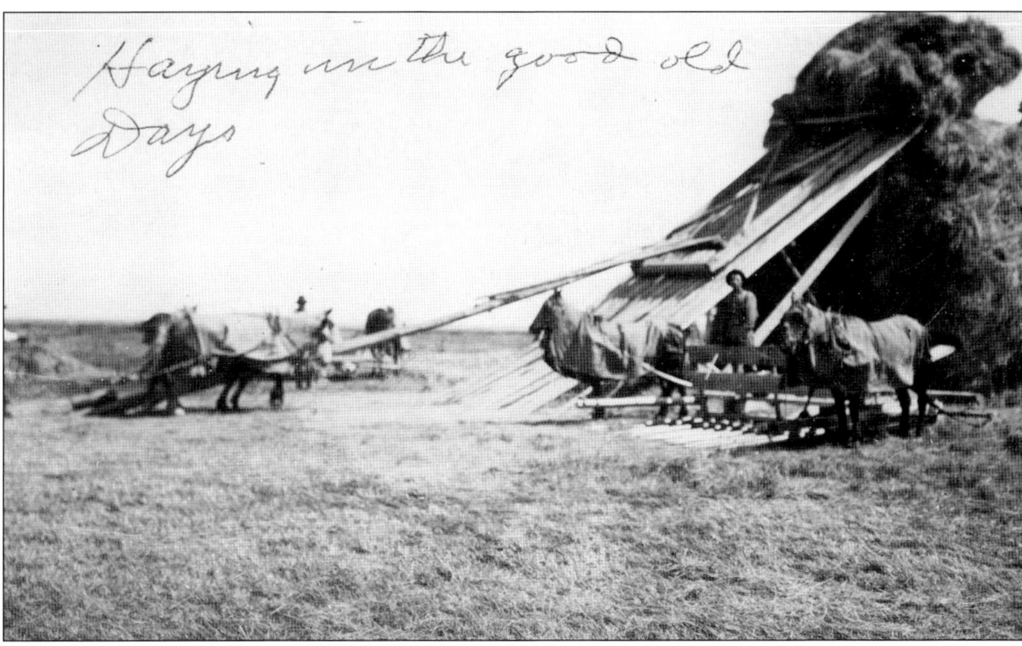

Each animal working in the hay field had a net made of a burlap sack over its head and neck. The body was covered with a large burlap wool sack, even though the sacks were designed to be used to store wool. This was to give some protection from horse flies and other biting insects. (Courtesy of Nancy Budd Espenscheid.)

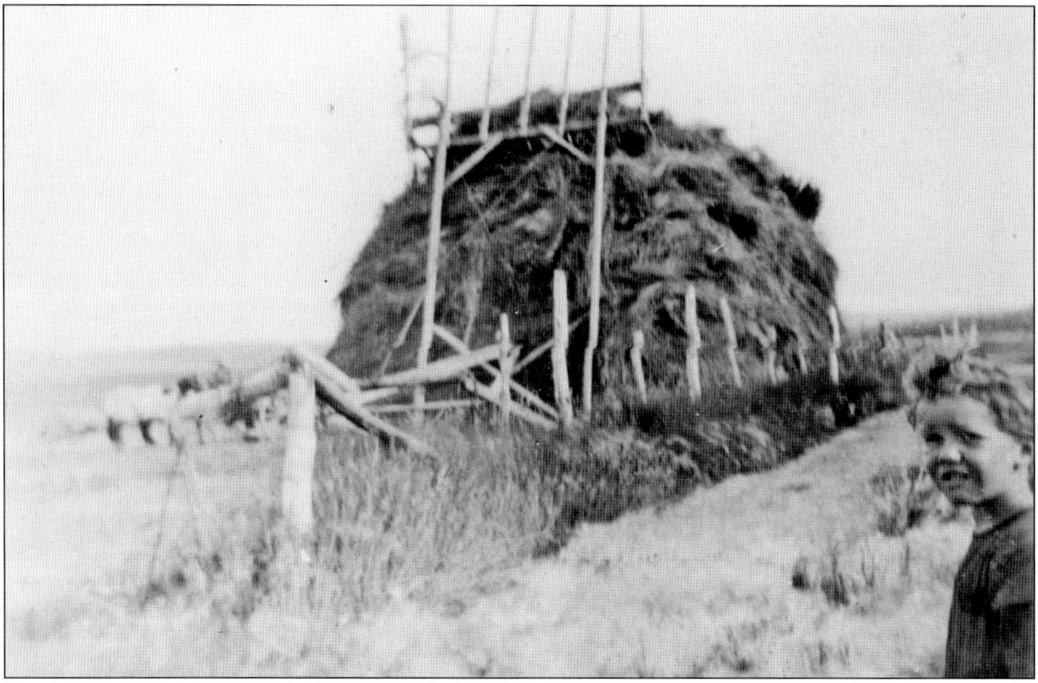

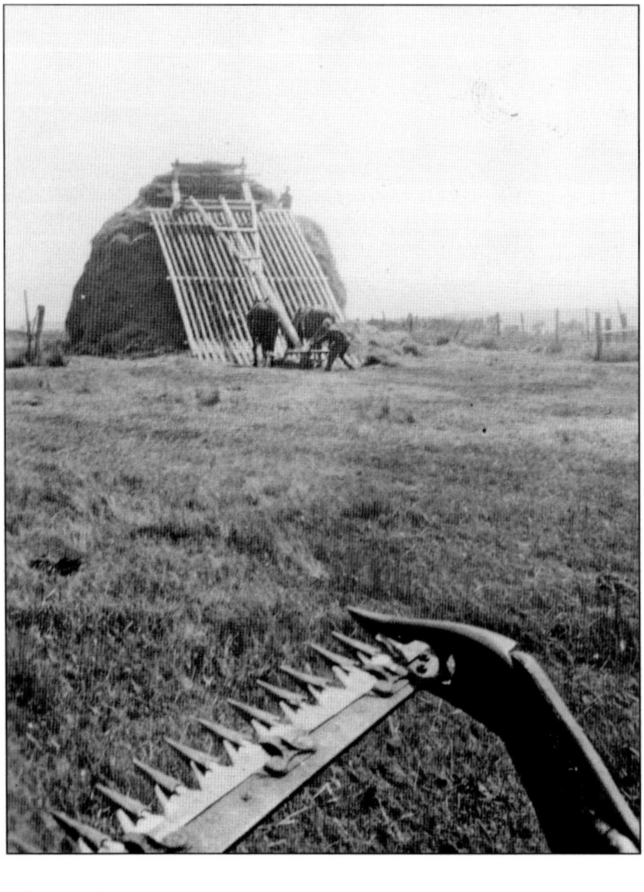

One early method of getting hay onto the stack was by the use of the overshot stacker. Hay was placed on the forklift and pulled up the slide by a team and cable. Looking into the camera from the bottom right of the photograph is Bud Sommers in 1920. Only seven years of age, he started haying by driving the plunger team. (Courtesy of Sommers family.)

The plunger has pushed another load of hay up the beaver slide stacker and on top of the hay stack at the Sommers Ranch in the late 1930s. In the front of the photograph is the mower cutter bar. In the dry, high altitude climate, hay usually could be stacked only a day after being cut. The cut grass has to cure, or dry, before being stacked to avoid getting moldy. (Courtesy Sommers family.)

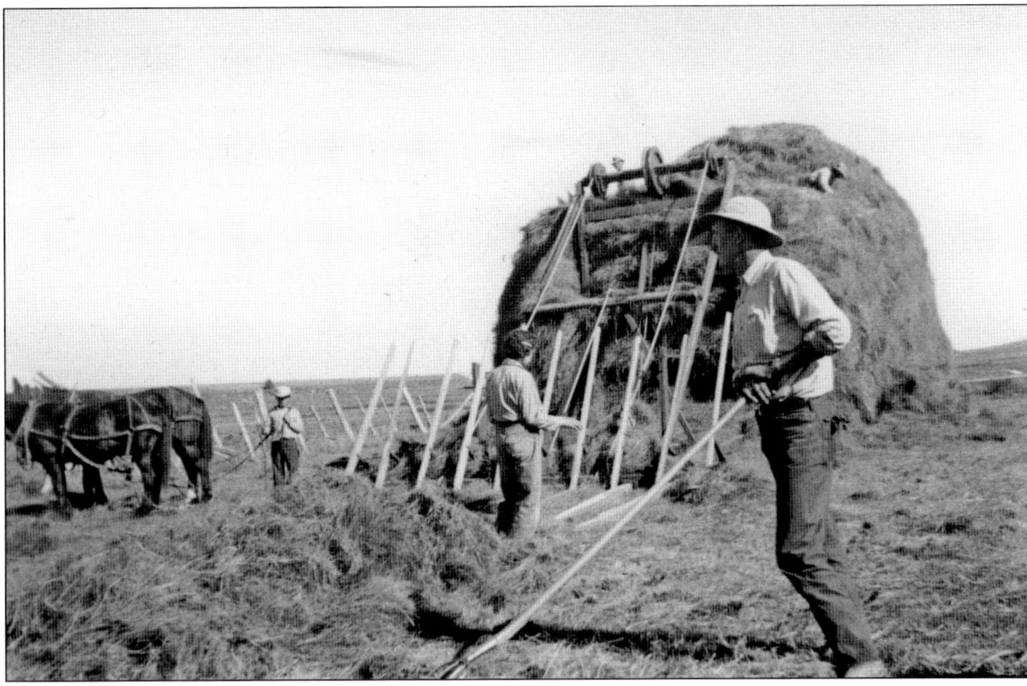

The Circle Ranch used an overshot stacker for its haying. Jim Mickelson Jr. stands with his pitchfork. Despite the raking, sweeping, and stacking equipment, a pitchfork was still used throughout the stacking process. (Courtesy of Mike and Tara Miller.)

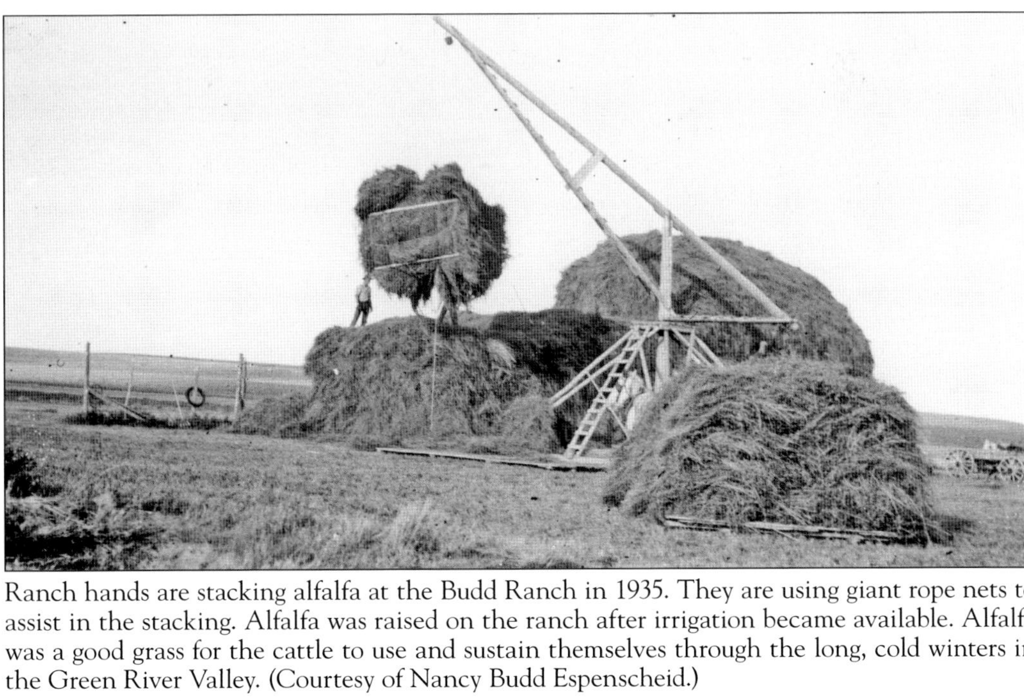

Ranch hands are stacking alfalfa at the Budd Ranch in 1935. They are using giant rope nets to assist in the stacking. Alfalfa was raised on the ranch after irrigation became available. Alfalfa was a good grass for the cattle to use and sustain themselves through the long, cold winters in the Green River Valley. (Courtesy of Nancy Budd Espenscheid.)

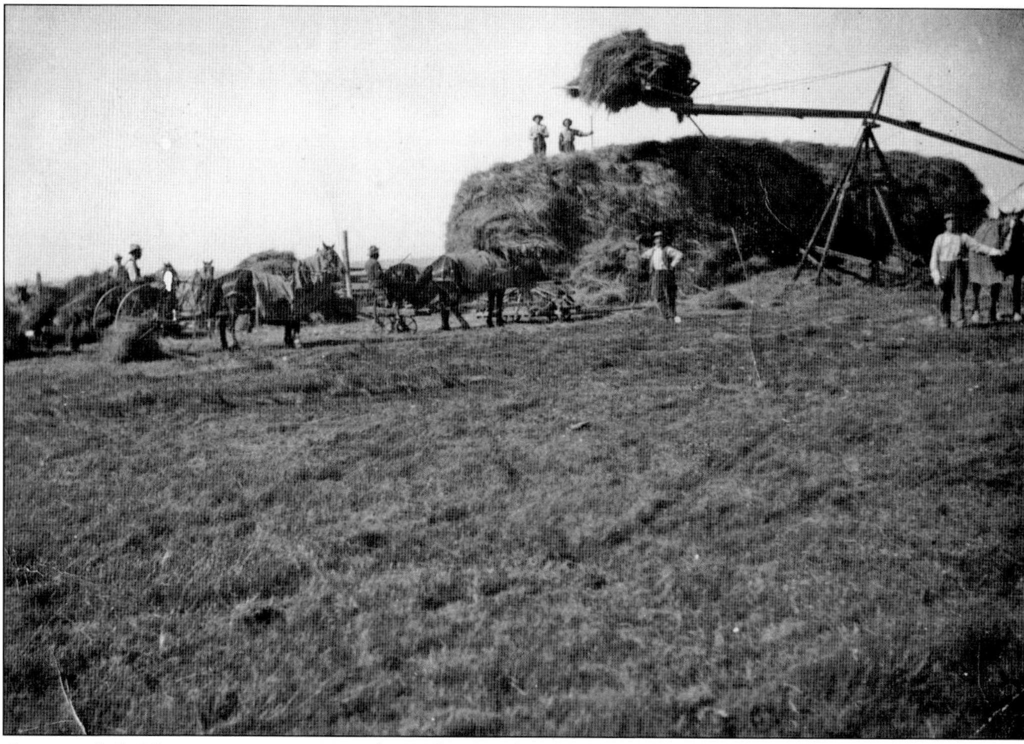

A giant fork-like instrument is used on the Circle Ranch in the early 1900s, when it was owned by Jim Mickelson. In addition to the stacking crew, other haying hands are pictured, such as the rakers and sweepers. (Courtesy of Mike and Tara Miller.)

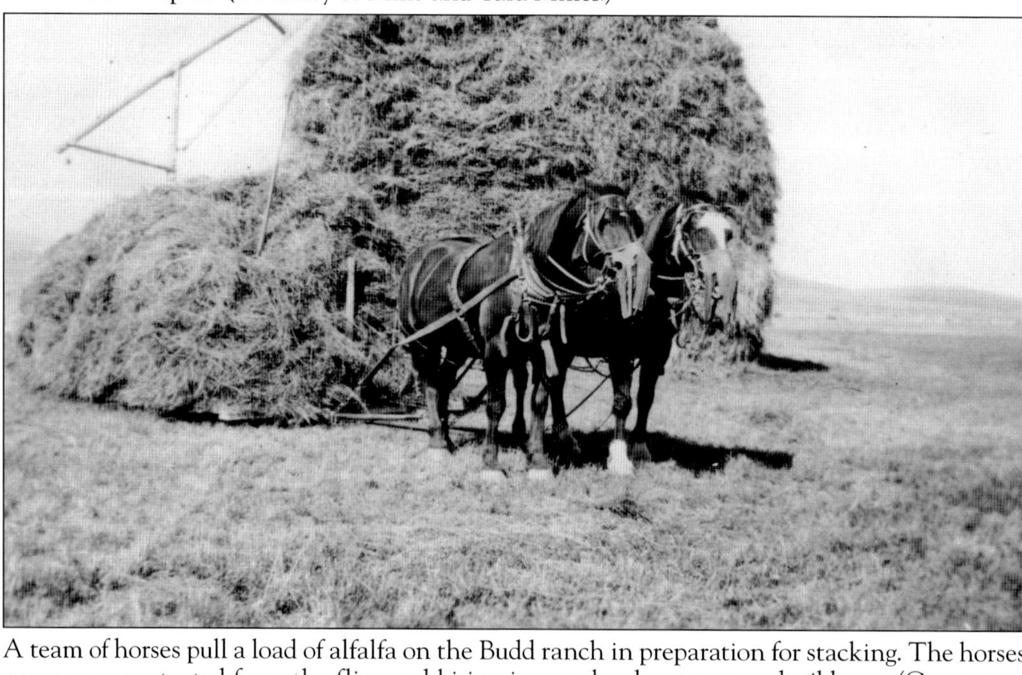

A team of horses pull a load of alfalfa on the Budd ranch in preparation for stacking. The horses' noses were protected from the flies and biting insects by the gunny sack ribbons. (Courtesy of Nancy Budd Espenscheid.)

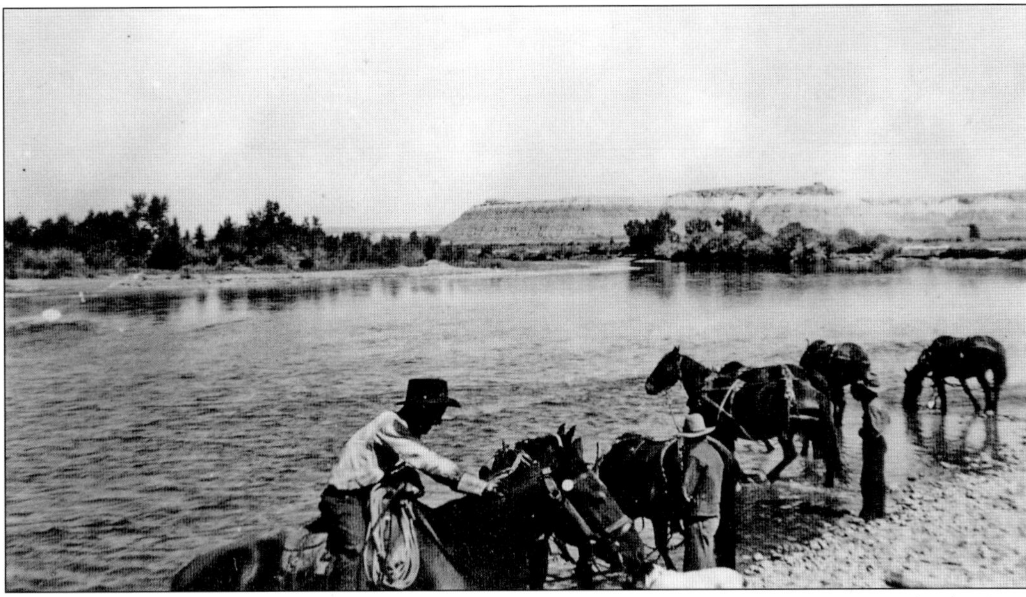

Herb Booth, on horseback, brings the haying teams down to the Green River for a drink after a long day in the hay fields. A rancher needed several horses in order to get his hay crop up every year. (Courtesy of Jay and Sandy McGinnis.)

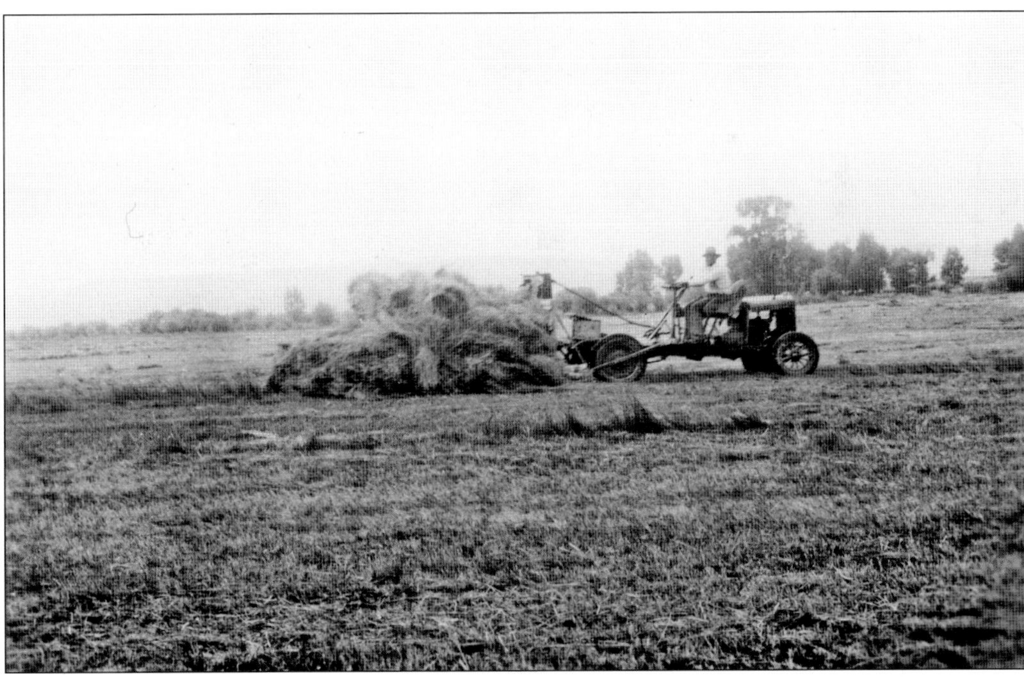

Starting in the 1940s, some Green River Valley ranchers transitioned from horsepower to trucks and tractors to get their hay crops in. In 1943, on the Sommers Ranch, Charlie McAlister is driving a truck that has been modified to drive backwards, making it work well as a hay sweep. It was common for ranchers to modify their equipment in this manner. (Courtesy of Sommers family.)

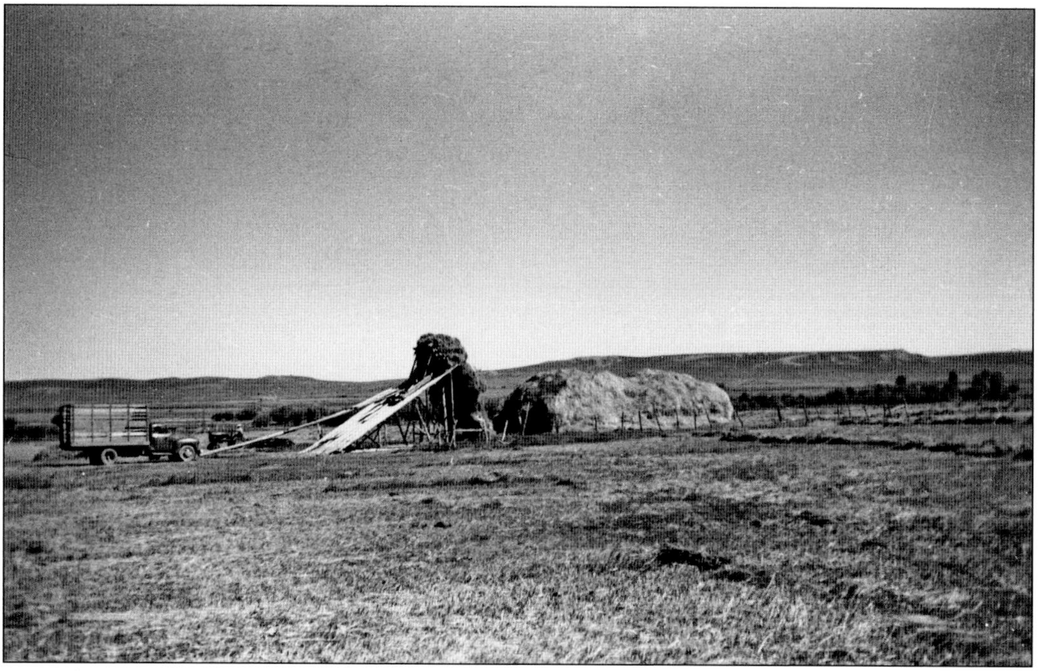

A stock truck is being used as the "plunger truck" on the Sommers Ranch in 1952. The truck has replaced the team of horses that previously moved the hay up the beaver slide. (Courtesy of Sommers family.)

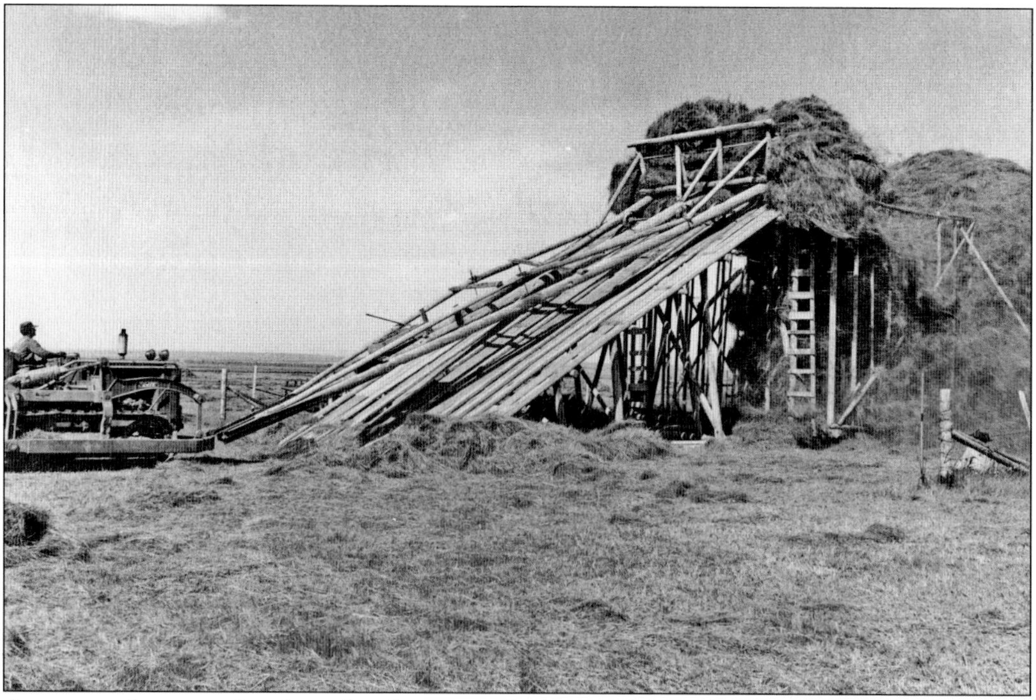

A tractor is being used to drive the plunger up the beaver slide at the Circle Ranch in the 1940s. Attached to the slide are swinging wings to assist the stackers building the stack by holding up the sides. (Courtesy of Mike and Tara Miller.)

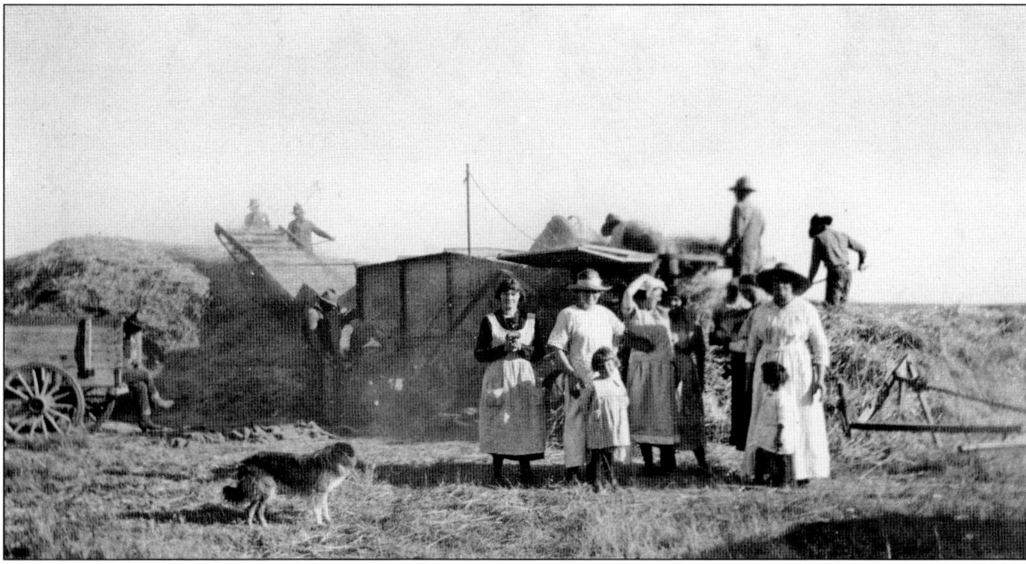

Members of the Wardell family stand in front of a thresher at their ranch on the Green River in the early 1920s. At far left is Belle and next to her is Jane Wardell. The threshing machine is making grain for the ranch animals. (Courtesy of Sprout and Jane Wardell.)

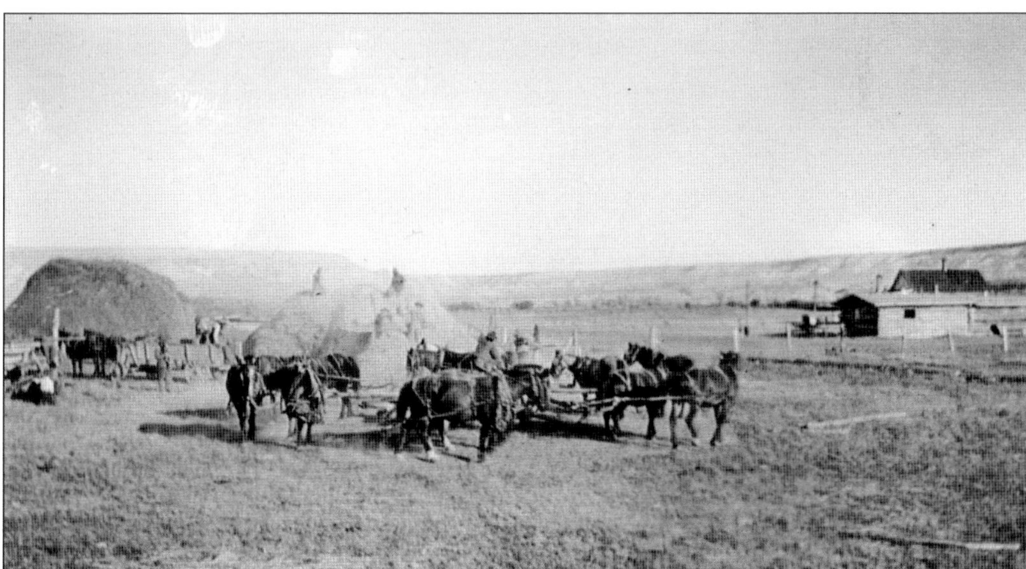

The horses are the power for the thresher at the Murdock Ranch on the Green River in 1920. They are making grain for the livestock and other animals raised on the ranch. (Courtesy of Sprout and Jane Wardell.)

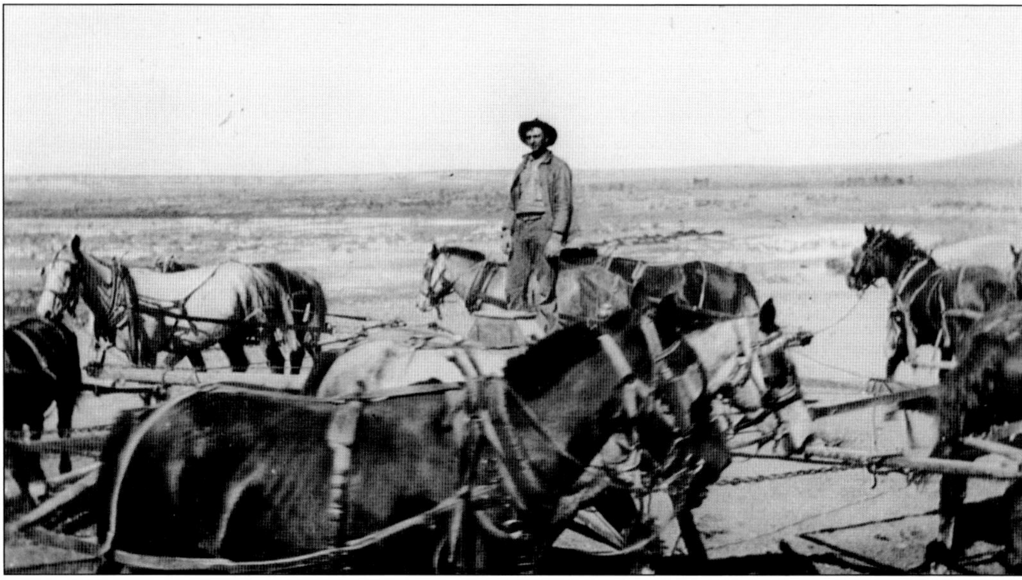

Rone Wardell stands on the thresher powered by the 12 horses attached to it. The grain produced will be an important food supplement for the ranch animals. Rone would later be hit in the head by the hoof of a horse, killing him and leaving a widow and orphans. Ranchers were skilled with their horses, but accidents with the animals were not uncommon. (Courtesy of Sprout and Jane Wardell.)

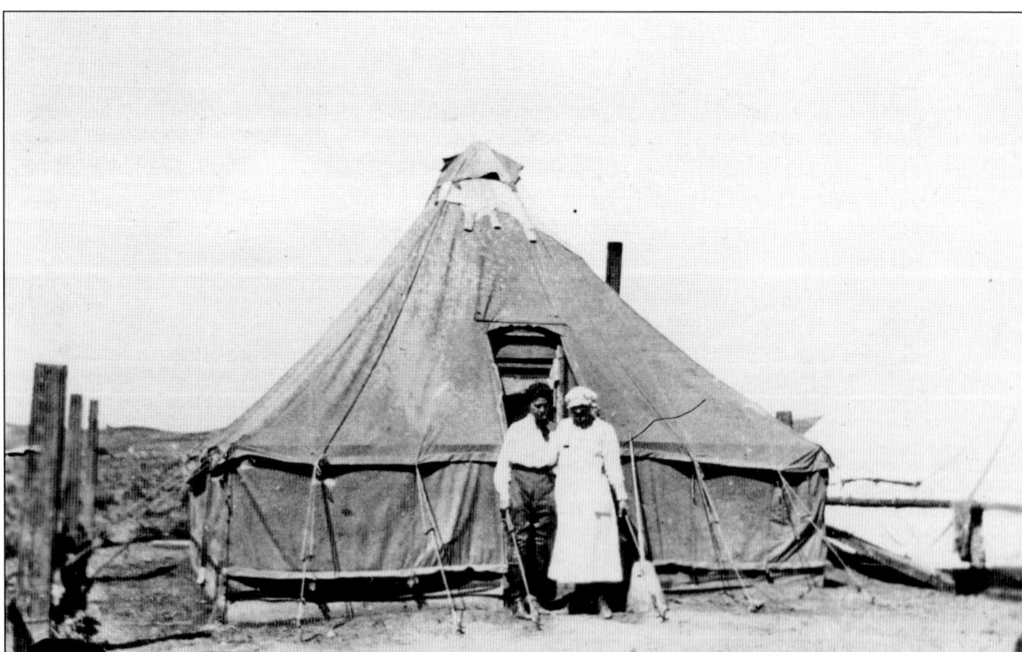

Lil Luster (in the white dress), a relation to May Sommers, stands in front of the cook tent for the workers on the Green River Supply Canal. It was erected through the Sommers Ranch along the Green River. This was part of the Uinta County Irrigation Company's plan to bring water to the desert lands north of Big Piney, which never materialized. (Courtesy of Sommers family.)

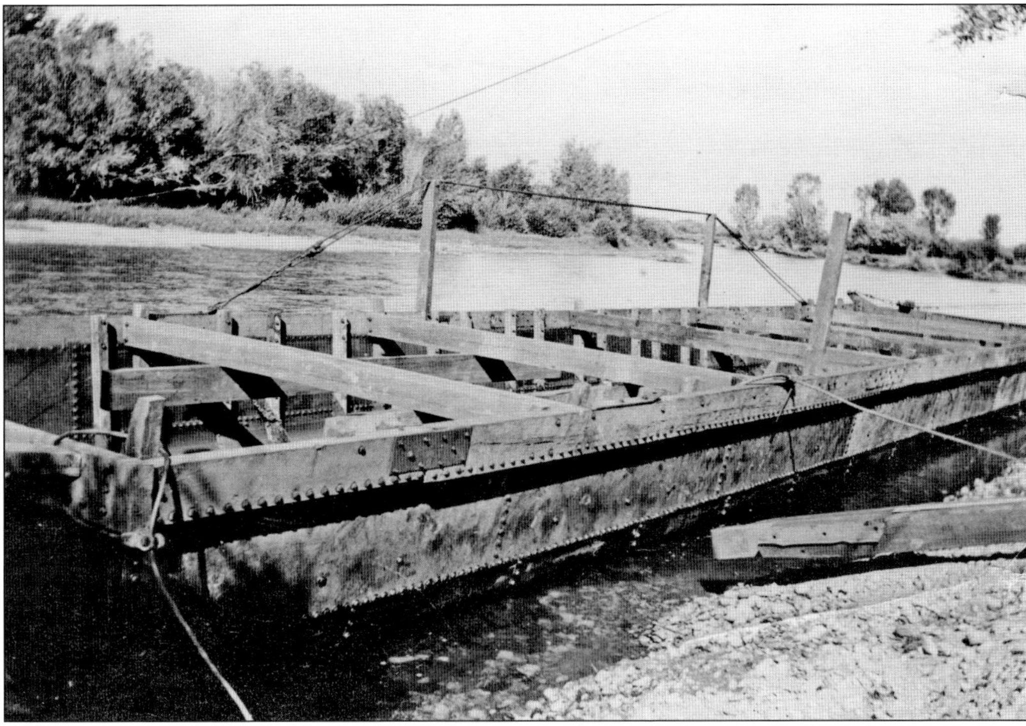

The Carey Land Act of 1894 allowed private companies to build irrigation systems in the western semiarid states and profit from the sales of water. Hoping to take advantage of this new law, the Uinta County Irrigation Company devised a plan to dig a canal system in Sublette County that would bring water to some of the desert lands. The dredge boat pictured here is digging the Green River Supply Canal with hopes that it, and the North Piney Canal, would bring settlers to the Big Piney and Marbleton area. Unfortunately, the project was not immediately successful, as the company was unable to complete the canal system when it failed to acquire all the rights-of-way through private property. In the 1930s, Jim Mickelson acquired the project and completed the work, supplying several ranches with water in the 1950s and 1960s. (Above, courtesy of the Green River Valley Museum, Pearl Budd Spencer Collection; below, courtesy of Sommers family.)

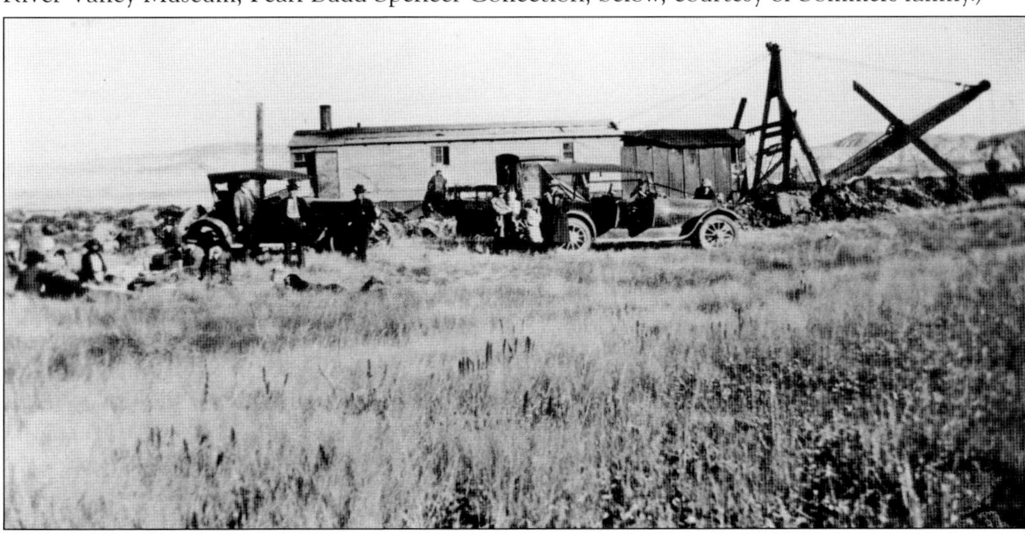

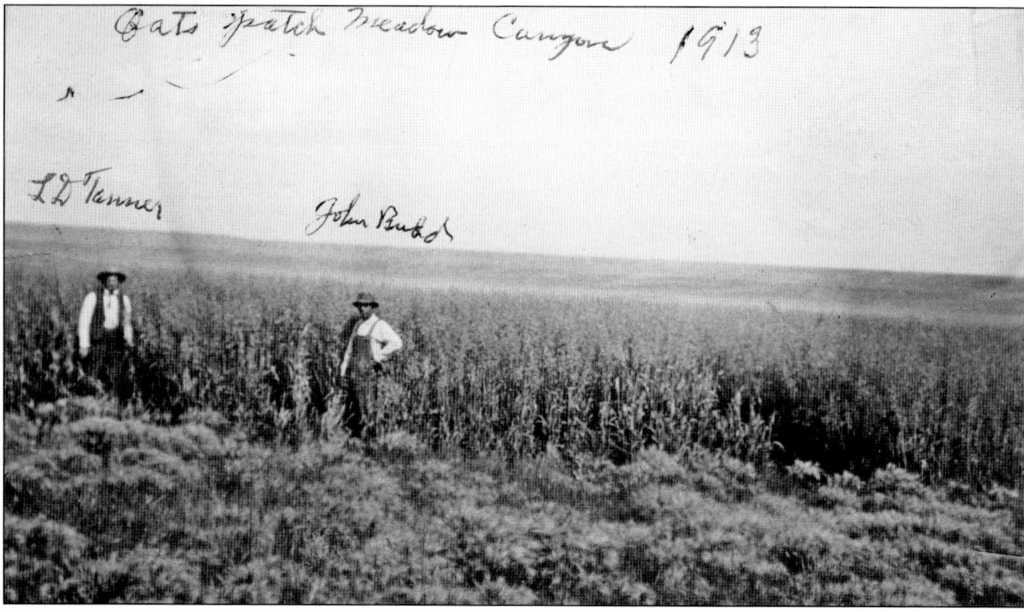

John C. Budd surveyed a large canal west of town. The success of that canal is shown here in 1913, with L.D. Tanner standing to the left of John Budd in the oat field in Meadow Canyon. Other irrigation projects in the area, such as the Green River Supply Canal, were not initially successful and led to financial ruin for some families who had relocated. (Courtesy of Nancy Budd Espenscheid.)

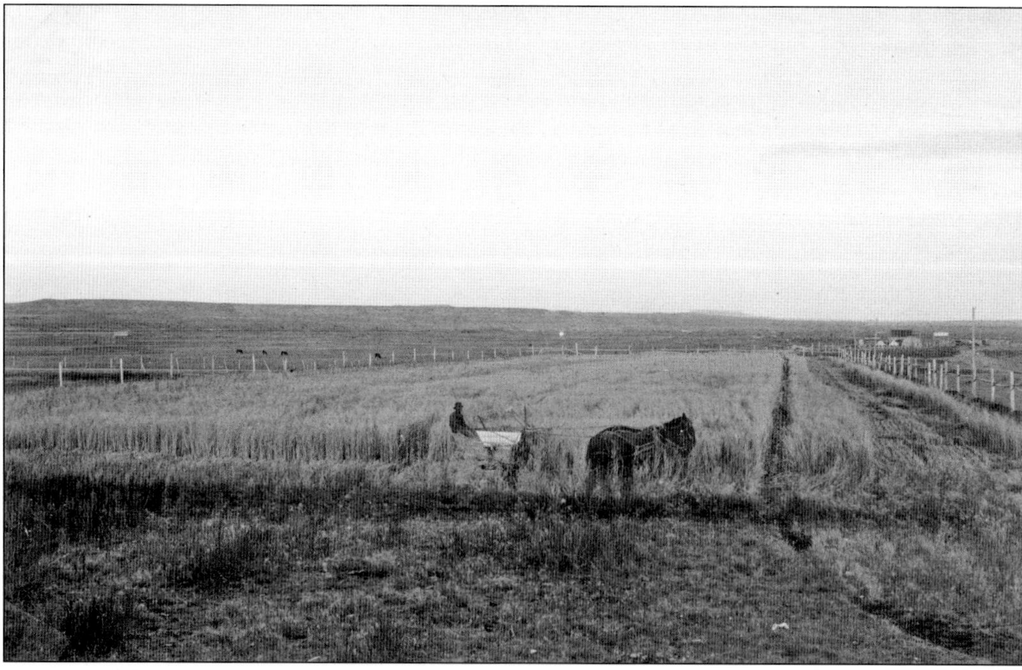
An oat patch is being cut at the Budd ranch in 1905. The oats, which would be important feed for the livestock, would not have been possible without irrigation. On the horizon to the right are the Budd ranch buildings and home. Rangers were as self-sufficient as possible, especially given the great distance (100 miles) to a supply center. (Courtesy of Nancy Budd Espenscheid.)

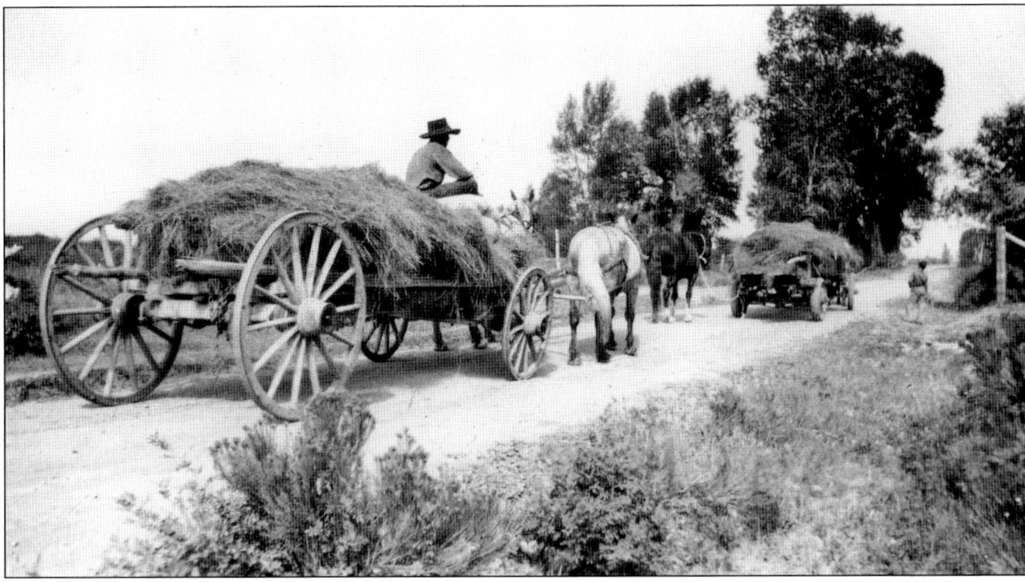

Hugh Carter is driving the back wagon and following Bill Budd Sr. while Bill Budd Jr. stands on the road about 1940. The men are hauling hay to the mountain for horse feed while they are getting their winter wood supply. Gathering a winter's worth of wood from the mountains was an important annual chore that often took a few days. (Photograph by Pearl Budd Spencer; courtesy of Bill and Carrie Budd.)

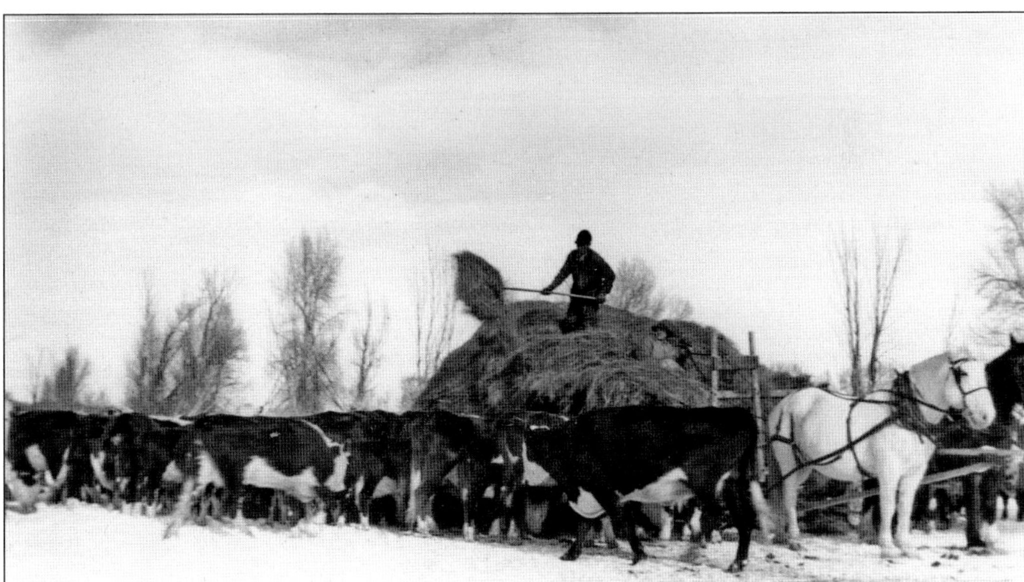

Henry Budd is feeding cattle on his ranch about 1920. The team of horses pulls the feed wagon while Budd makes a feed line with the hay. The team knows where to walk on the feed ground. The rancher then pitches hay off the wagon to the cows all by hand with a pitch fork. Ranchers took pride in their well-trained horses. (Photograph by Pearl Budd Spencer; courtesy of Bill and Carrie Budd.)

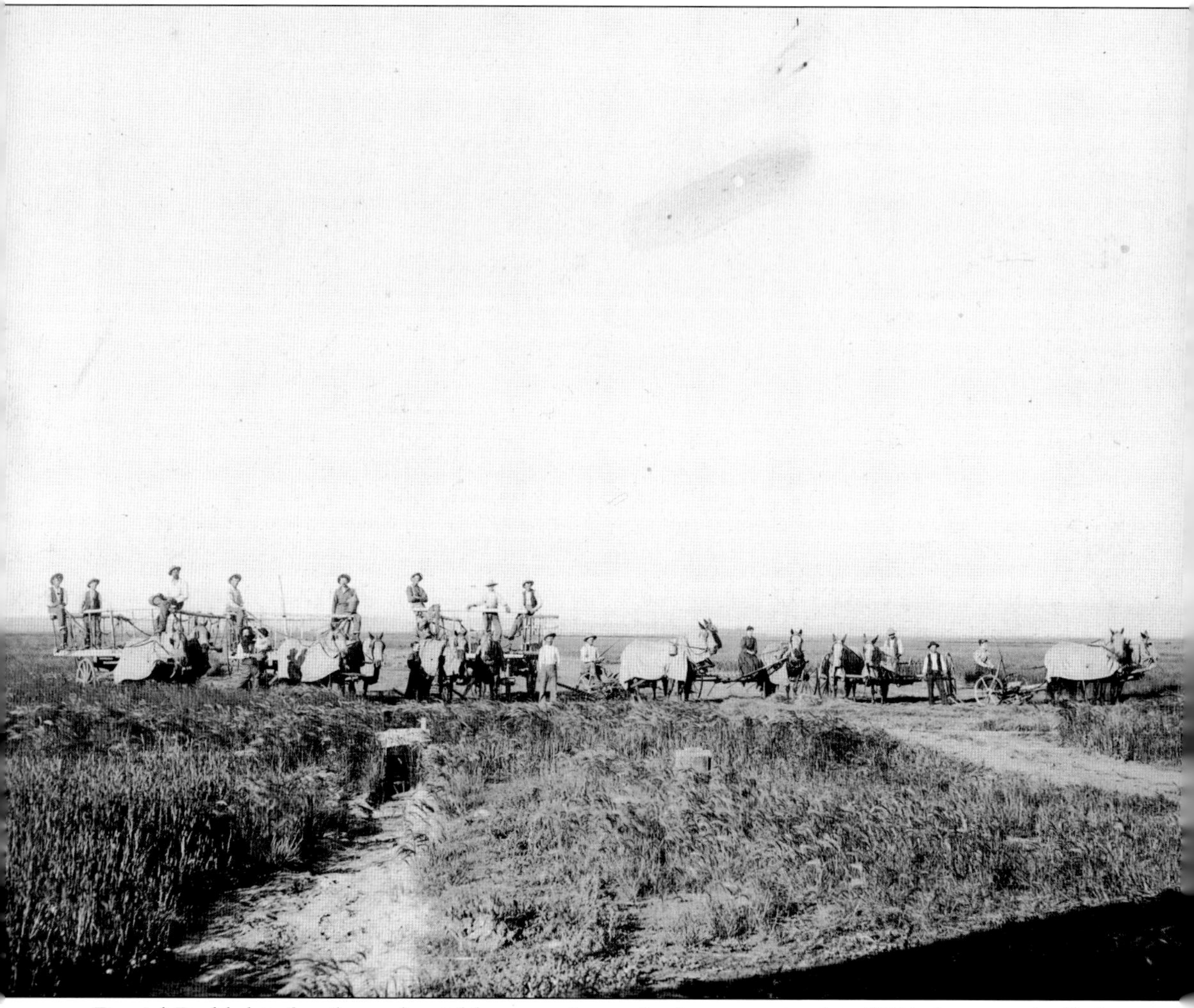

Daniel Budd, his family, and neighbors made up the hay crew in this 1897 photograph. Sadie Budd Osterhout is on the mower, Daniel Budd sits with his grandchild Chester Osterhout, and Josephine is standing by the team. Daniel had cleared sagebrush for hay meadows, developed an irrigation system with the ditch visible at the bottom of the photograph, and had built a home by now. Thanks to a roving photographer, this event has been captured. Neighbors Mr. and Mrs. Wilfred Nichols are on the two hay rakes. Manning three wagons with hay racks are the five Budd boys, son-in-law Al Osterhout, and a ranch hand or two. The earliest hay crews were family-oriented with perhaps two or three neighbors helping out. This was necessary because both manpower and money for wages were scarce. (Courtesy of Bill and Carrie Budd.)

Six

Growing Up in the Country

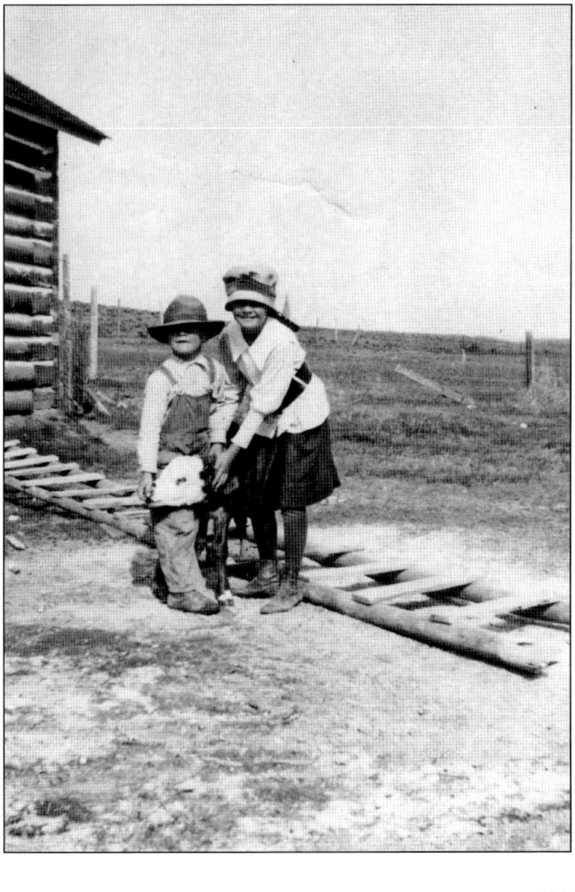

Siblings Joe and Helen Budd pose with their pet calf for this photograph taken around 1916 at the family ranch near Big Piney. The ranch yard lacks foliage and would appear bleak to many, yet the children are happy. Note how stylishly they are dressed, especially Helen, despite living in an isolated area. (Courtesy of Nancy Budd Espenscheid.)

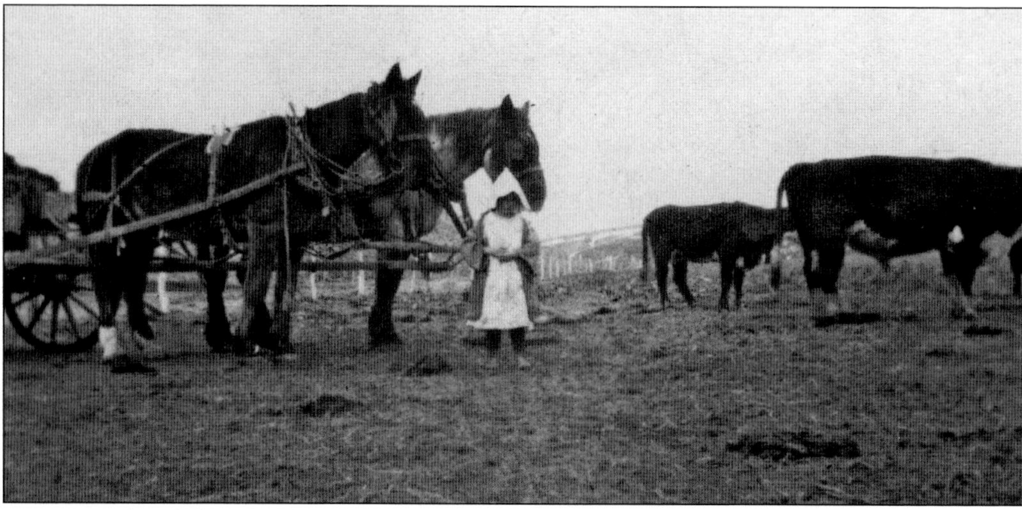

A young girl and the schoolteacher from the Sommers Ranch stands in front of a roan stallion in about 1918. The child appears comfortable standing with the large horses and cattle, suggesting she is with them regularly. (Courtesy of Sommers family.)

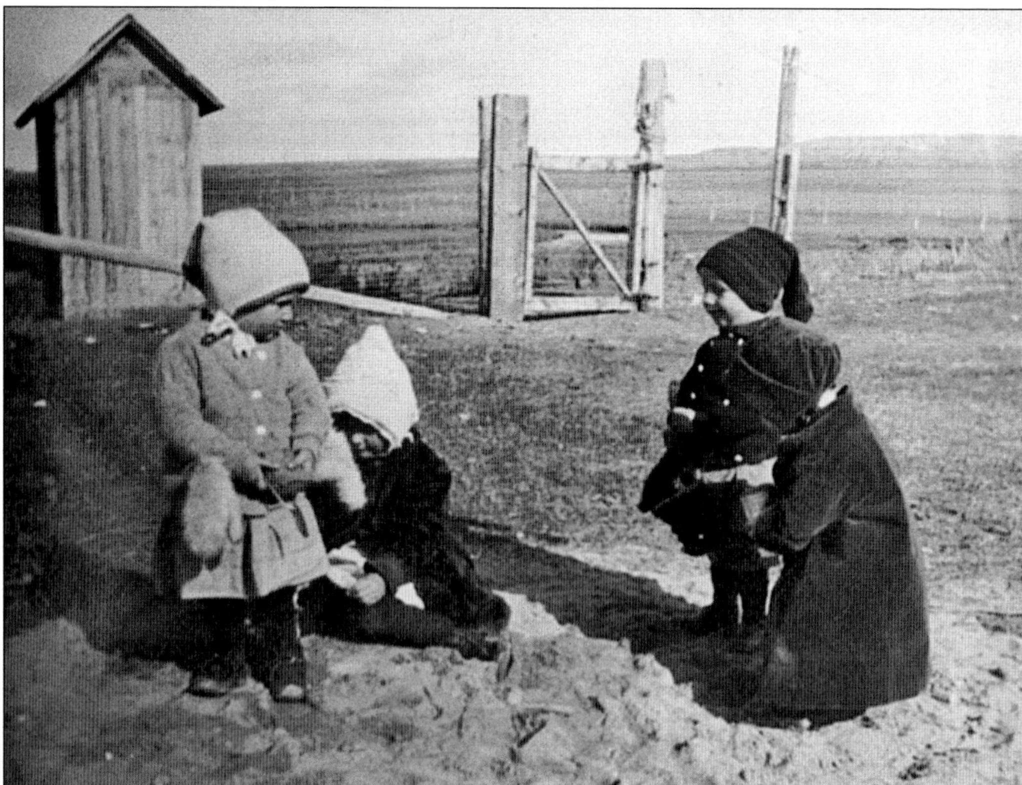

The caption accompanying this photograph in the Budd family album says, "The Ladies Twentieth Century Club, Big Piney, Wyoming," referring to the girls' birth dates in what was then the new century. They are well dressed and bundled up with hats and coats to ward off the cold typical in the high altitude mountain area. The family outhouse can be seen in the top left of the picture. (Courtesy of Nancy Budd Espenscheid.)

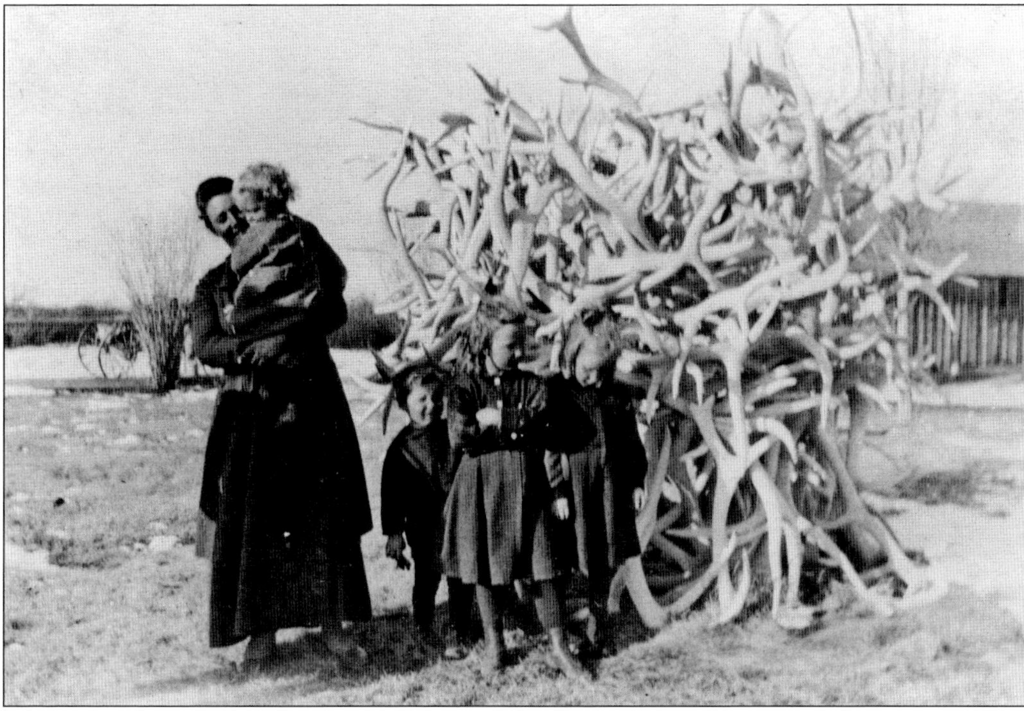

May McAllister Sommers is seen here with her four children in 1918. She is holding John and standing next to her are, from left to right, Bud, Martha, and Florence. The family ranch was on an elk migration route, and it was common to find antlers shed by the elk on the ranch as they moved north every spring. (Courtesy of Sommers family.)

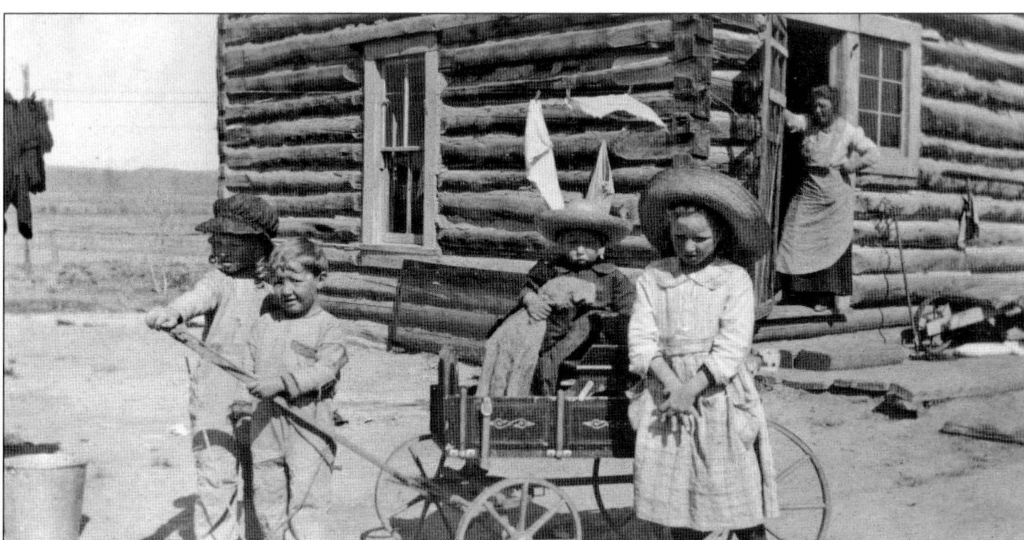

Sommers children pose with their wagon in the Sommers Ranch yard while their mother, May Sommers, looks on from the house. Note the large hats on all of the children except one, to ward off the hot summer sun. Laundry flops in the Wyoming wind behind the children. (Courtesy of Sommers family.)

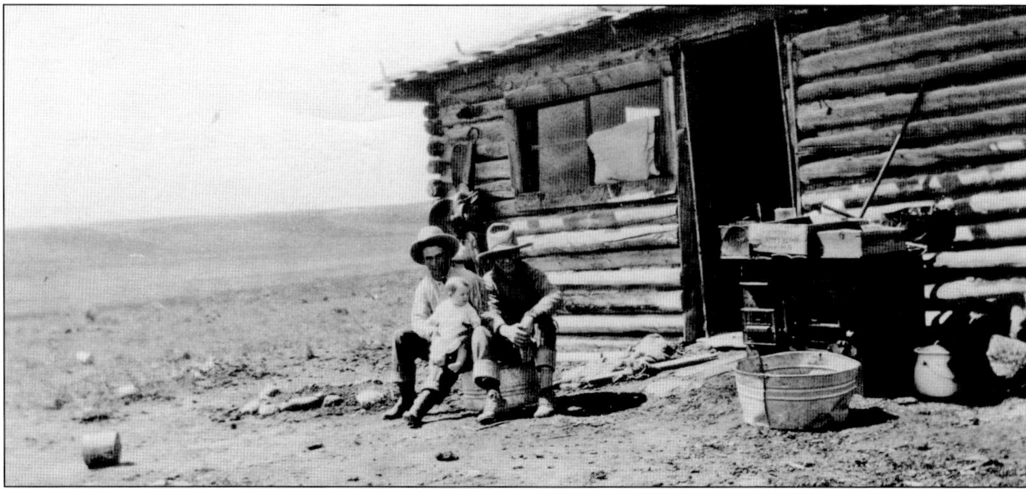

Hired man Al Shaffer holds his young child in front of the cabin Jim McAlister built for his homestead at the Sommers Ranch. This cabin is typical of the small living quarters for folks living on the Wyoming prairie in the early 20th century. Most people, including the children, would therefore spend time outdoors when the weather permitted. (Courtesy of Sommers family.)

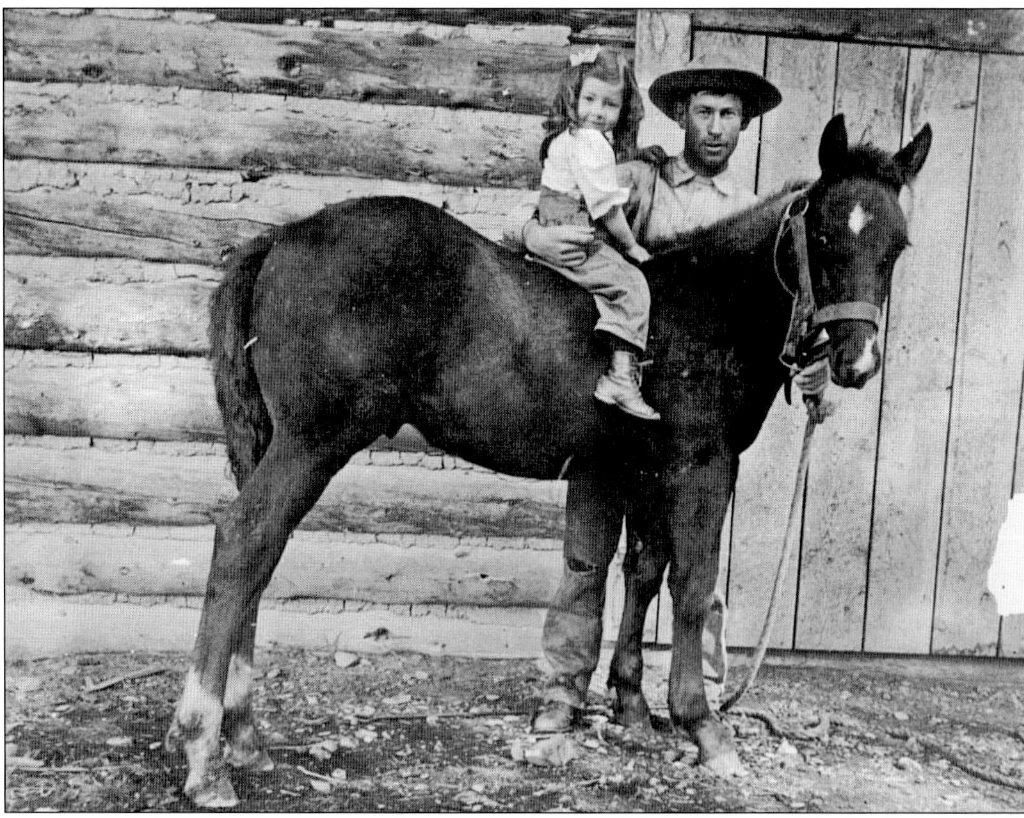

Pearl Budd sits on the family horse, Felix, while being held by her father, Henry Budd. Children learned to ride horses at a young age. They often were not given saddles, in order to avoid injury when they fell. It was easy to get hung up on a saddle during a fall, which could lead to an injury. (Courtesy of Nancy Budd Espenscheid.)

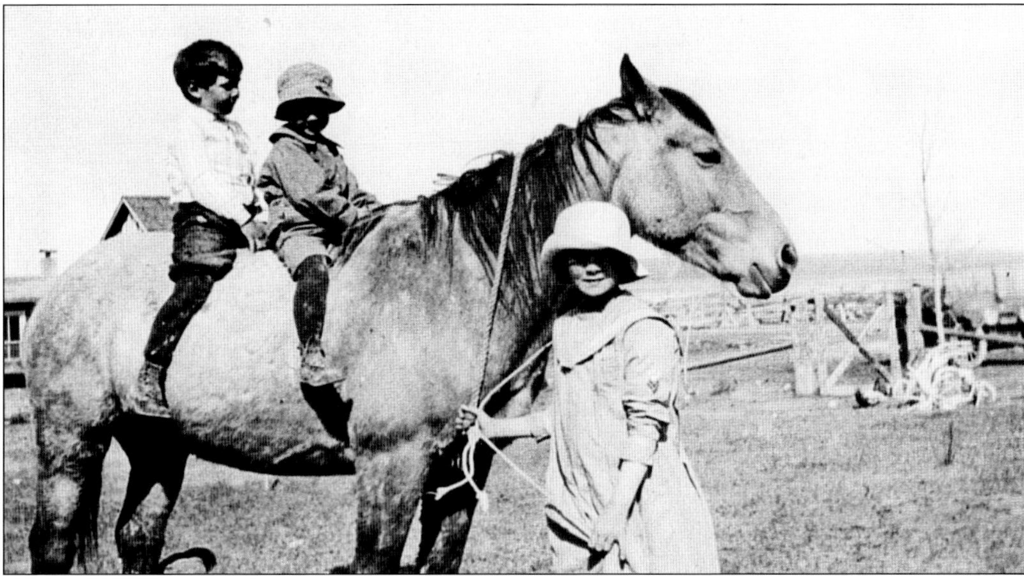

"Makings of a cowboy" reads the caption on this Budd family photograph. Cousins Joe, Burr, and Helen Budd play with a horse in the ranch yard. The children were riding without a saddle and little more than a rope was used to lead the animal. This was typical entertainment for ranch children. (Courtesy of Nancy Budd Espenscheid.)

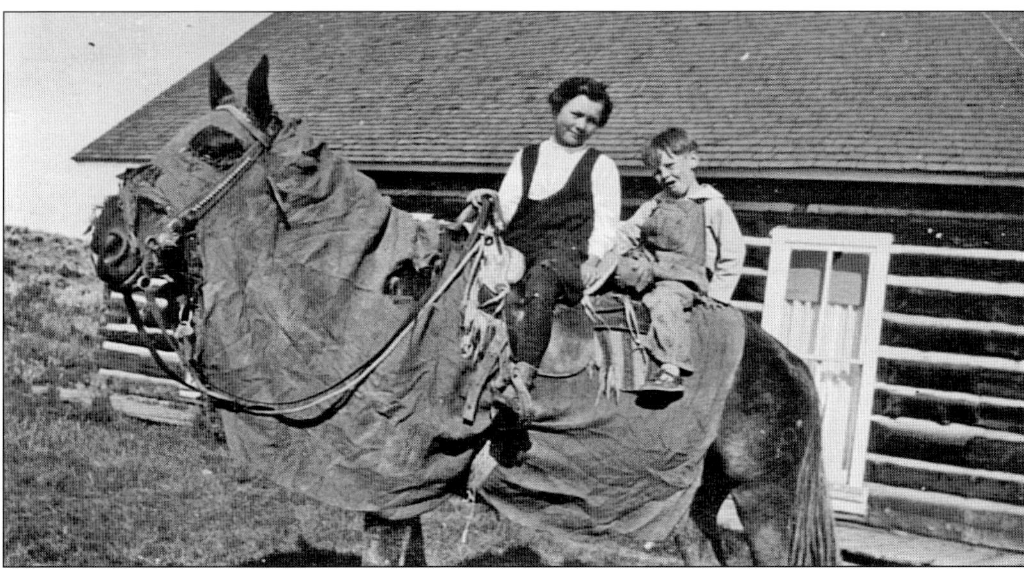

Josephine and Chester Osterhout sit on a horse that is draped in loose burlap to keep off the fierce biting horse flies during the summer. The saddle was placed over the sack. Chester was killed as a young boy traveling to school. The horse he was riding bucked, resulting in a fall that took his life. (Courtesy of Nancy Budd Espenscheid.)

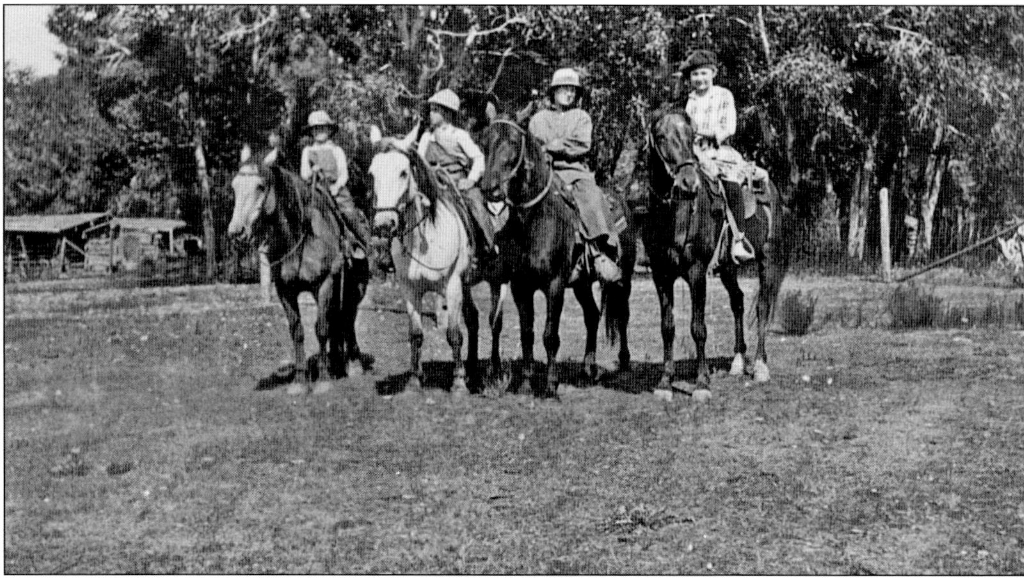

The Budd cousins are, from left to right, Joe, Bill, Pearl, and Helen. Throughout the summer, the four would entertain themselves often riding the length of North Piney Creek. It was common for children to take off riding by themselves all day. (Courtesy of Nancy Budd Espenscheid.)

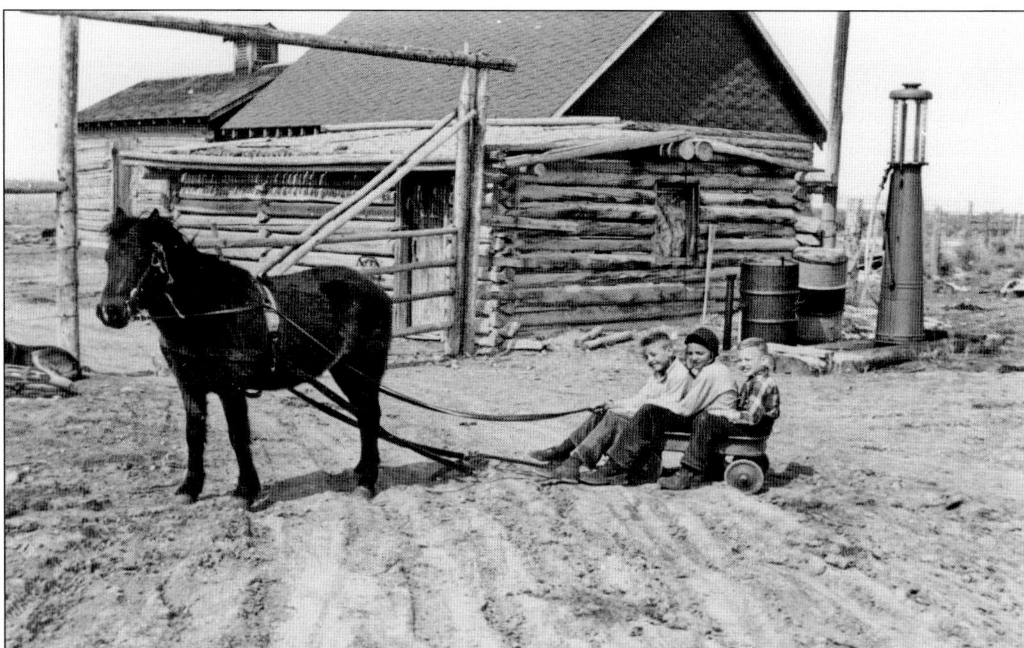

In 1940, Bobby Miller (left), Johnny Erbin (center), and a friend are entertaining themselves at the Miller Land and Livestock ranch yard by having a pony pull their wagon. Ranch children often used horses and ponies for their play. (Courtesy of Mike and Tara Miller.)

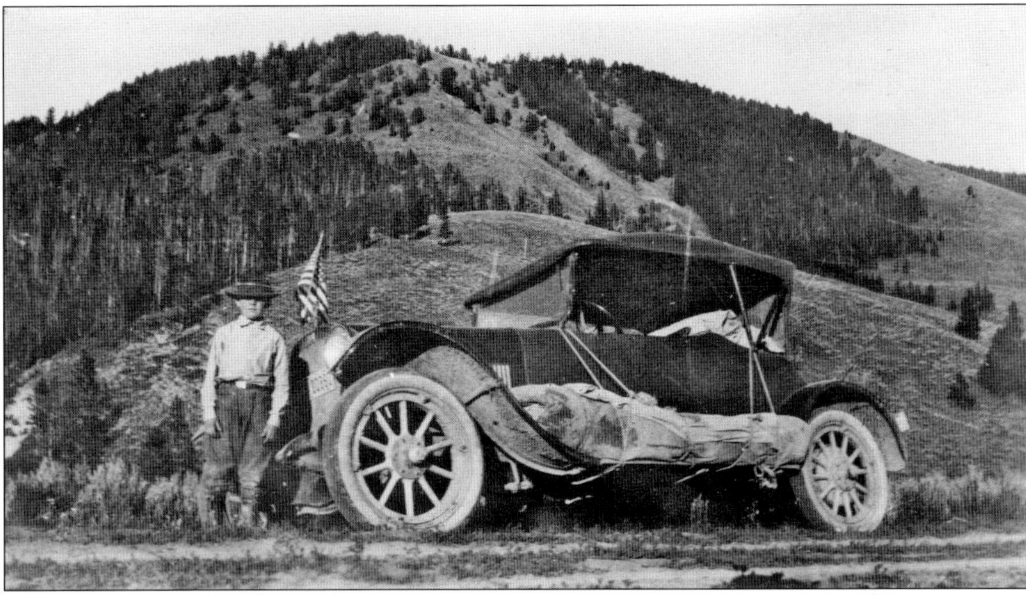

Joe Budd stands next to the family car at Middle Piney. Attached to the sideboard of the vehicle is a canvas tent. The family is likely taking the car for an extended trip to the mountains. Note the flag attached to front hood. It was common to attach a flag to a vehicle, especially at this time, which was during World War I. (Courtesy of Nancy Budd Espenscheid.)

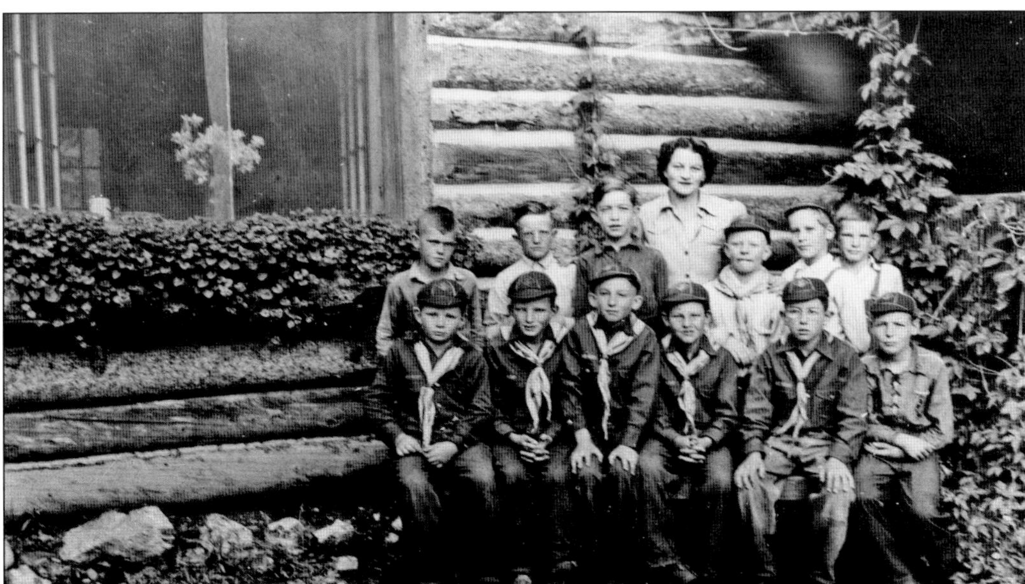

Big Piney and Marbleton's Cub Scouts Pack 269 pose with their den mother, Cap Looney, at her cabin in 1941. As guests of Cap's for a week, according to the caption, they were busy "passing ranks, fishing, camping, and having fun." The towns had several organized groups throughout their history, such as the Cub Scouts. (Courtesy of Green River Valley Museum.)

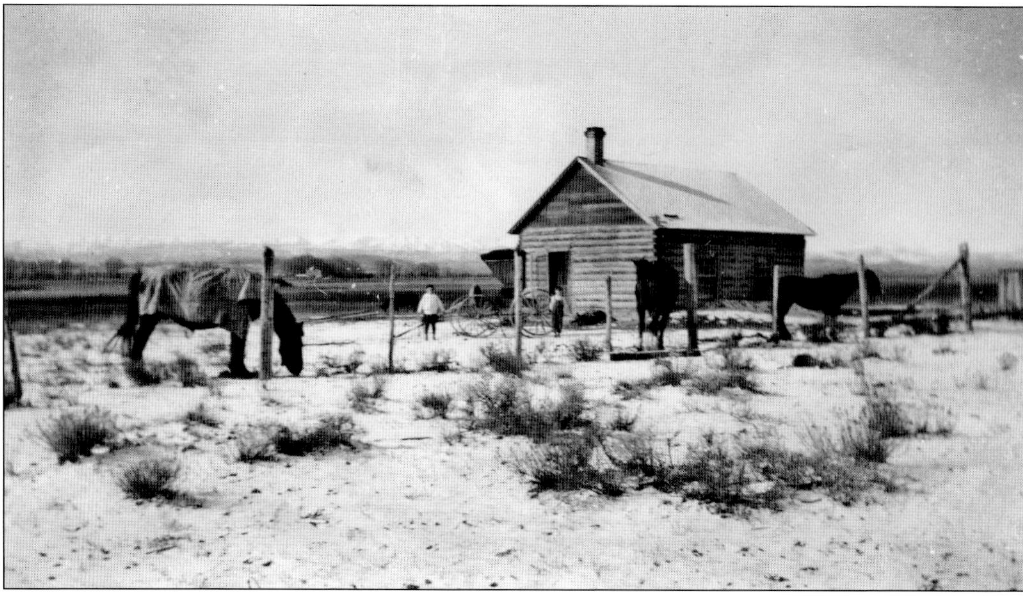

The first school built on North Piney Creek had furnishings made of rough lumber. The desks were tables with a shelf underneath for books and a bench long enough to seat two children together. Each family was responsible for getting their children to school. In this photograph, the children had taken a horse-drawn buggy. The horses patiently waited, tied to the fence, while the children attended class. (Courtesy of Nancy Budd Espenscheid.)

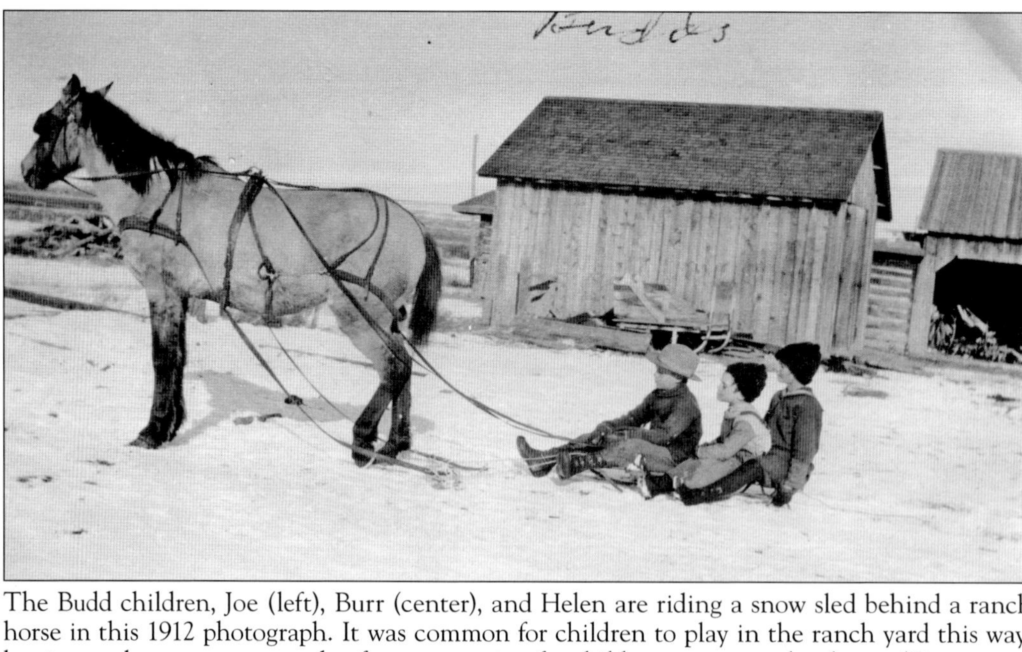

The Budd children, Joe (left), Burr (center), and Helen are riding a snow sled behind a ranch horse in this 1912 photograph. It was common for children to play in the ranch yard this way, but it was also a common mode of transportation for children to get to school, too. (Courtesy of Nancy Budd Espenscheid.)

"We road three miles—my trusty steed, Beauty and I," wrote Marjorie McGinnis on this photograph. She is referring to the ride she took daily on the horse to attend school at Dry Piney. Note the tin can on her arm. Children had to bring their lunches to school, which they did in flour sacks tied to the saddle or in tin lard pails or tobacco cans. (Courtesy of Jay and Sandy McGinnis.)

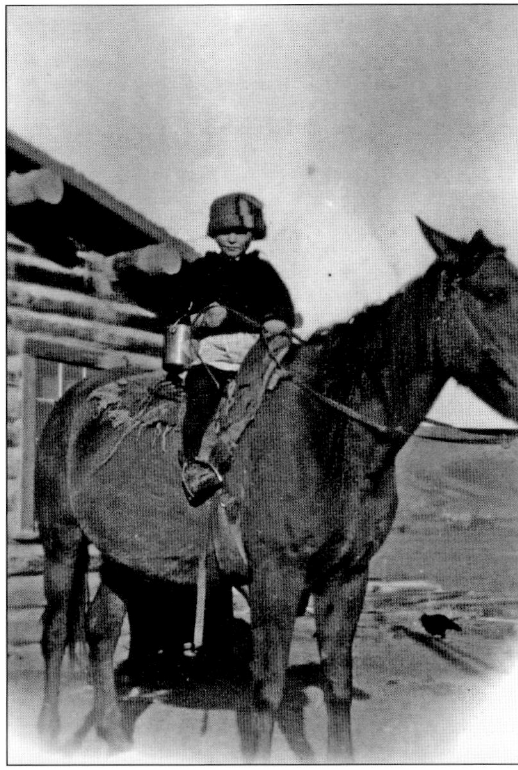

Pearl Budd Spencer reads to her class during Christmastime. The town schools were is session during the winter, but some rural schools were in session beginning in June and ending in November, with August out for haying, a time when the older children were needed in the hay fields. While not teaching, Pearl documented the early Big Piney and Marbleton history with her writings and photographs. (Courtesy of Nancy Budd Espenscheid.)

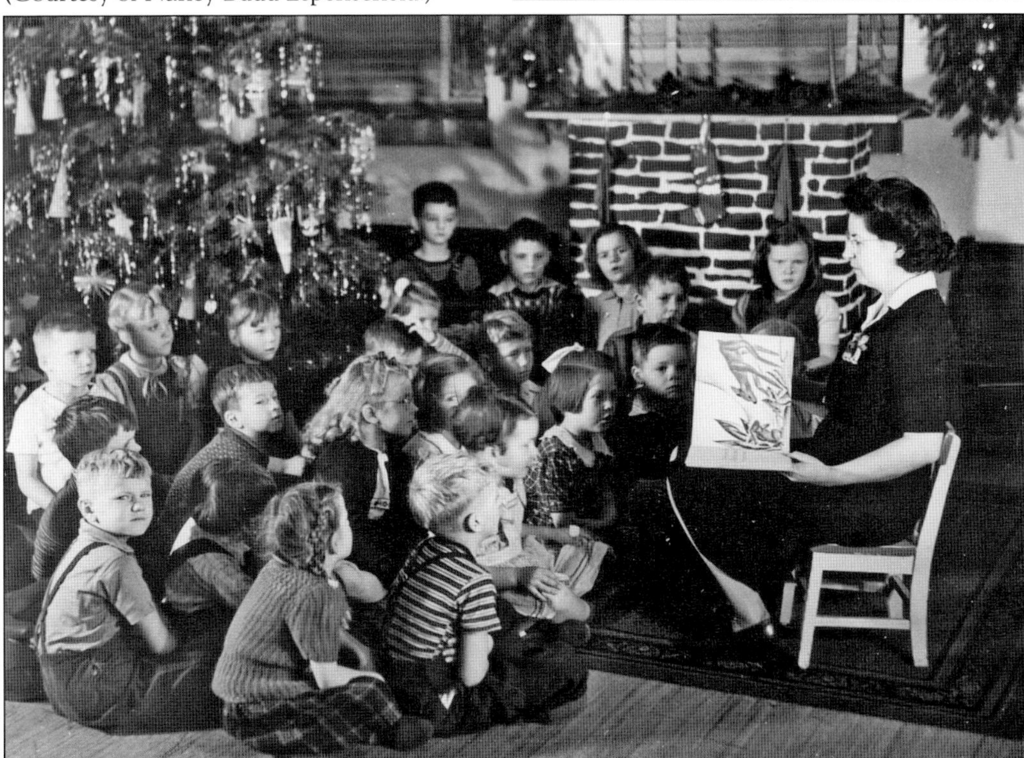

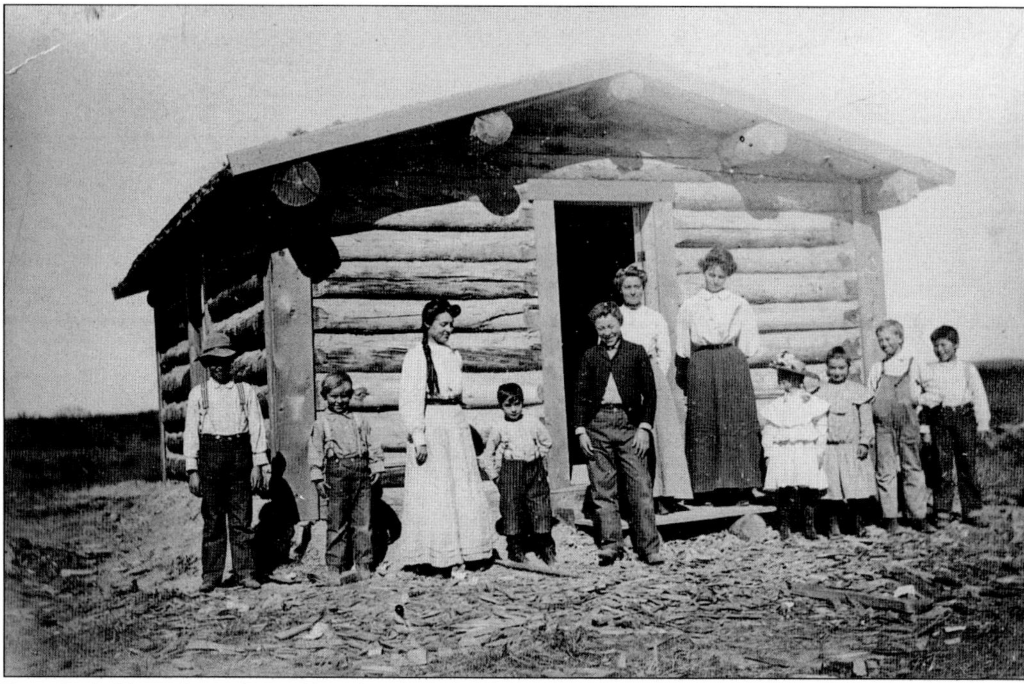

Ranch children from the Ball and Dunham families are pictured in what was then known as the Ball/Dunham School. It would later be removed to another location and referred to as the Price/Sommers School after children from those families. Eddie Edwards numbered the logs before taking the structure apart and moving them in a wagon to the next location, where it was rebuilt in the same log order. (Courtesy of Green River Valley Museum.)

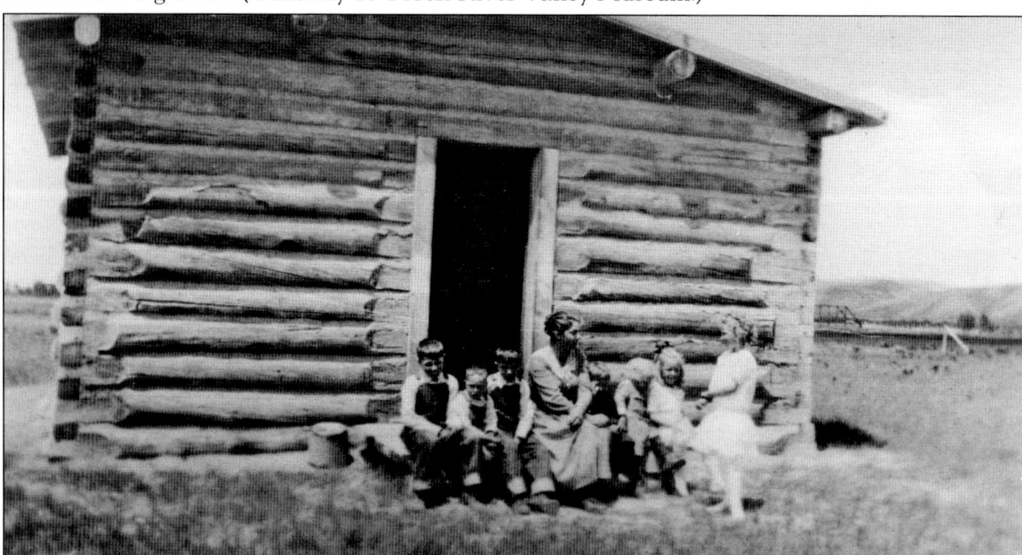

Sitting in front of the Price/Sommers School around 1919 are children from the ranch families. From left to right are Clay, Bill and Doug Price and Bud, John, Martha and Florence Sommers. In the middle is their teacher, Lydia Tanner. The schoolhouse was placed on the boundary between the Price and Sommers land, so that both families had about the same distance to travel to attend. (Courtesy of Sommers family.)

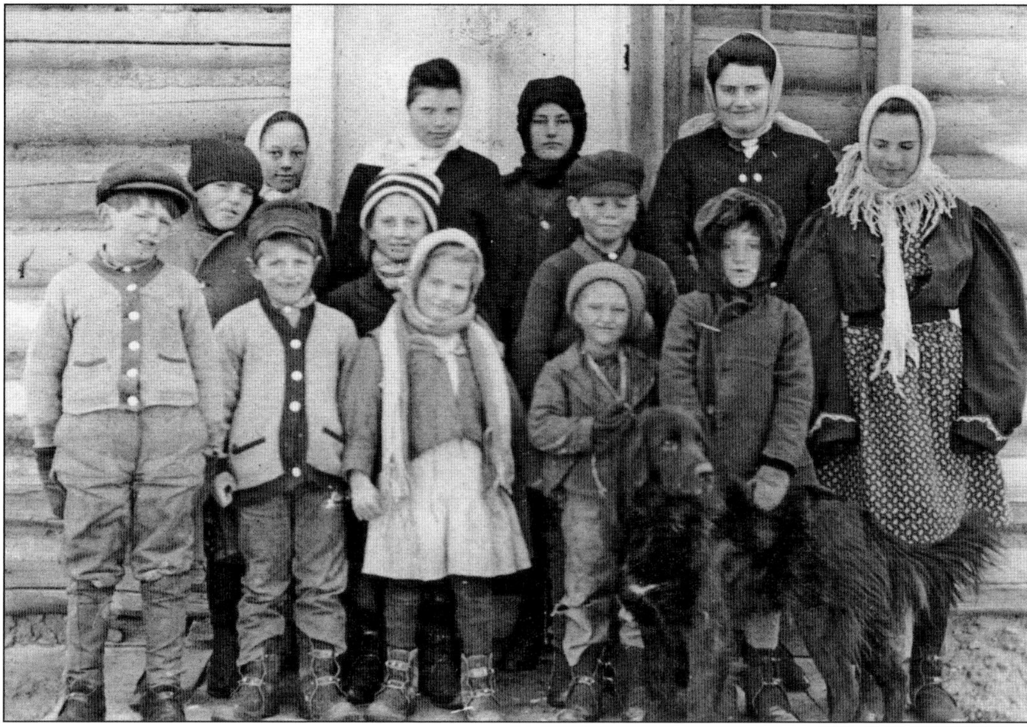

The children attending Midway School are bundled against the cold in their school picture. It appears that a family dog has joined them. Severe cold winters and snow made some rural schools try summer terms, though this was not always possible, especially with older children needed on the family ranch. (Courtesy of Nancy Budd Espenscheid.)

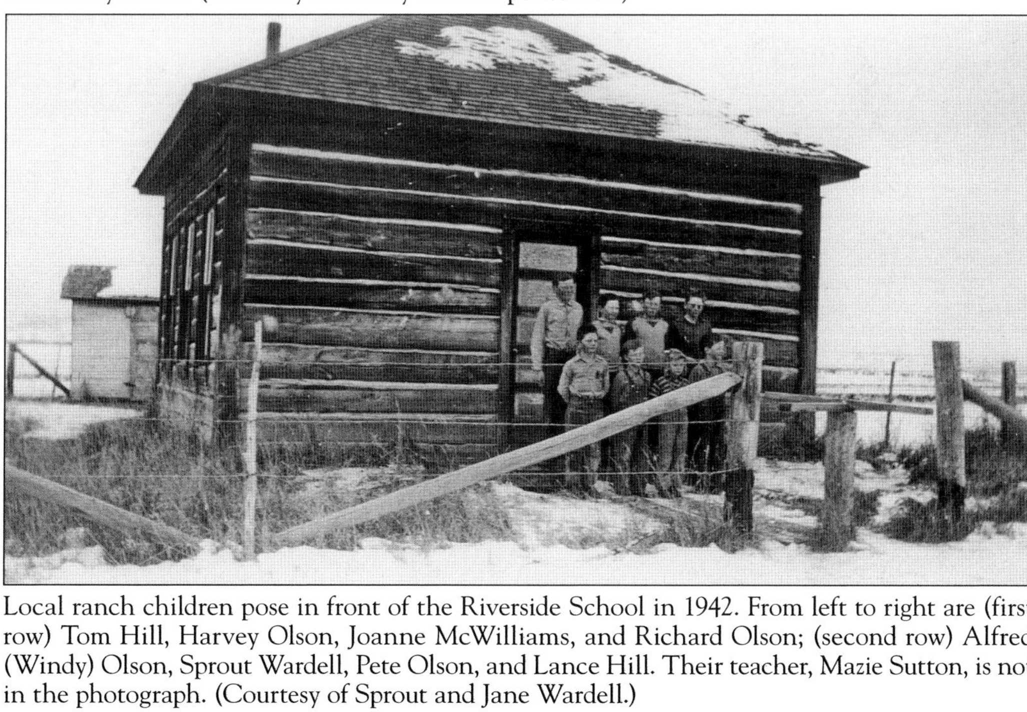

Local ranch children pose in front of the Riverside School in 1942. From left to right are (first row) Tom Hill, Harvey Olson, Joanne McWilliams, and Richard Olson; (second row) Alfred (Windy) Olson, Sprout Wardell, Pete Olson, and Lance Hill. Their teacher, Mazie Sutton, is not in the photograph. (Courtesy of Sprout and Jane Wardell.)

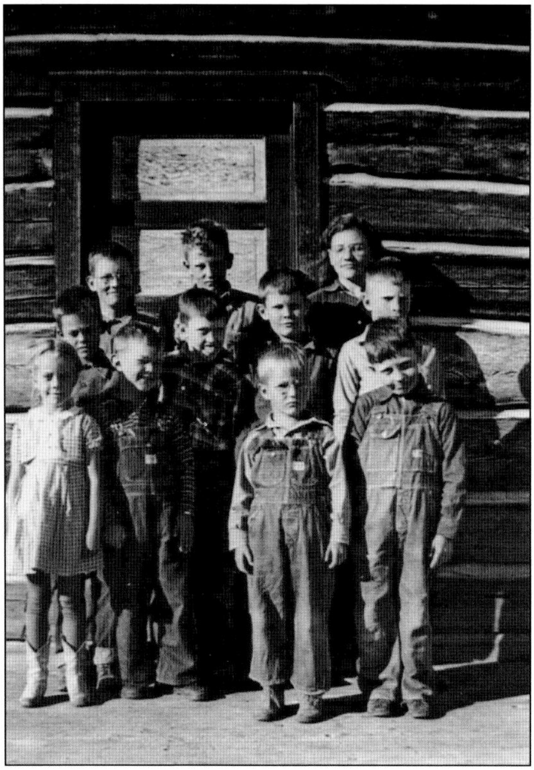

Children from the Olson, Wardell, and Hill ranch families stand in front of their school, Riverside, in 1942. The school was located in the Murdock Ranch field, as equidistant as possible among the ranches. Early schoolhouses were often moved from year to year to be closest to the most students. (Courtesy of Sprout and Jane Wardell.)

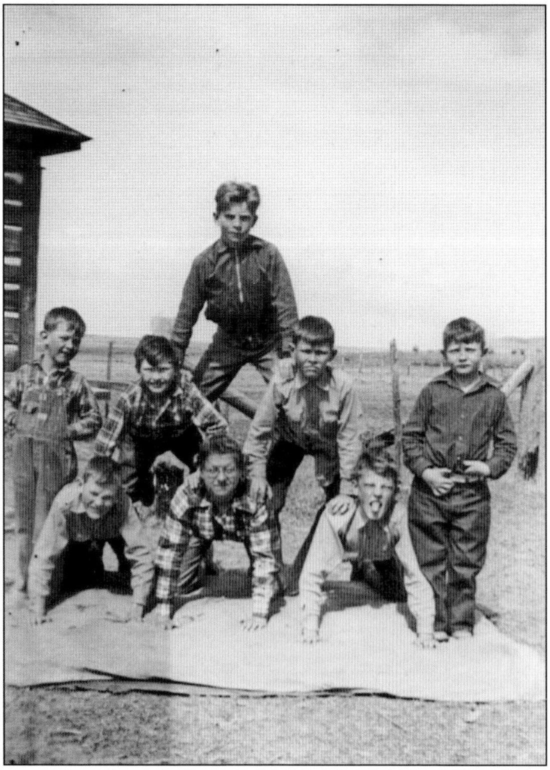

Children from the Riverside School in 1942 are demonstrating the tumbling exercises they learned in gym class at their one-room schoolhouse. At the bottom in the plaid shirt is their teacher, Mazie Sutton. (Courtesy of Sprout and Jane Wardell.)

Seven

Ties, Ice, and Rigs

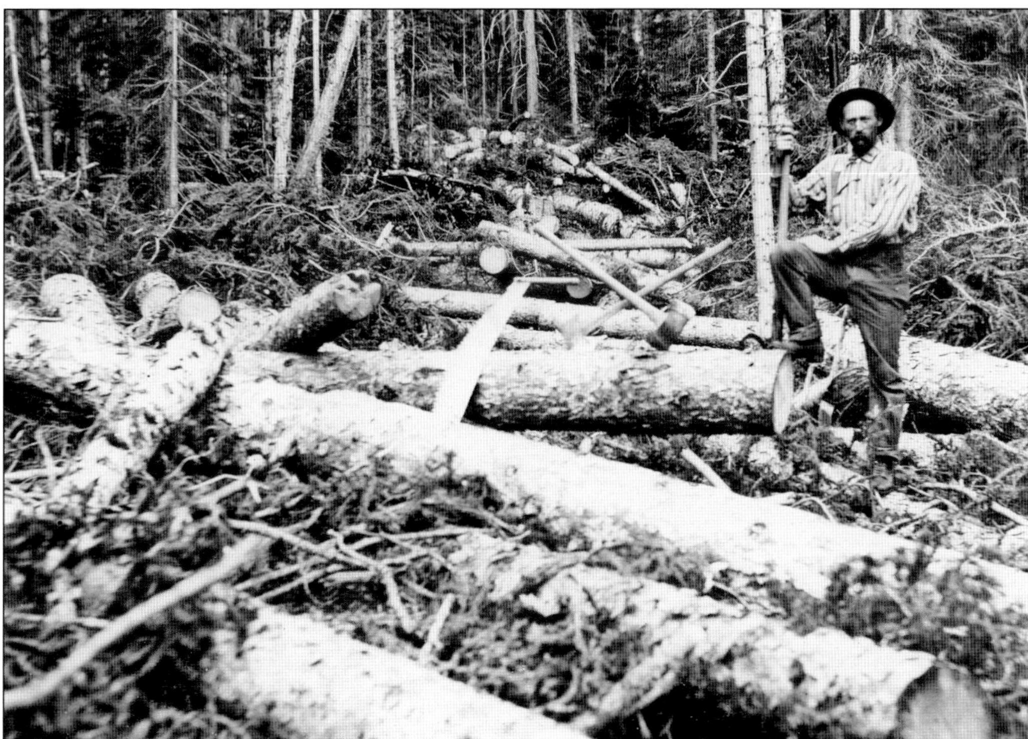

Wesley Vickrey stands with felled logs in the Wyoming Range northwest of Big Piney and Marbleton. Many of the logs would be hewn by skilled men into railroad ties. The demand for the ties was brought on by the building of the transcontinental railroad across southern Wyoming. Ties were cut for the initial railroad construction, but eventually an enduring replacement industry developed and lasted into World War II. (Courtesy of Bill and Carrie Budd.)

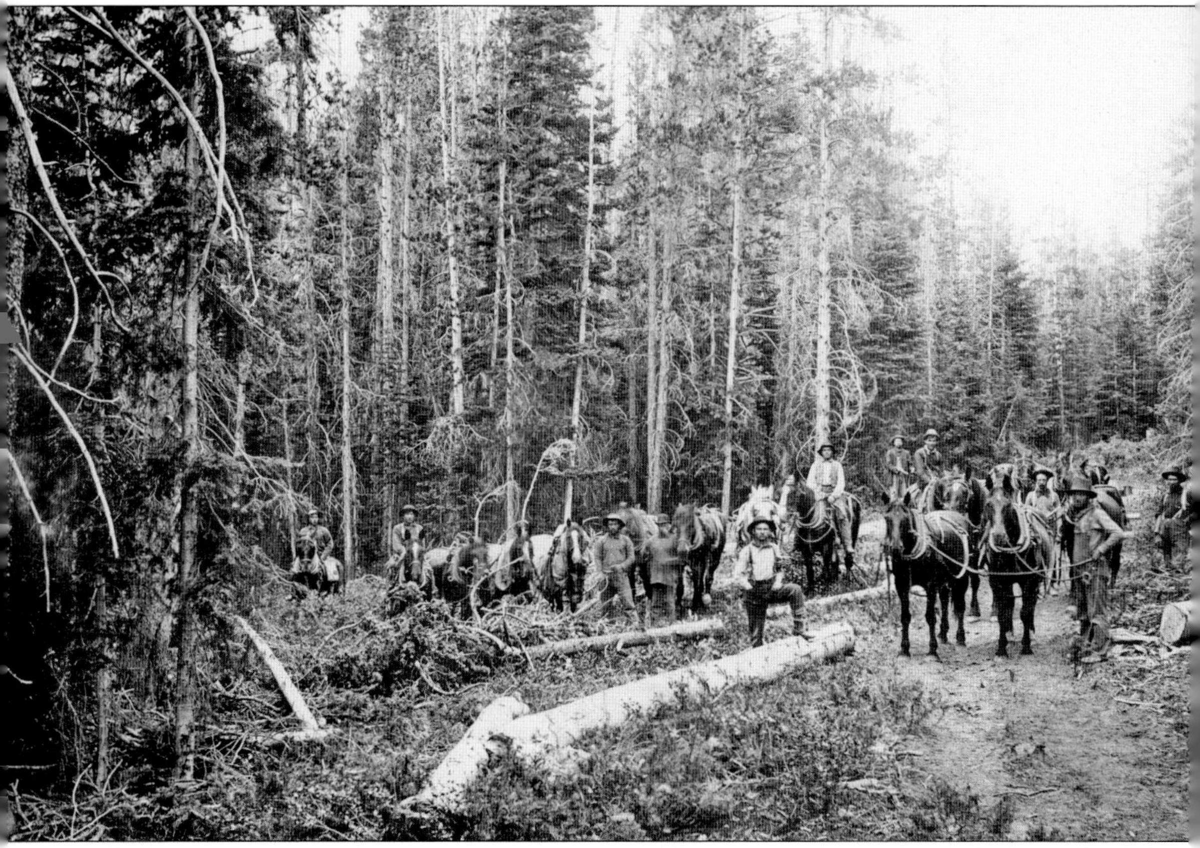

Harvested logs were skidded down the hillside behind teams of work horses. Some of these logs ended up at a local mill for local use. Most of the logs, though, were hand hewn into railroad ties by skilled "tie hacks." Two important factors enabled this industry: large stands of lodgepole pines in the mountains and numerous drivable streams and rivers for floating ties to Green River City, Wyoming, where the Union Pacific crossed the Green River coming from the Big Piney area. (Courtesy of Bill and Carrie Budd.)

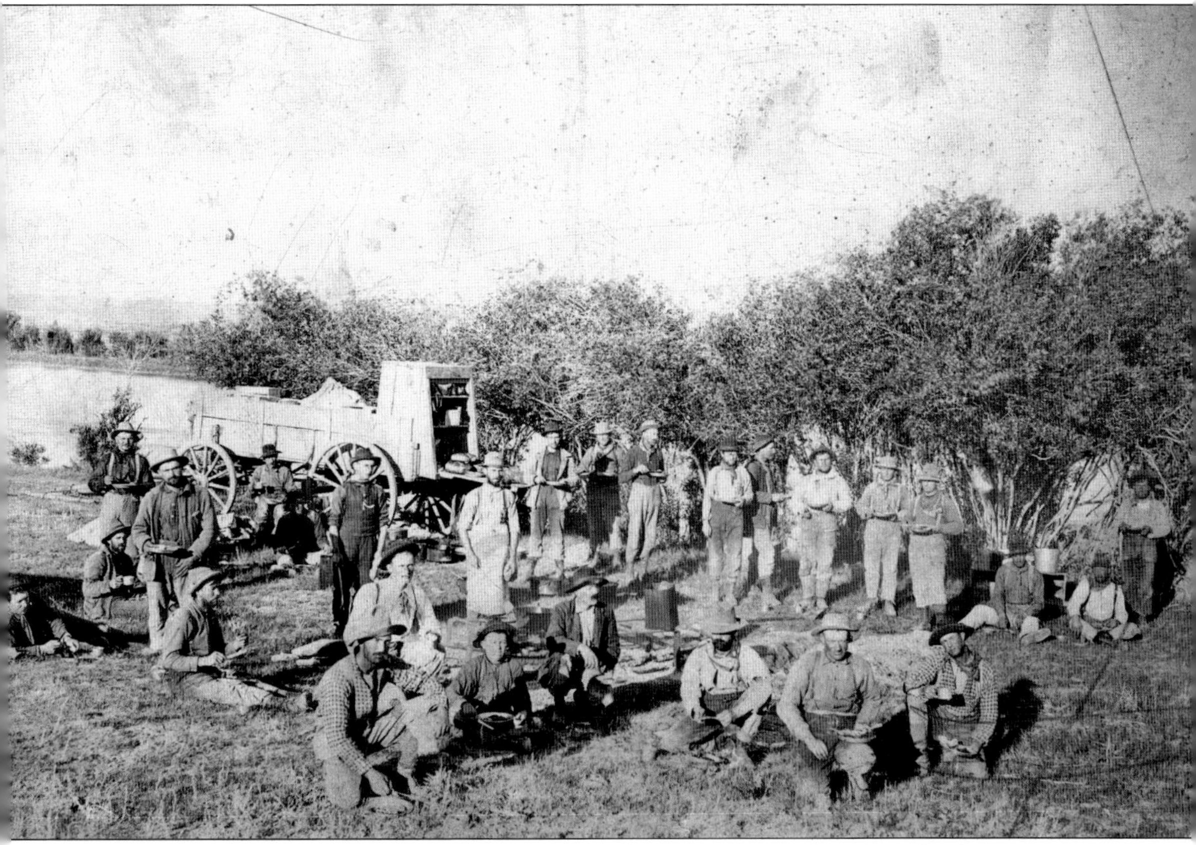

Timber men are taking a break for lunch on a river drive. Ties were placed on the frozen rivers in the winter and held in the river during the initial thaw until the water was high enough for the drive, usually in mid-July. A typical drive had approximately 250,000 ties. The drive, over 100 miles, took 27–40 days. (Courtesy of Bill and Carrie Budd.)

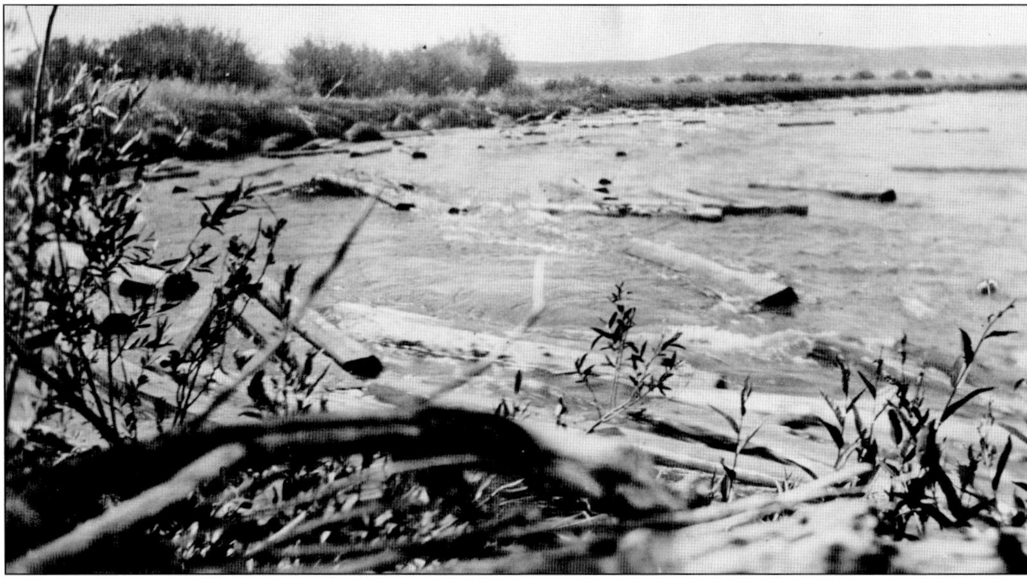

Logs from the forest were floated down the Green, Horse, and Cottonwood Creeks, tributaries of the Green River. Shown here are logs floating down the Green River where it meets the New Fork River. The hewn ties were delivered to market by huge tie drives, when the ties were floated down the Green River and its tributaries with help from the tie hacks. (Courtesy of Sprout and Jane Wardell.)

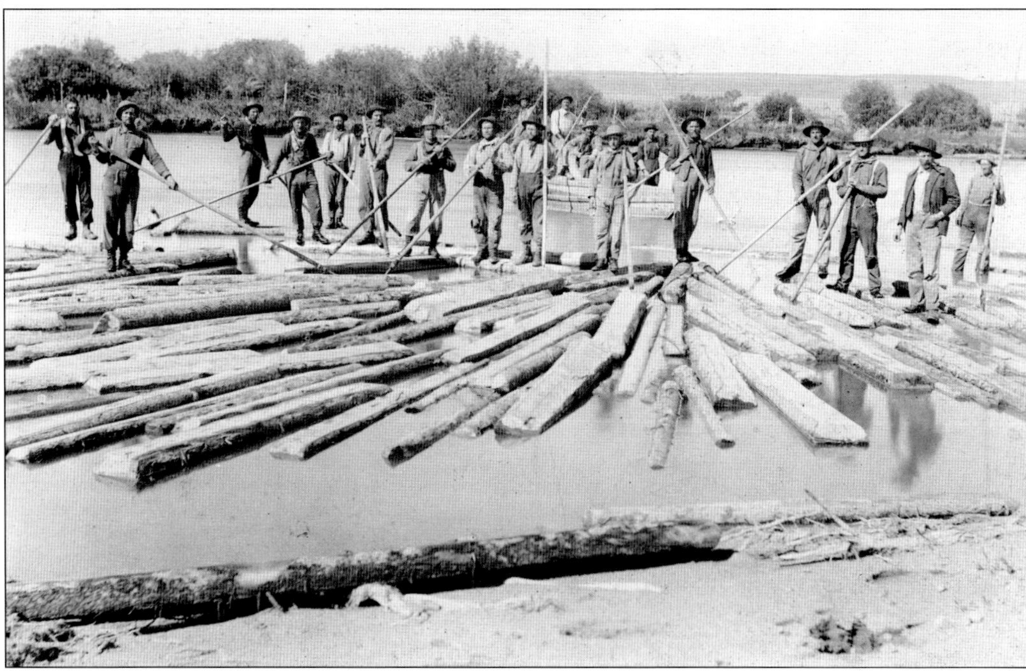

The ties were hand hewn by skilled tie-hacks from Sweden, Norway, Finland, and Austria. These "river rats" were paid well for their dangerous, back-breaking labor. Shown here are a group of river rats moving ties down the Green River with the aid of a long stick to assist in keeping the logs moving. Behind the workers is one of the boats that followed the crew with supplies. (Courtesy of Bill and Carrie Budd.)

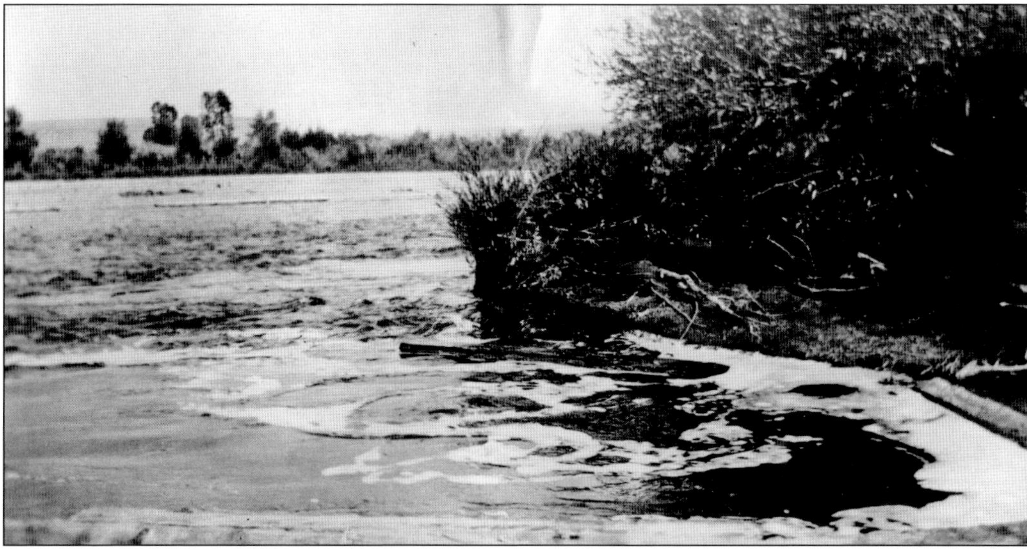

Some days, the ties and their crews traveled 10 very crooked miles on their way; some days less than half that much. After a rainstorm, when the water level was higher, the ties floated midstream and made good speed. When the water was dropping, everything drifted to the edges and got hung up, as shown here. (Courtesy of Sprout and Jane Wardell.)

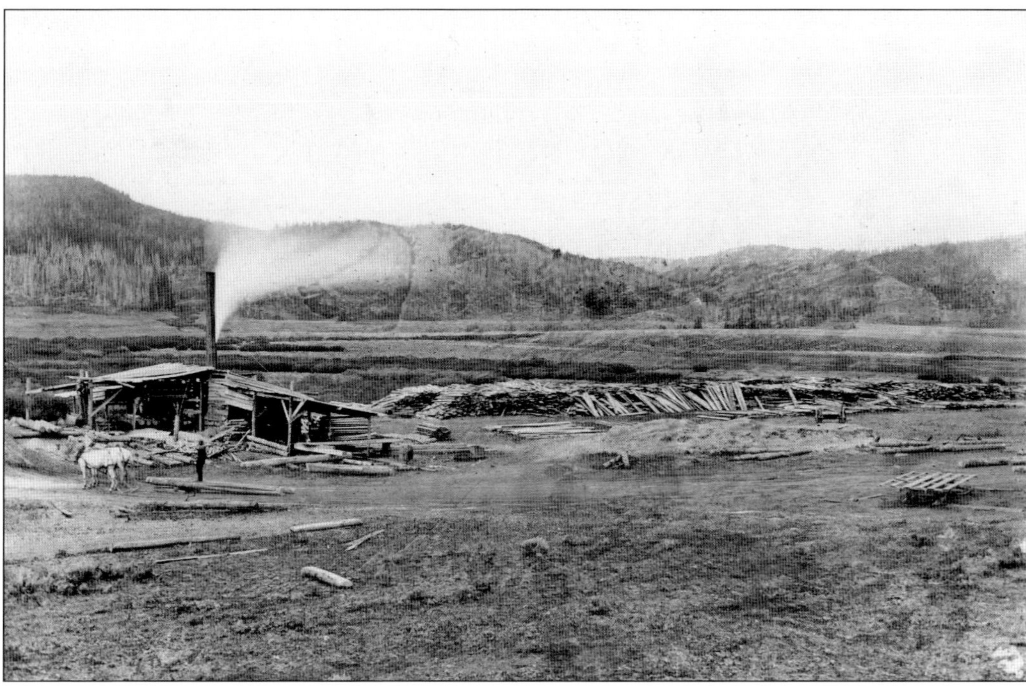

Wesley Vickrey's sawmill on Horse Creek is seen here in 1898. Logs were brought to the mill from the hills in the background. Loggers often cut the trees in the winter and then skidded to the mill by horsepower, as seen on the left side of the picture. This local source of wood would be used to build area ranch structures, as well as the buildings and fences in the towns. (Courtesy of Bill and Carrie Budd.)

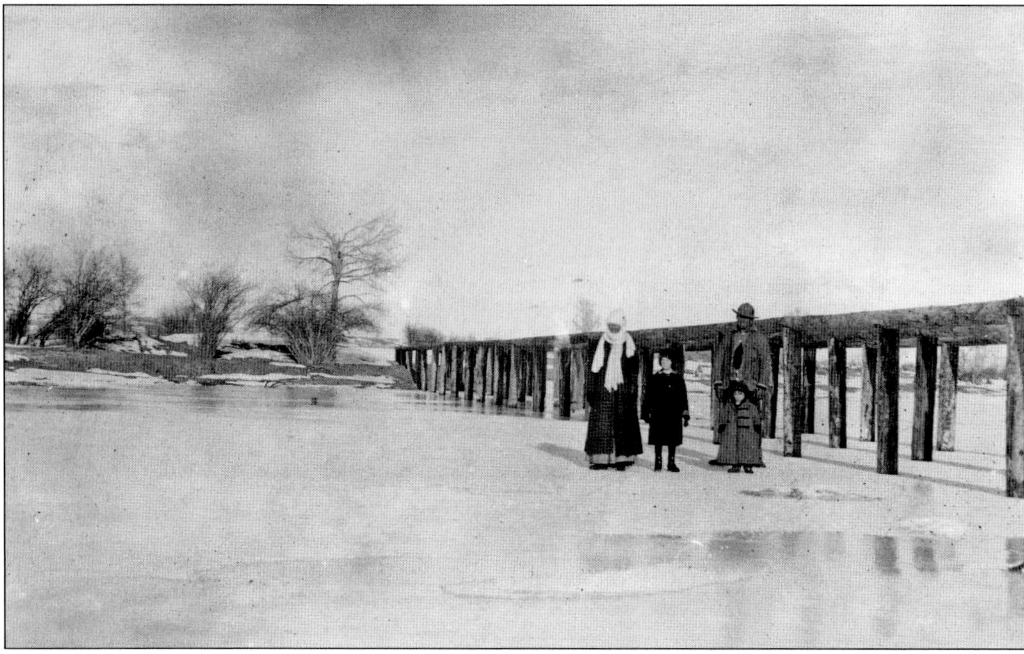

A typical winter in Big Piney and Marbleton lasted at least half of the year. Locals had to regularly bundle up for the outdoors, as are the Vickrey family, pictured here. Lewis Vickrey is seen here standing on the frozen Green River with his wife, Mary, and daughters Beulah (left) and Lois. (Courtesy of Bill and Carrie Budd.)

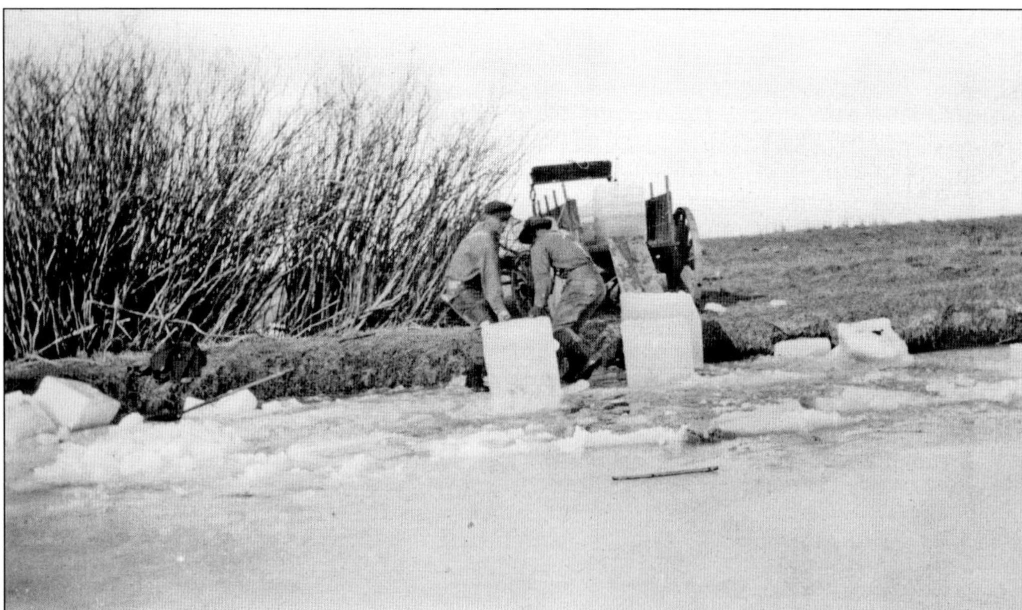

"Putting up ice" was an important winter chore before the time of refrigeration. Pictured here are Fred Beck (left) and Billie Mills Jr. cutting blocks of ice from North Piney Creek in 1915. The giant ice blocks were stored in icehouses, special wood buildings with sawdust insulation to keep the ice frozen. The blocks of ice were later used in the summer in iceboxes to keep food cool. (Courtesy of Bill and Carrie Budd.)

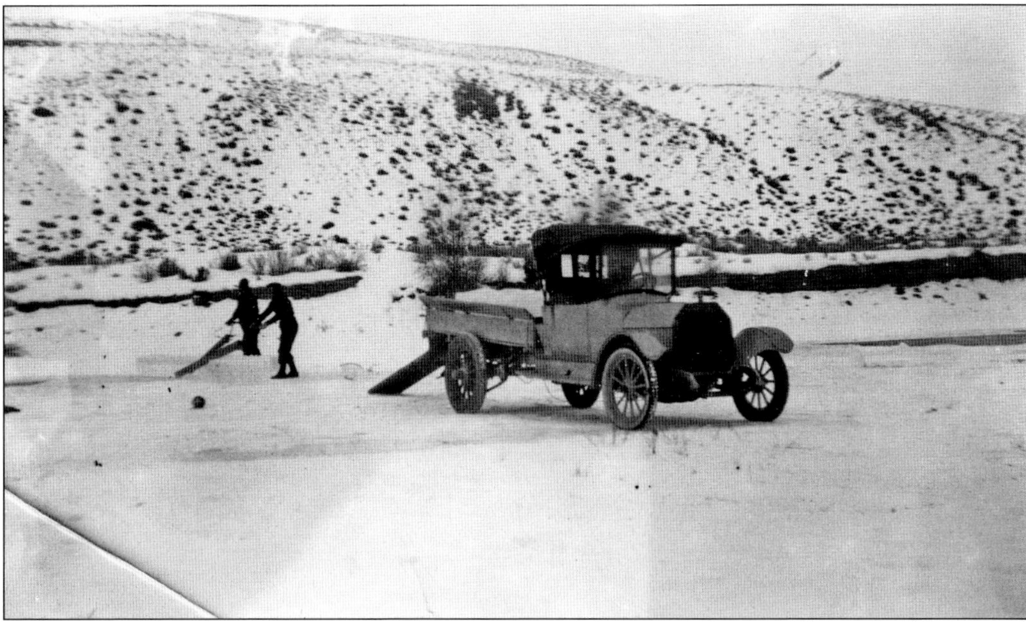

Wesley Vickrey and a helper are cutting ice from the local creek during the wintertime. This was a common chore for locals, but for some, it was also a job. Selling ice, especially in the summer time, could be lucrative. The ice blocks were slid up a ramp to the back of the pickup. Obviously the ice is thick enough on the creek to hold a vehicle. (Courtesy of Bill and Carrie Budd.)

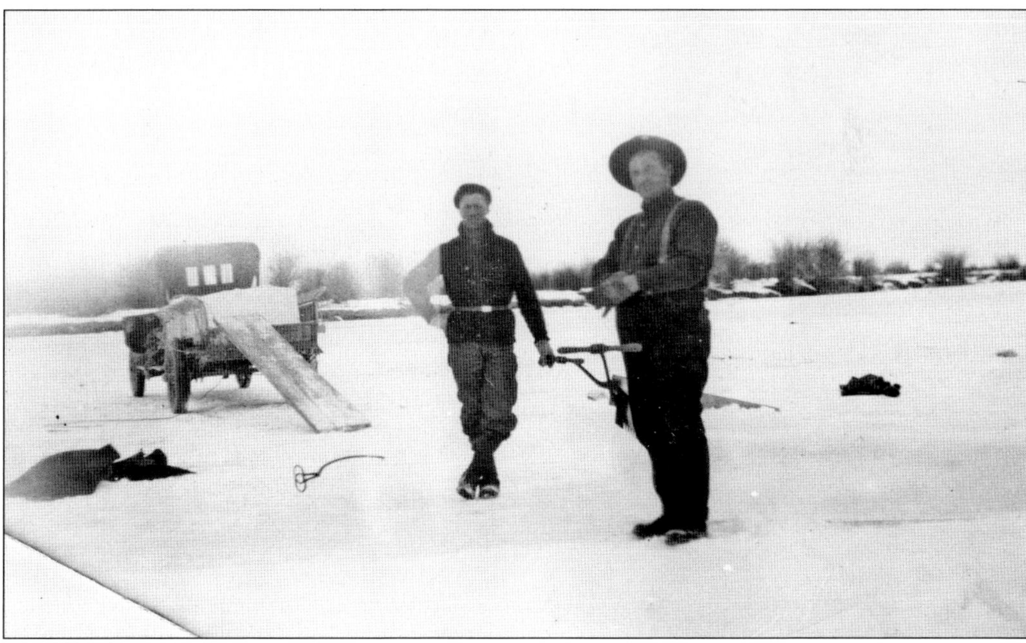

Wesley Vickrey and a helper take a break while putting up ice. The men have shed their coats (seen lying on the ice), no doubt from overheating while doing this physically demanding work. After sawing blocks of ice in the creek, giant ice tongs, seen on the frozen river next to the man at center, are used to lift the blocks. (Courtesy of Bill and Carrie Budd.)

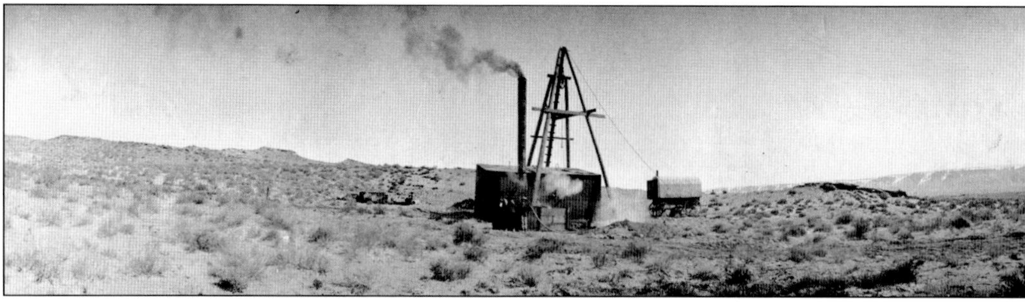

Signs of oil were reported in the Big Piney and Marbleton area by early immigrants in the 1840s, who used it to grease their wagon wheels. Oil was first drilled south of the towns in 1907 in what became the La Barge Oil Field. Pictured here is one of the early oil wells. Note the sheep wagon, used to house the early oilmen. (Courtesy of Mike and Tara Miller.)

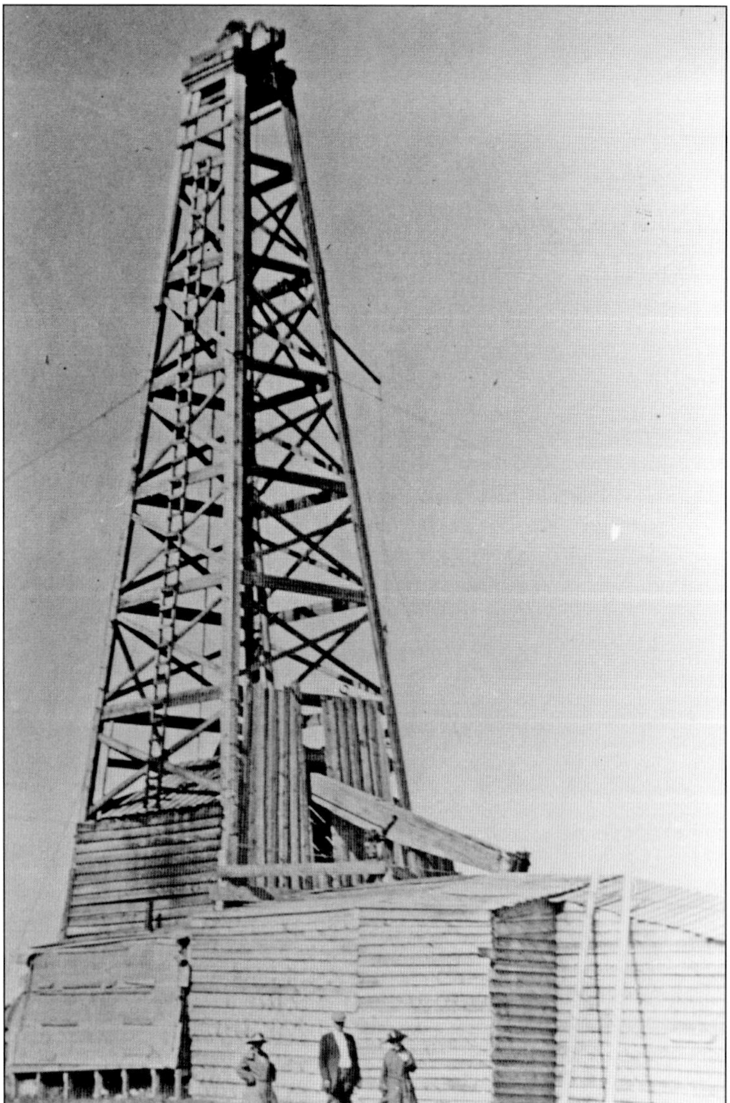

The Big Piney Gas Field extends from eight miles west of Big Piney to one-and-a-half miles north of the North La Barge Field. It is 15 miles long and from one to three miles in width. Drilling for oil started in 1919, with some success in producing oil and natural gas. Not all wells were successful, though, such as the one pictured here on the Henry Budd ranch. (Courtesy of Green River Valley Museum.)

Charlie Budd had this oil derrick on his ranch at the Corder place. Called the Budd No. 1 and operated by the Wyoming Petroleum Corporation, this well would mark an important discovery for oil and natural gas production in the area. It ultimately produced from numerous geological layers in the formations below. (Courtesy of Nancy Budd Espenscheid.)

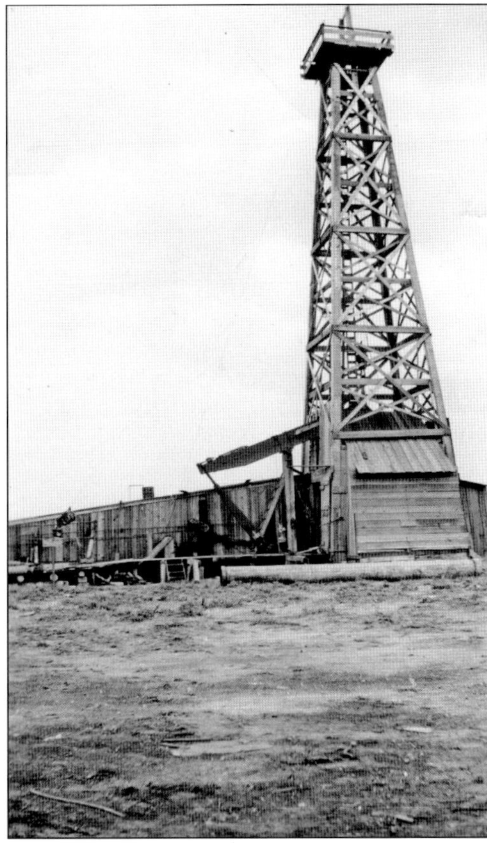

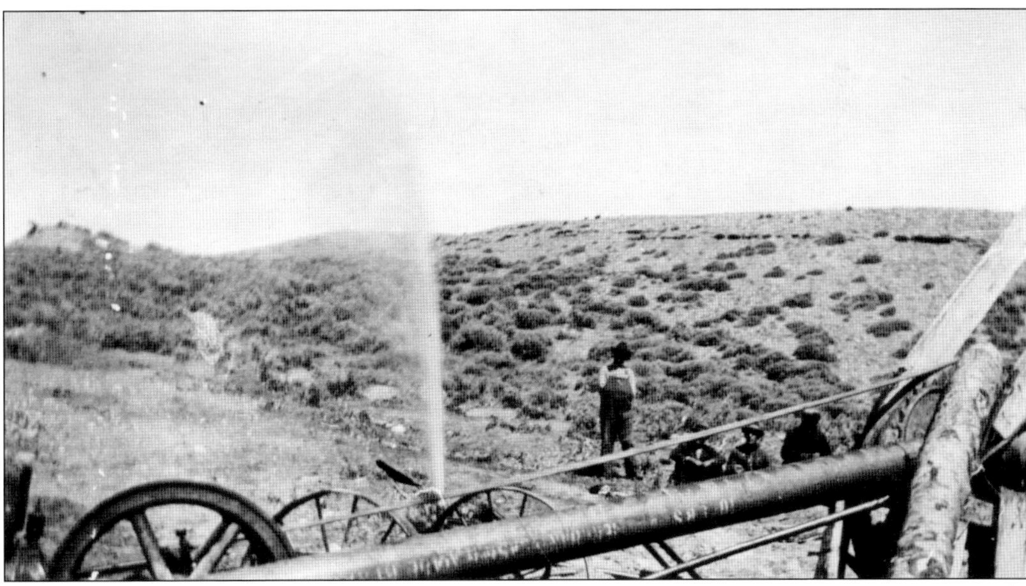

Early Big Piney and Marbleton oilmen look on as natural gas shoots from a transport pipe. The gas is coming from the Cretaceous Field, named for the prehistoric period also known as the age of dinosaurs. Natural gas was plentiful in this area, but unfortunately, there was no market for the product. Consumers were using mostly oil. (Courtesy of Nancy Budd Espenscheid.)

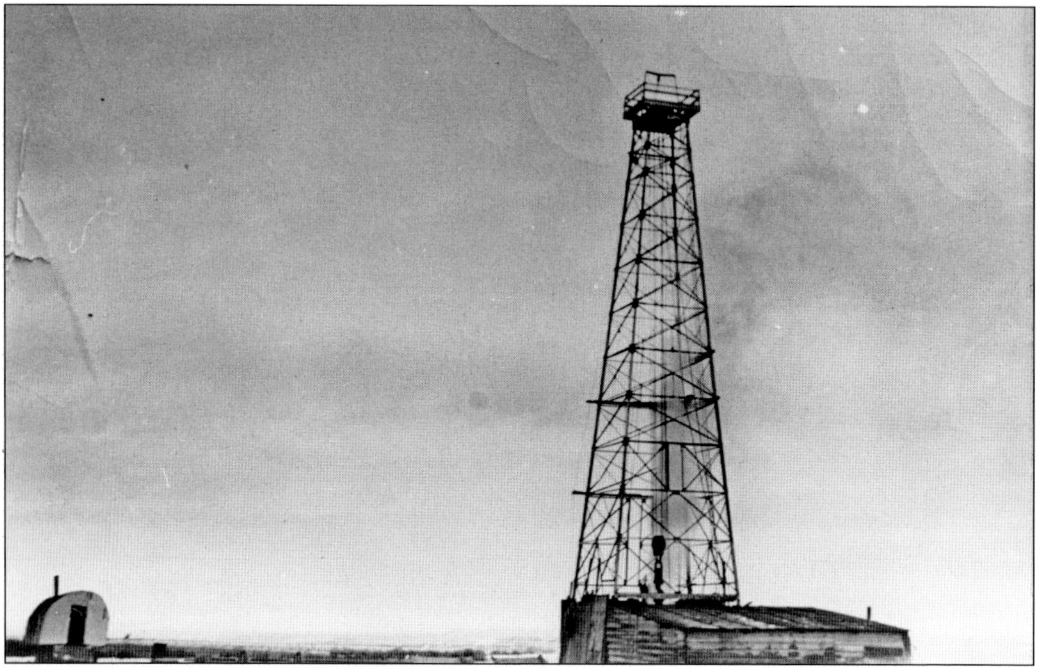

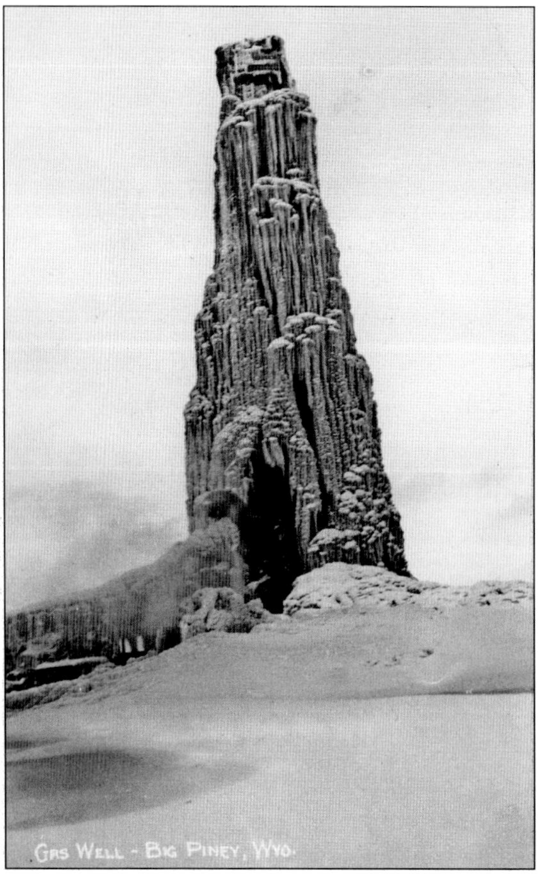

Charlie Budd's sheep wagon was parked near Wyoming Petroleum Corporation's Budd No. 1 well on December 4, 1938, when it began to blow. It had been idle for three weeks at a depth of 1,695 feet when it unexpectedly blew. Eventually the blowout would mark the discovery of the Big Piney Shallow Field. (Courtesy of Green River Valley Museum.)

Natural gas and water from Wyoming Petroleum Corporation's Budd No. 1, known as the ice well, blew out for six weeks. The derrick was encased in an estimated 700 tons of ice before the workers were able to shut in the well. It was also thought somewhere between .75 and 1.5 billion cubic feet of natural gas escaped into the atmosphere during the blowout. (Courtesy of Jonita Sommers.)

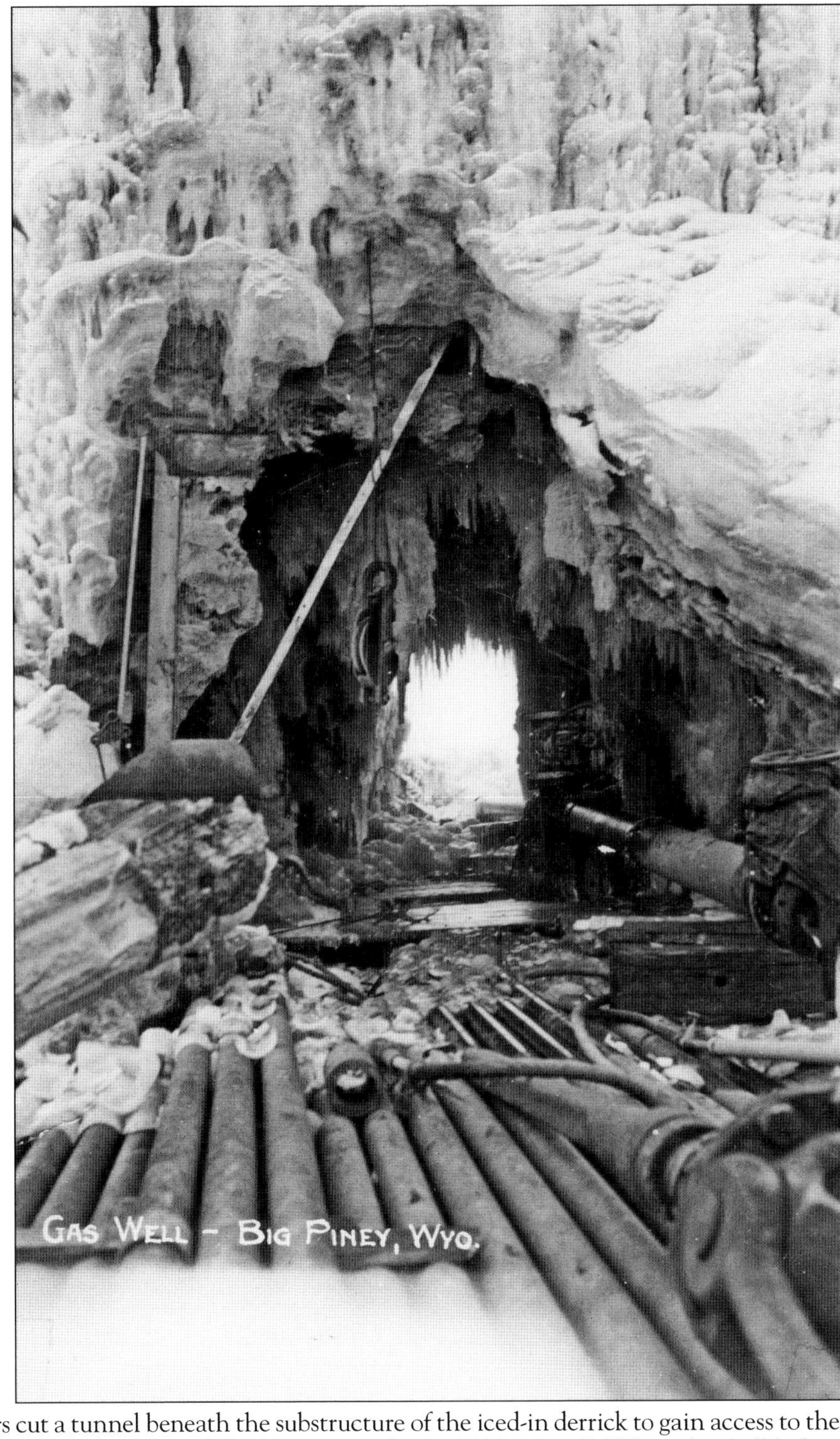

Workers cut a tunnel beneath the substructure of the iced-in derrick to gain access to the drill hole as they struggled to control the blowout at the Budd No. 1 well. When the drill hole was finally uncovered, workers forced logs over the hole to deflect the gas in attempts to stop the blowout. Eventually, they were successful. (Courtesy of Nancy Budd Espenscheid.)

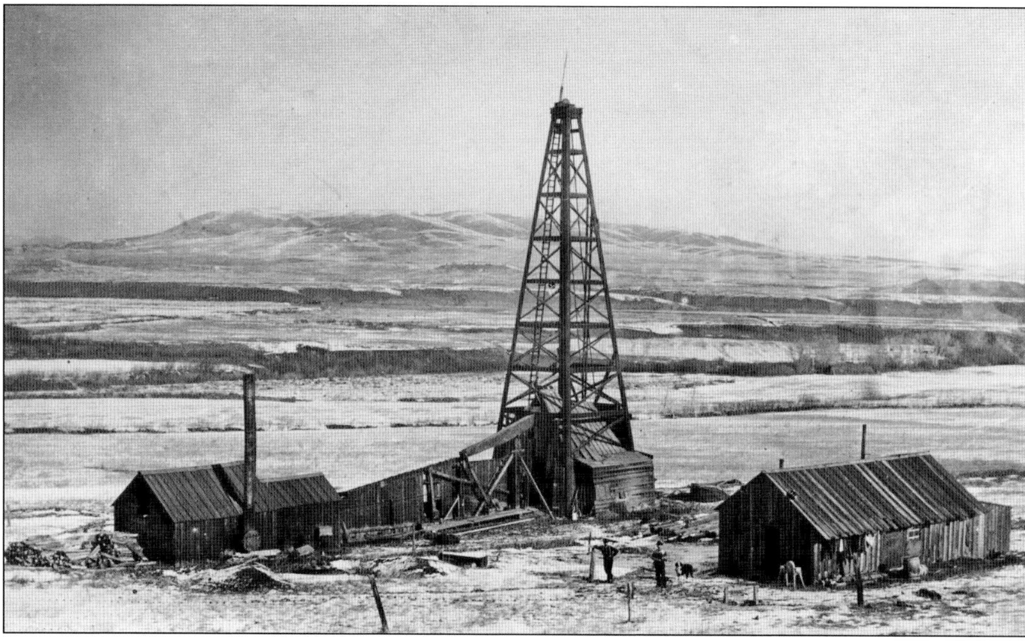

The derrick and support building at one of the earliest Big Piney and Marbleton area wells are constructed from wood. Early attempts at drilling in the area were minimally successful when more natural gas was produced than oil. Unfortunately for the early drillers, there was not a market for the gas. (Courtesy of Joe Murdock.)

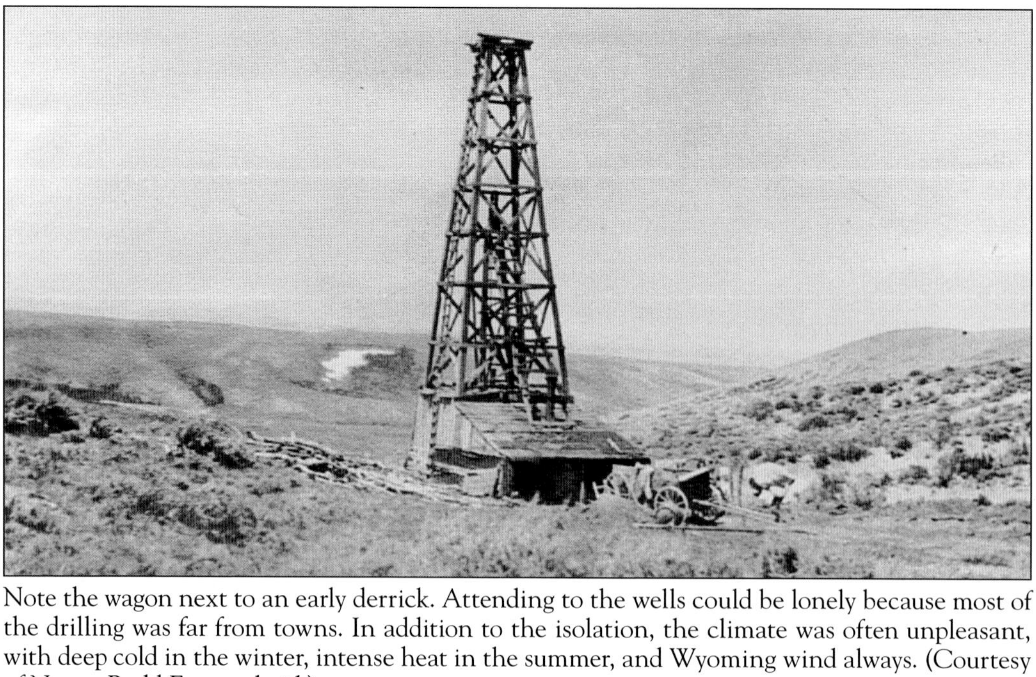

Note the wagon next to an early derrick. Attending to the wells could be lonely because most of the drilling was far from towns. In addition to the isolation, the climate was often unpleasant, with deep cold in the winter, intense heat in the summer, and Wyoming wind always. (Courtesy of Nancy Budd Espenscheid.)

Eight

Serving the Country

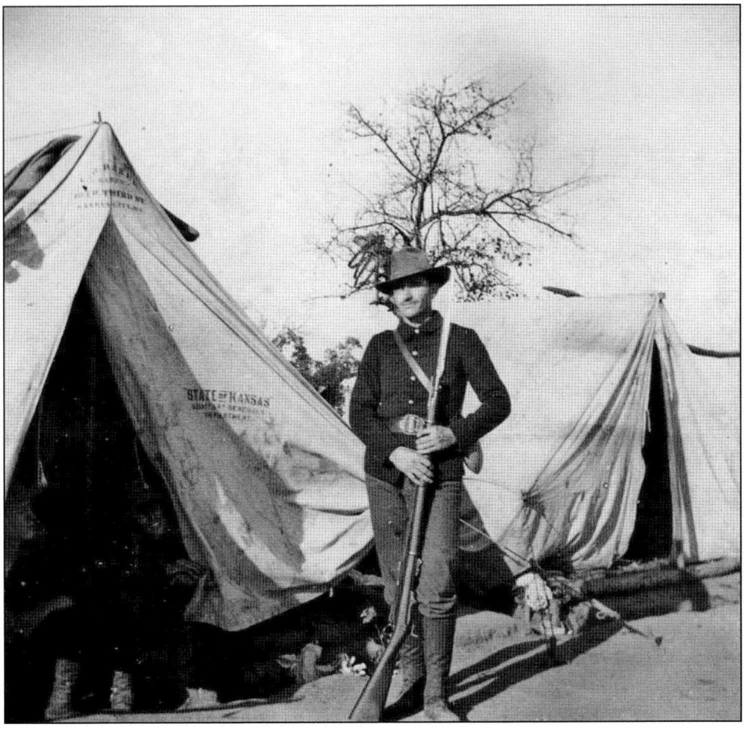

Albert Pomeroy Sommers is shown here in 1898 while in service during the Spanish-American War. Sommers was a member of the 22nd Regiment Kansas Volunteer Infantry, Students' Company H. After the war, he graduated from college, moved to Wyoming, and eventually homesteaded northeast of Marbleton, where he raised his family and Hereford cattle. (Courtesy of Sommers family.)

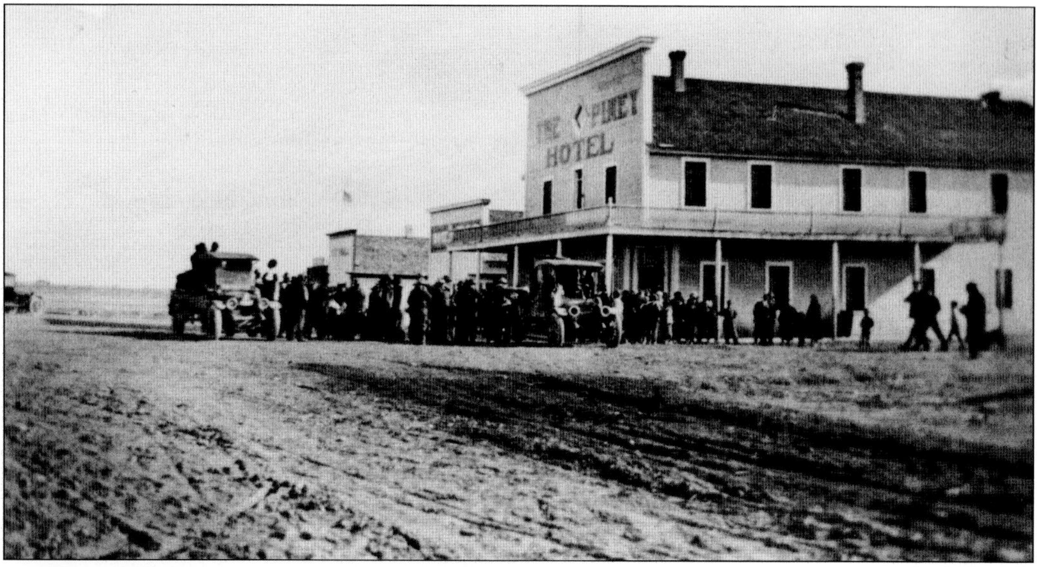

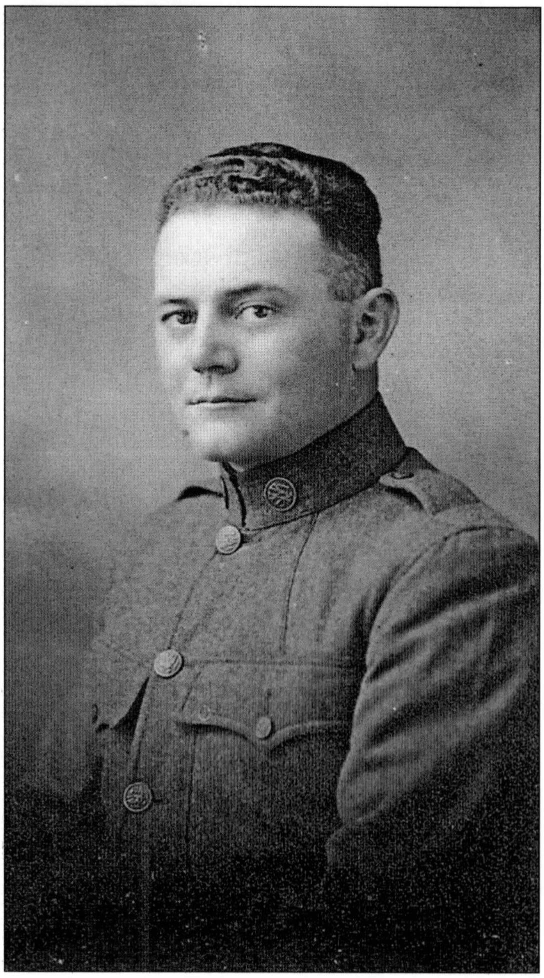

Young men from the Big Piney and Marbleton area gathered in front of the Piney Hotel to leave for service in the Great War, later called World War I. They would join other Wyoming volunteers to serve in the Machine Gun Platoon, Sunset Division, in France. Tragically, Russell Daniels was killed on November 28, 1918, leaving a wife and three children in Big Piney. (Courtesy of Green River Valley Museum.)

William Elmer "Billie" Sherman is shown here in his official military portrait. Bill was working as a cowboy on a local ranch for Buster McIllvain when he volunteered for the service during World War I. He was part of a group of local men to enjoy a big farewell dance given in their honor in April 1917 at Budd Hall. Sherman was stationed at Camp Lewis, Washington, as a member of the military police force. (Courtesy of Green River Valley Museum.)

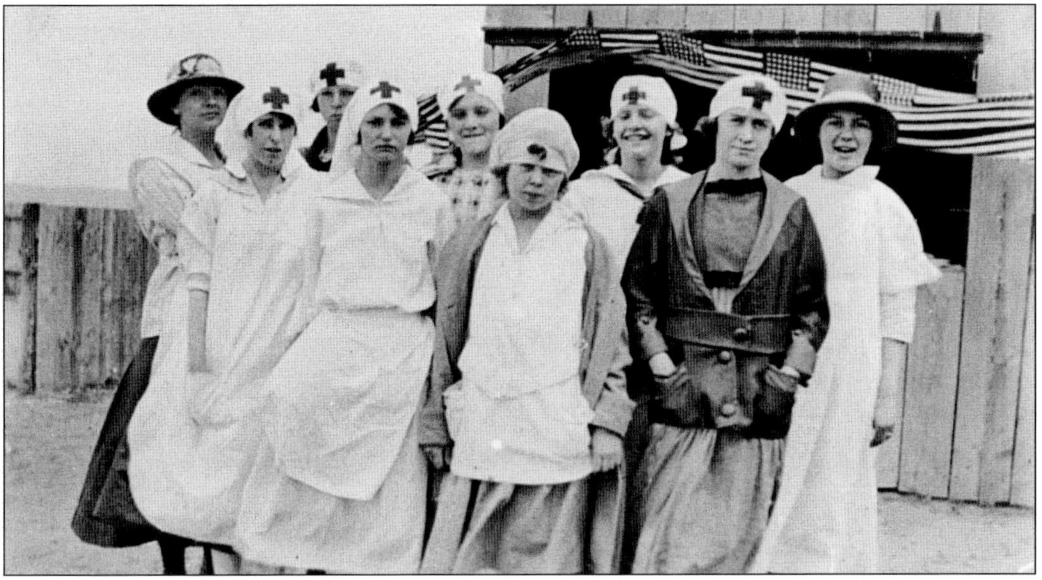

On April 22, 1917, a chapter of the American Red Cross was formed in Big Piney with participating members from throughout the Green River Valley. Shown here are members from the chapter in uniform. From left to right are (first row) Dorothea Budd, Effie Stout, Florence Huchinson, and Pearl Vickrey; (second row) Lydia Tanner, Valerie Harmison, Charlotte Fields, Opal Hakes, and Doris McGlashan. (Courtesy of Green River Valley Museum.)

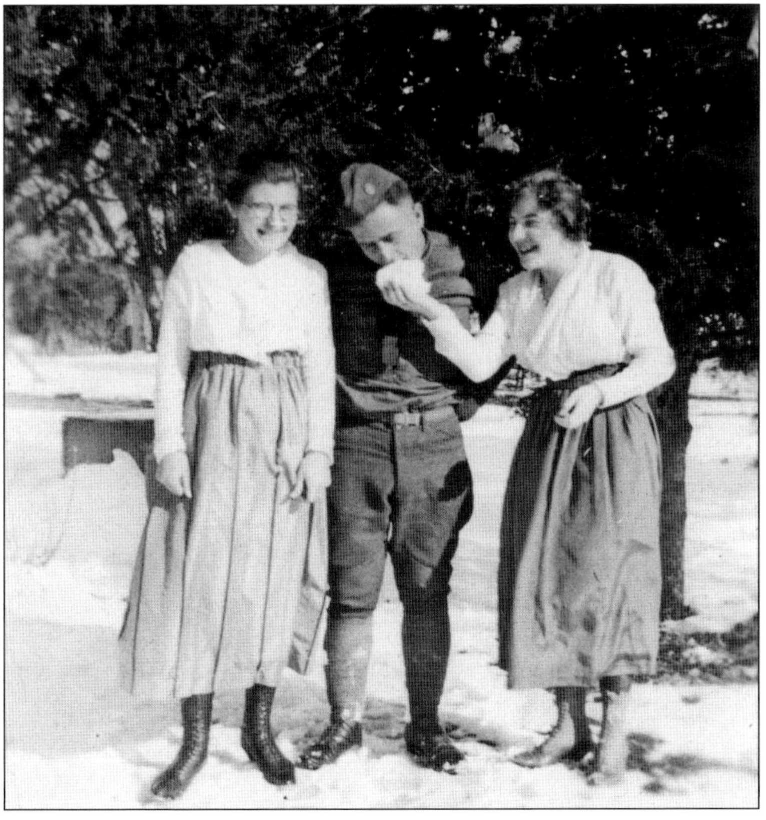

"Have a bit of snow," reads the caption of this photograph. Returning World War I veteran Melvin eats snow while posing with Sylvia Marks (on right) and a friend. Fortunately, most of the local soldiers returned from the European conflict, but some carried the deadly Spanish flu virus, which took several local victims, including the sheriff and nearly all the George Hereford family on Cottonwood Creek. (Courtesy of Green River Valley Museum.)

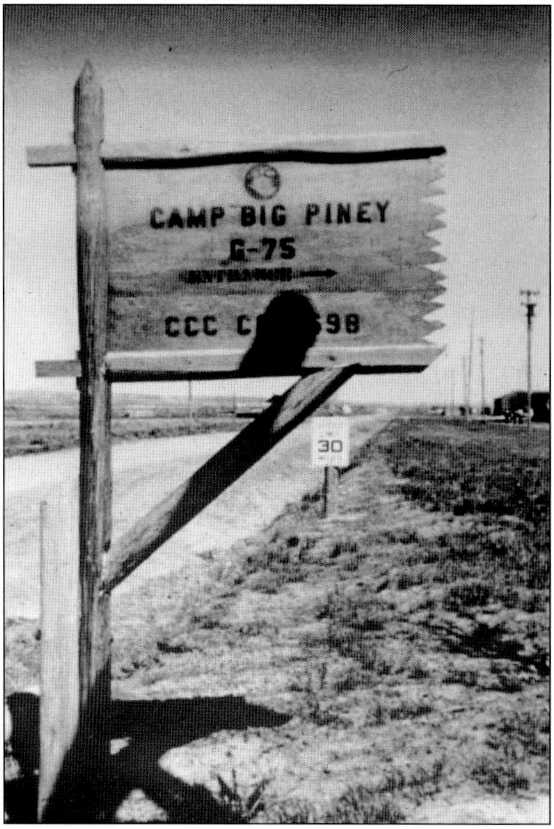

One of the most popular and successful New Deal programs during the Great Depression was the Civilian Conservation Corps (CCC), which combined work relief with the preservation of natural resources. Big Piney was home to a CCC spike camp, headquartered near Pinedale on Fremont Lake. The spike camps enabled the workers to be closer to their job sites. (Courtesy of Mildred Bertram and Wildman Haynie.)

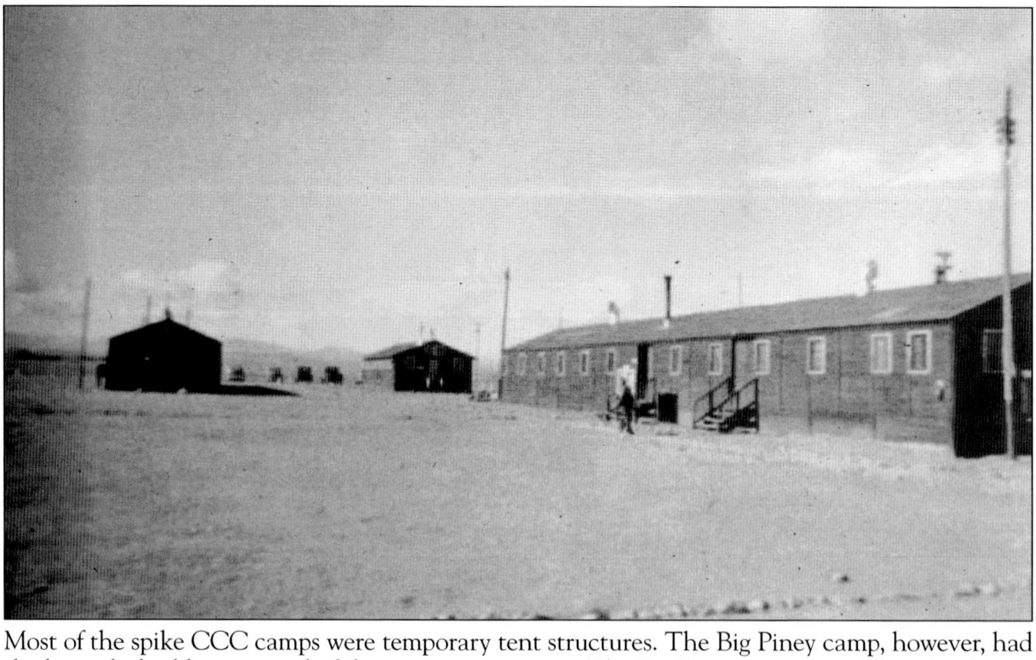

Most of the spike CCC camps were temporary tent structures. The Big Piney camp, however, had the barracks buildings typical of the permanent camps. The Big Piney camp opened in April 1938 and was located one mile west of town on Wyoming Highway 350. (Courtesy of Marjorie Guio.)

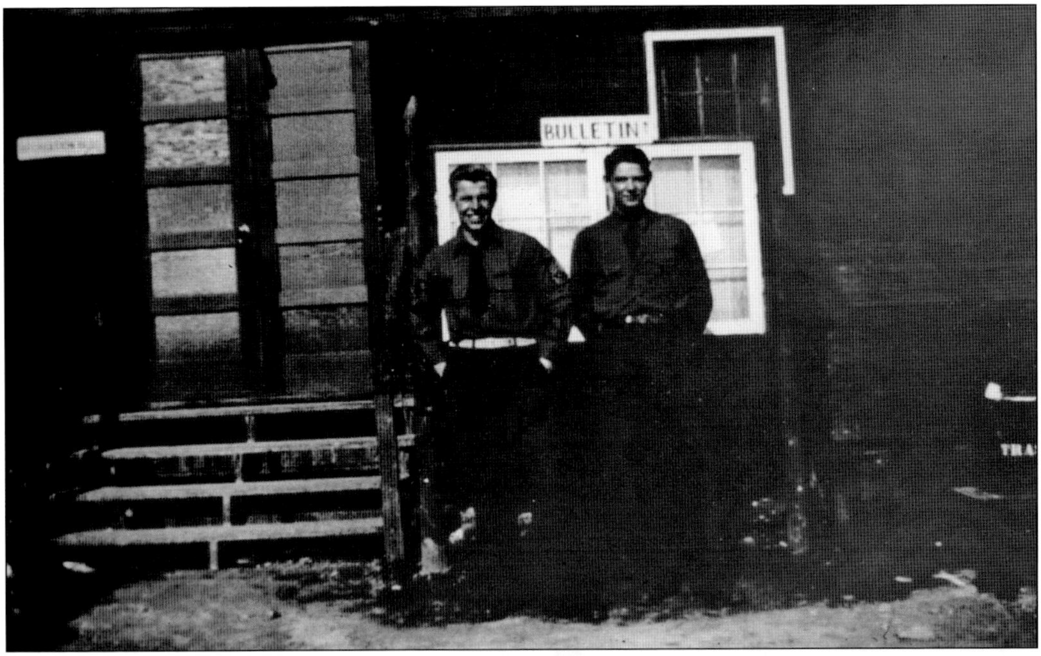

CCC enrollees Earl Wildman (left) and a Mr. Wisniski stand outside the administration building at the Big Piney camp. One of the major jobs for the Big Piney enrollees was building fences, brought on with the passage of the Taylor Grazing Act of 1934. Grazing allotments in the mountains, managed by the US Forest were now fenced, including those in the Wyoming Range, near the Big Piney camp. (Courtesy of Mildred Bertram and Wildman Haynie.)

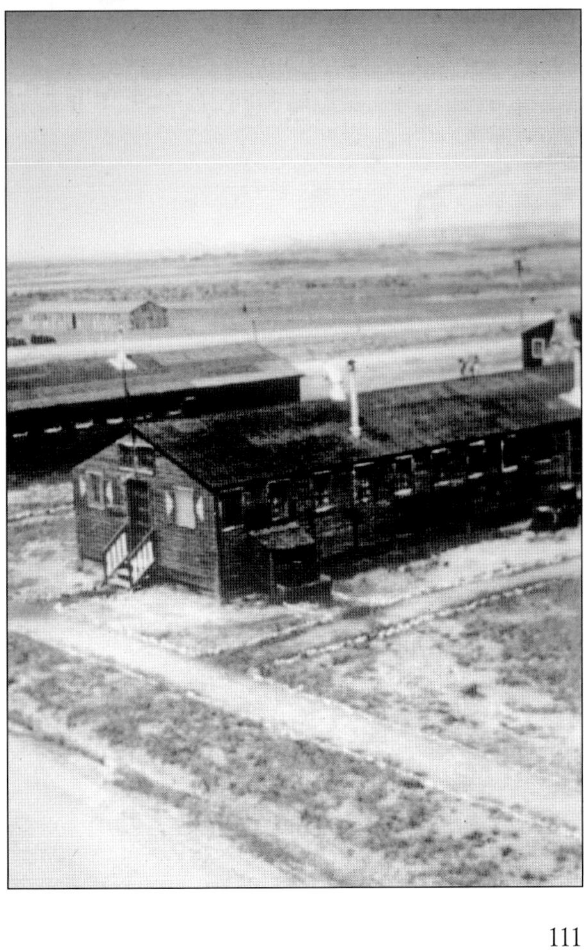

Building roads was a common undertaking for CCC members. Enrollees staying at the Big Piney spike camp helped with the construction of the road between La Barge and Star Valley, which was several miles long and a major undertaking. They also helped with road upgrades into the Wyoming Range on the former Lander Wagon Road of the Oregon Trail and assisted with fence building in the area. (Courtesy of Mildred Bertram and Wildman Haynie.)

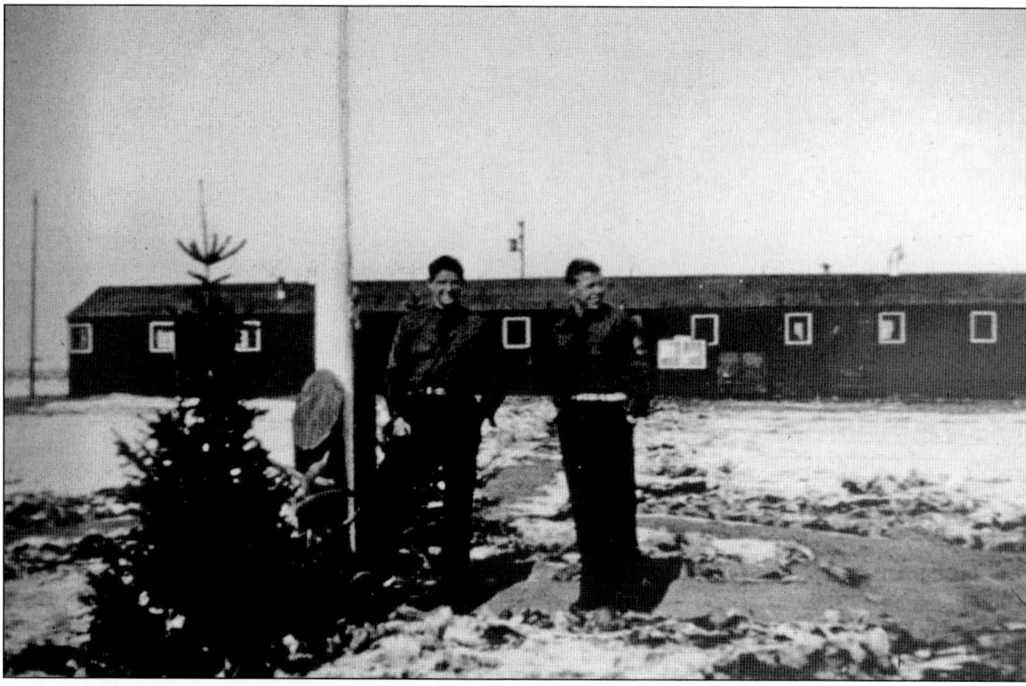

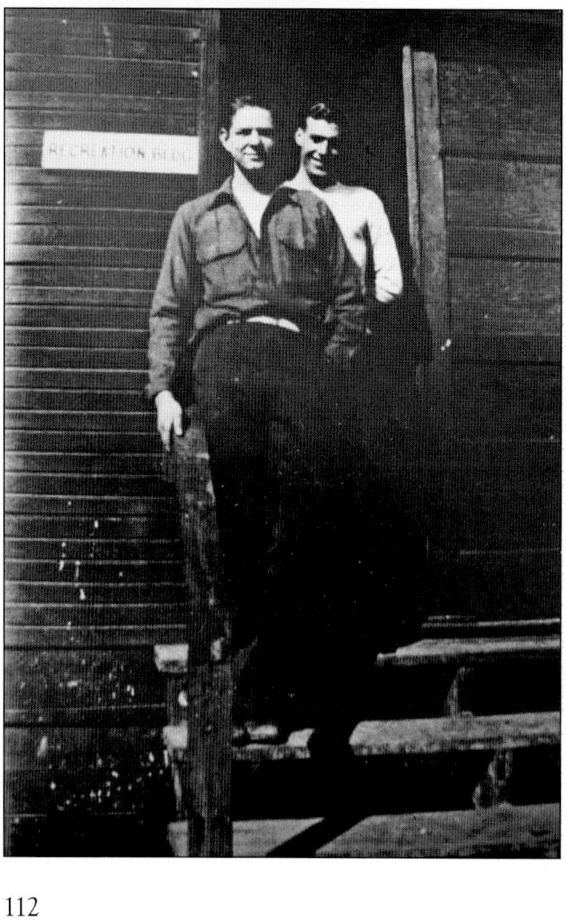

Enrollees at the Big Piney CCC camp stand next to the flag pole. Young men at the camp came from New York, California, Ohio, Illinois, Kentucky, Virginia, and Wyoming. (Courtesy of Mildred Bertram and Wildman Haynie.)

Earl Wildman, on left, and Max Schmidt stand outside the recreation hall at the Big Piney camp. When not working, camp administration provided a wide array of activities for the young men in the recreation hall, including "talkies" or movies, board games, a small library, lectures, and sometimes classes. It was also a good place to gather and visit during off hours. (Courtesy of Mildred Bertram and Wildman Haynie.)

CCC enrollee Mickey Kriel, stationed at the Big Piney camp, is pictured here in town in front of the Big Piney Drug Store. His relaxed dress and pose suggests he was not working. The army truck he is leaning on was typical transportation for the young men to job sites usually in the Wyoming Range to the west of the towns. (Courtesy of Marjorie Guio.)

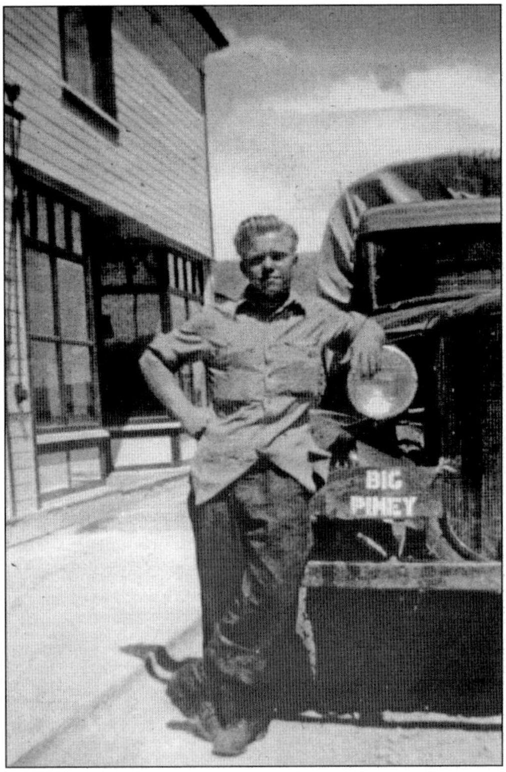

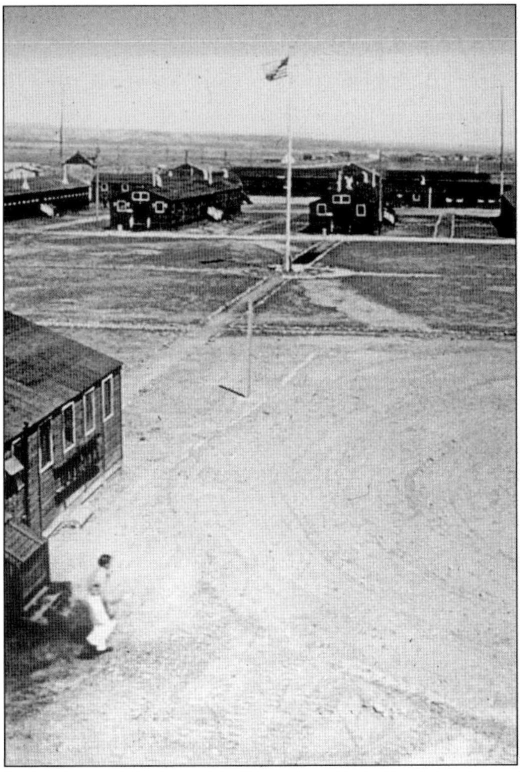

Building US Forest Service ranger stations was also an undertaking for CCC enrollees. Those at the Big Piney camp assisted with the construction of the Big Piney station, as well as ones in Snyder Basin and in Merna, located in the Wyoming Range west of town. (Courtesy of Mildred Bertram and Wildman Haynie.)

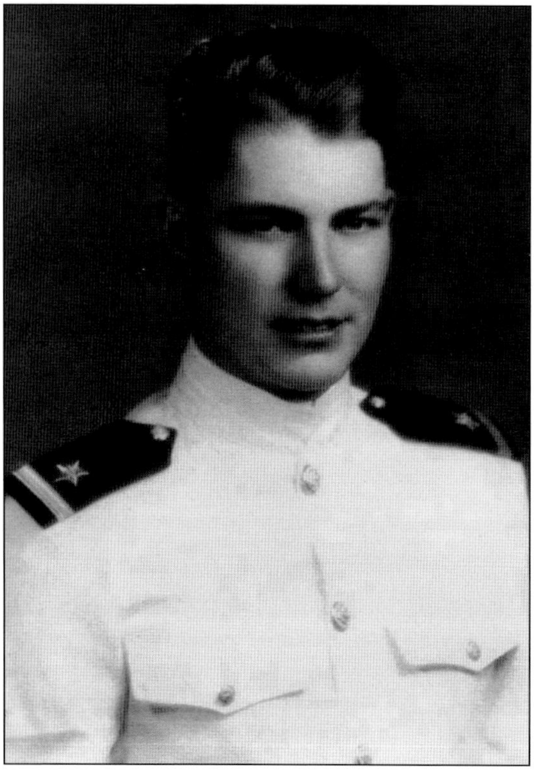

Paul Scherbel enlisted in the Navy on January 15, 1942, at age 24. Scherbel entered the service as an apprentice seaman in the beginning of America's involvement in World War II. When he was discharged, he was a commander, having served all his time in the Pacific theater. In 1946, after the war, Scherbel moved to Big Piney, where he worked his entire career as a surveyor. (Courtesy of Paul Scherbel.)

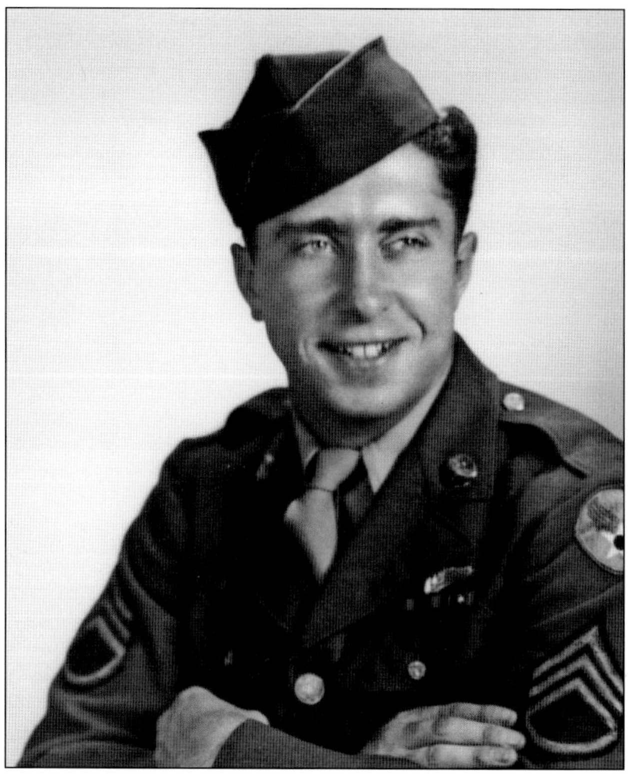

S.Sgt. Robert Linn was stationed in Italy during World War II. He enlisted in the Army Air Corps and served as a bombardier on B-17 bombers. Later, he would raise his family in Big Piney after working for the Soil Conservation Service. (Courtesy of Robert and Helena Linn.)

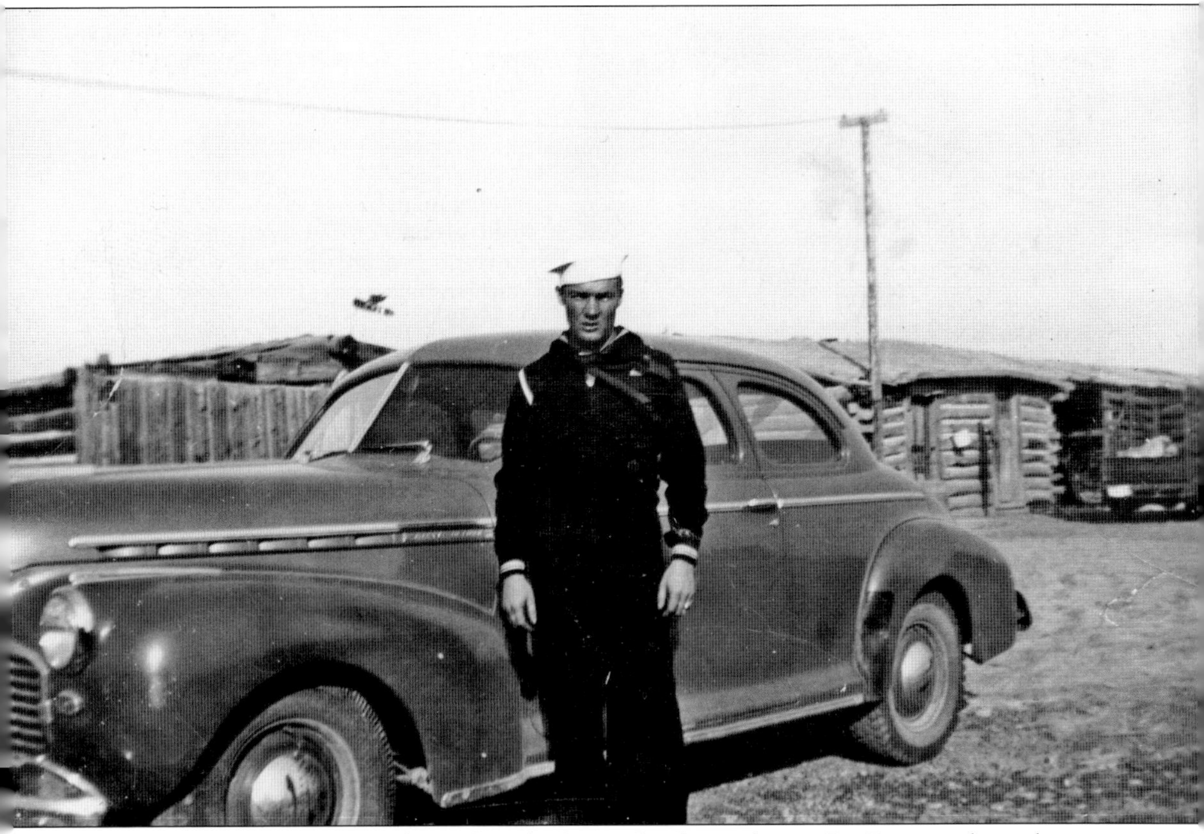

Dean Gordon Jewett, born and raised on the Jewett family ranch near Big Piney, is shown here in uniform at home during World War II. Dean enlisted between Christmas and New Year's, a few weeks after the bombing of Pearl Harbor in 1941. He joined the Navy and saw very active duty for almost four years on the flagship USS *Honolulu* in the Pacific. (Courtesy of Sommers family.)

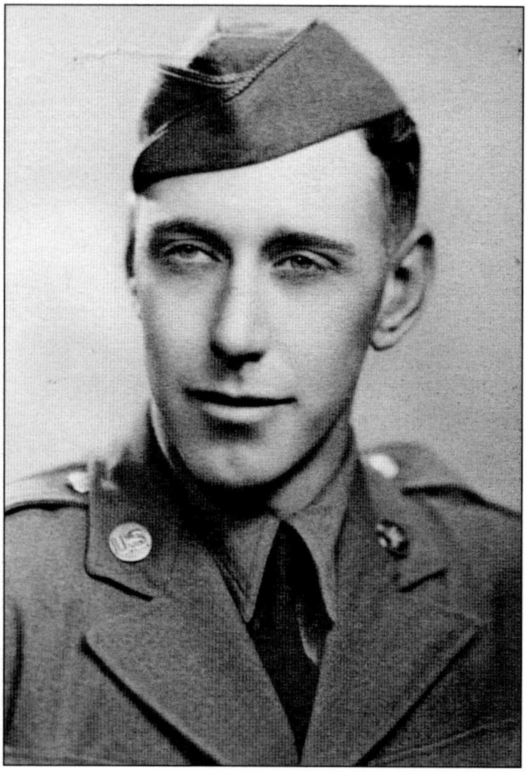

Born and raised on a cattle ranch near Big Piney, Sgt. John Sommers enlisted in 1941 to serve in the Army's 32nd Bomb Squadron during World War II. By war's end, he would serve in England, Italy, and North Africa. Sommers was typical of many young men his age who left the security of their homes to assist their county during the world conflict. (Courtesy of Sommers family.)

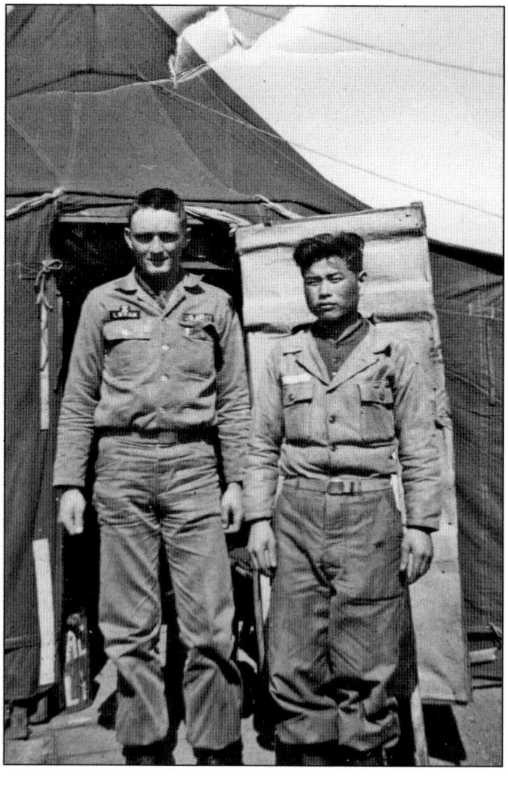

Abner Luman, the third generation of his family in western Wyoming, left the family ranch to serve in the Korean conflict in 1955 and 1956. As a member of the Army infantry 32rd Regiment 7th Division, Luman's unit served with Korean attached personnel, such as the one he is standing next to in this photograph. (Courtesy of Sommers family.)

Nine

COMMUNITY ENTERTAINMENT

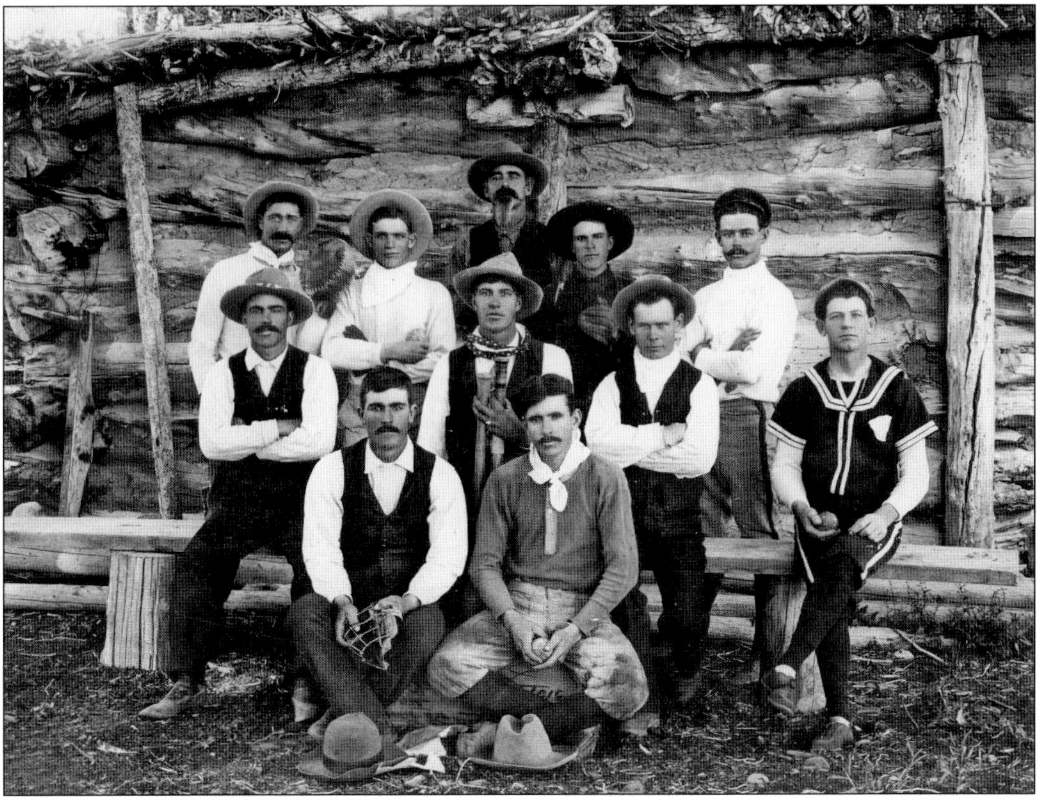

The Big Piney and Marbleton ball team is seen here in 1898. With few teams around to play against, they often played one another. From left to right are (first row) Will Mills Jr. and unidentified; (second row) Bill Fleming, Bob Snyder, Frank Larson, and Jerome Mills; (third row) Charley Hammond, Sol Trimball, W.E. Mills Sr., Less Mills, and Bill Hammer. (Courtesy of Nancy Budd Espenscheid.)

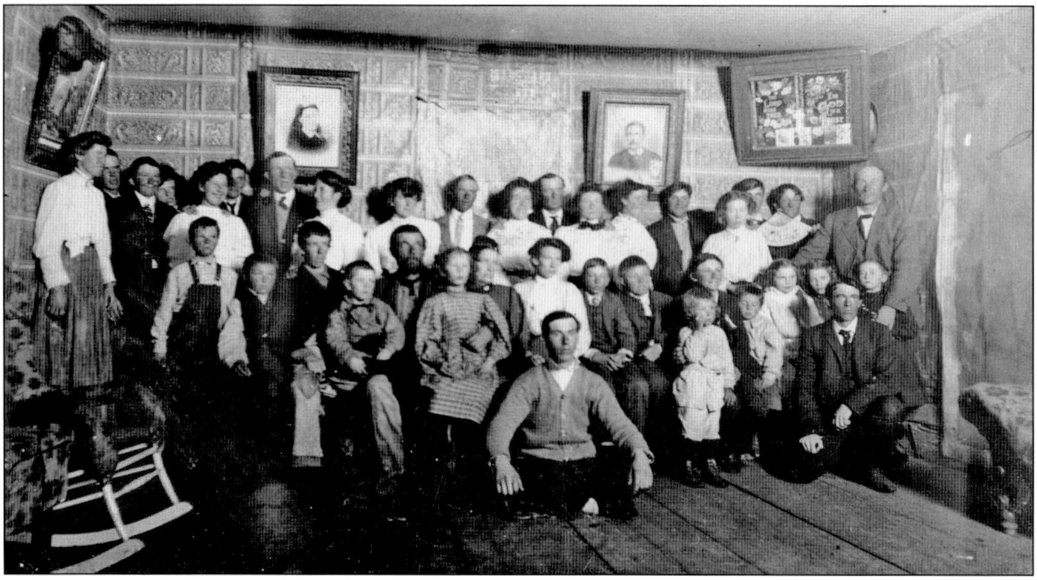

Dances were one of the most popular forms of entertainment during the early years. Pictured above are the guests at a dance at Frank Smith's place on February 4, 1911. Folks would arrive starting in the afternoon and not leave until daylight the following morning. A break from the dancing would usually take place at midnight for a meal prepared by the ladies. (Courtesy of Bill and Carrie Budd.)

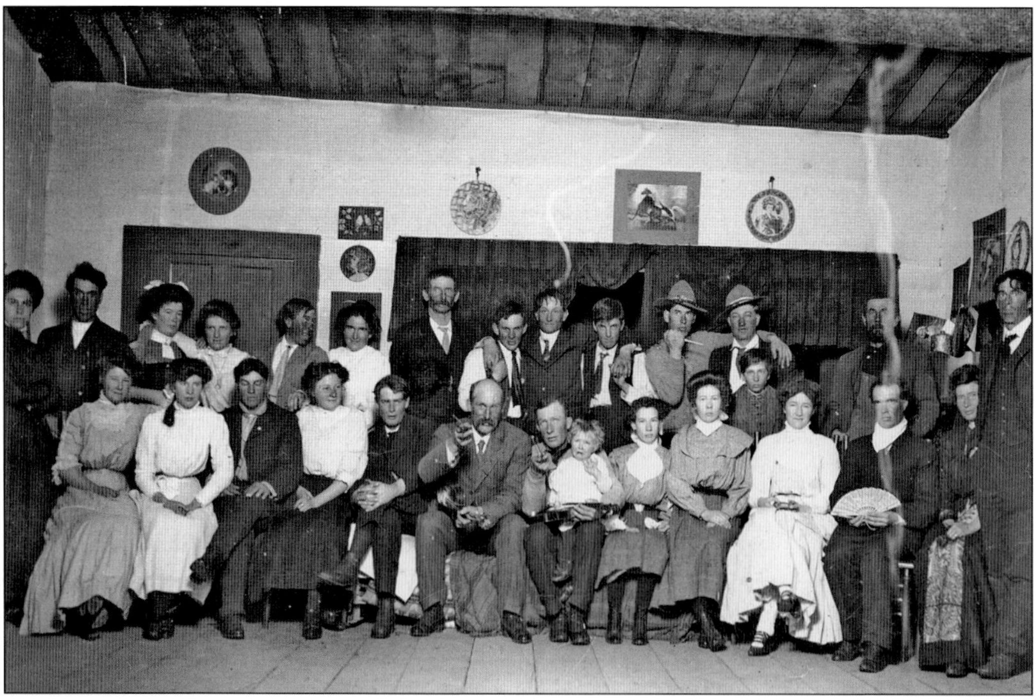

Guests pause for a photograph at a dance at Cottonwood in 1910. In the center sits Wes Vickery, holding his fiddle and a child he seems to be cheering up for the pose. Children were always brought to the dances and bedded down when they were too tired to stay up any longer. Their parents, however, danced the whole night through. (Courtesy of Bill and Carrie Budd.)

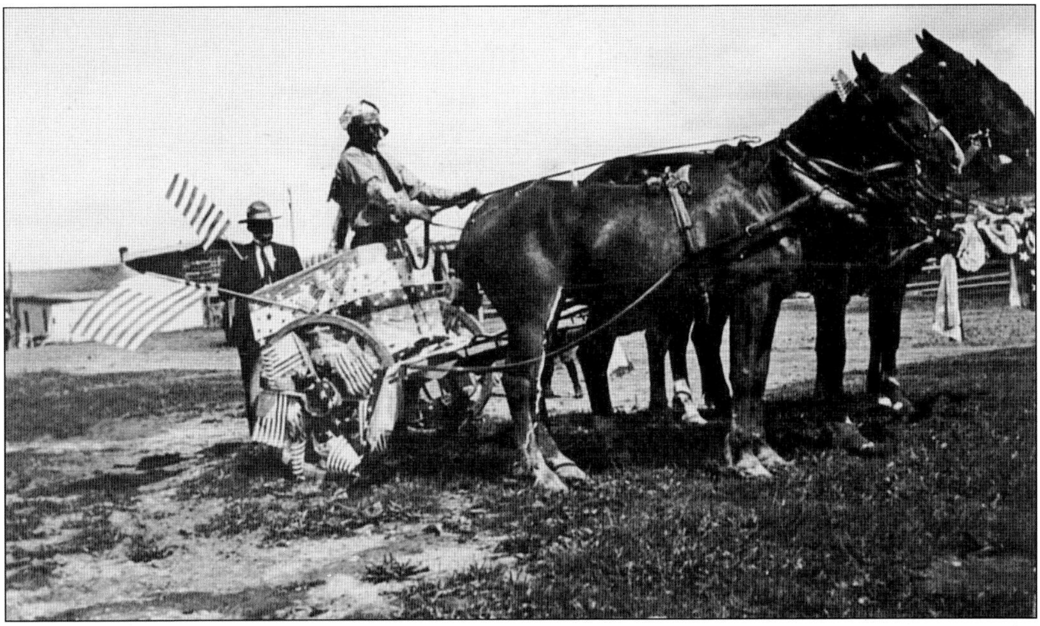

Chariots pulled behind horses were often seen at community gatherings. Pictured here are the winners of an event held in town on July 4, 1914. Note how patriotic the driver has made himself and his chariot. They are covered with American costume, decorations, and flags. Fourth of July gatherings were popular, complete with community picnics and many activities. (Courtesy of Nancy Budd Espenscheid.)

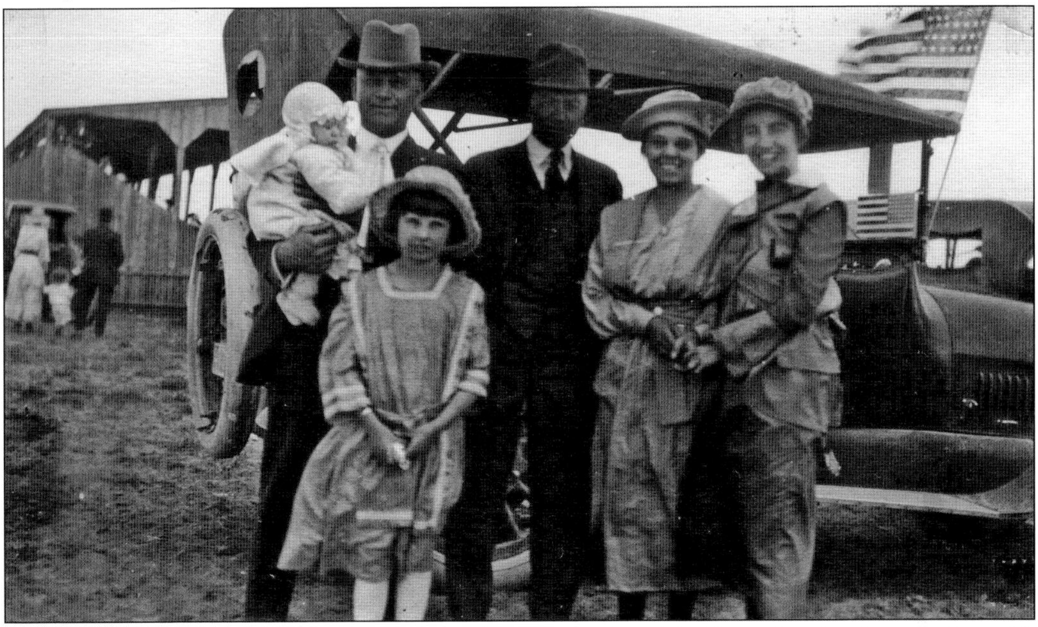

People came for miles to attend the local rodeos. Attending Marbleton Rodeo Days on June 20, 1919, are a Mr. Oswald of Omaha, Nebraska, holding local baby Clifton Fear Jr. Others gathered are Otto Hersig, Corene Murdock, Mrs. Joseph P. Jensen and Mrs. Clifton Al Fear. The group stands in front of the Frank A. Fear automobile, decorated with American flags. (Courtesy of Mardell Fear.)

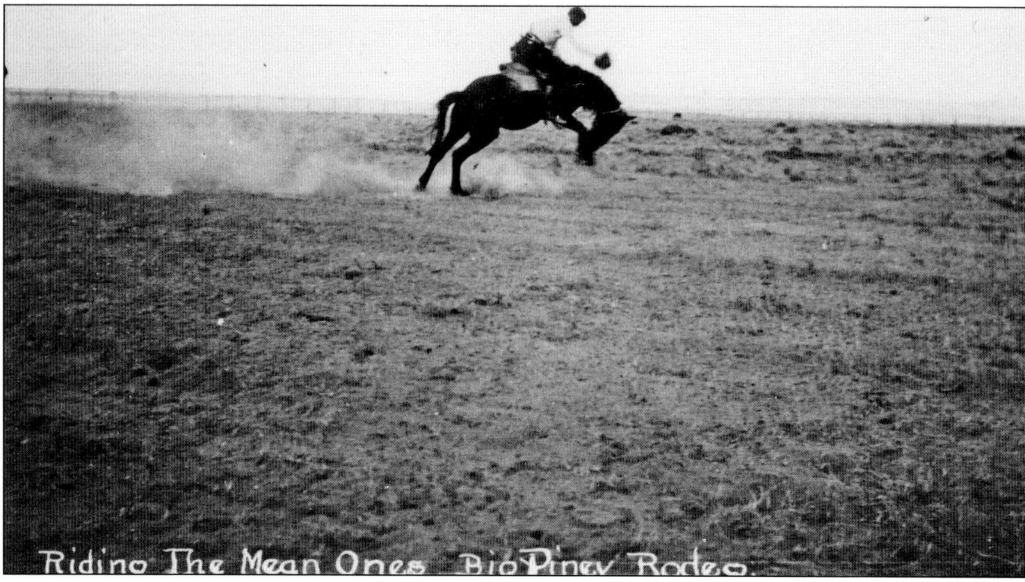

The cowboy is fanning the horse with his hat to show off. The big event of the year was the Big Piney Chuckwagon Rodeo, two days of fun and excitement held over the Fourth of July. On the first day, the citizens would have a big barbecue feed, served free to all. After eating, everyone went to the rodeo grounds to see a show put on entirely by local talent. (Courtesy of Mike and Tara Miller.)

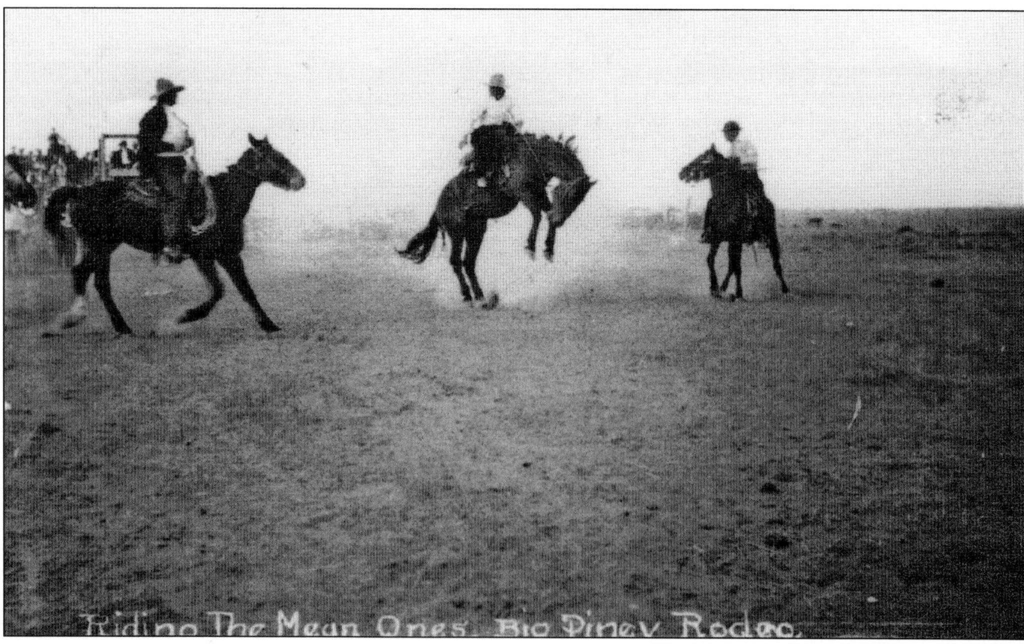

The early Big Piney rodeos used hard-bucking horses from the local ranches. There were also plenty of good riders among the local young men. Plenty of riders where willing to put on a good show in their attempts to win the first prize of $100. There were saddle bronc riding contests, roping contests, and all kinds of horse and pony races. (Courtesy of Mardell Fear.)

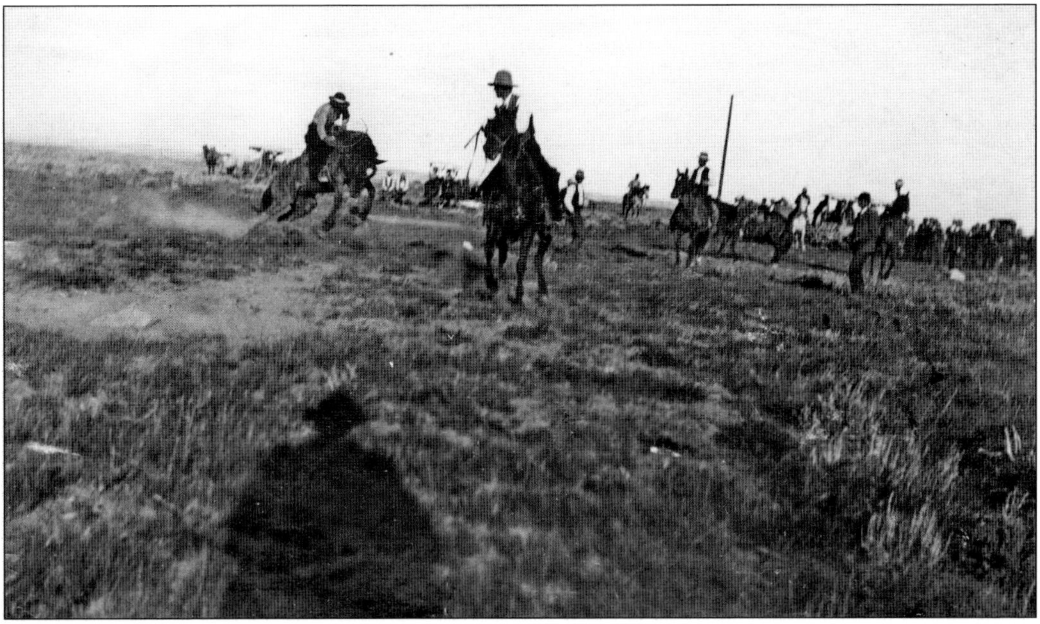

Rodeos have always been popular from the town's earliest days. Pictured here is one of the area's earliest rodeos, where cowboys are showing off their ability to stay on a bucking horse, or so they hoped. The men on horses near the bucking horse and cowboy are there to assist if the cowboy gets in trouble. This rodeo took place on the open range, with no fenced arena. (Courtesy of Sommers family.)

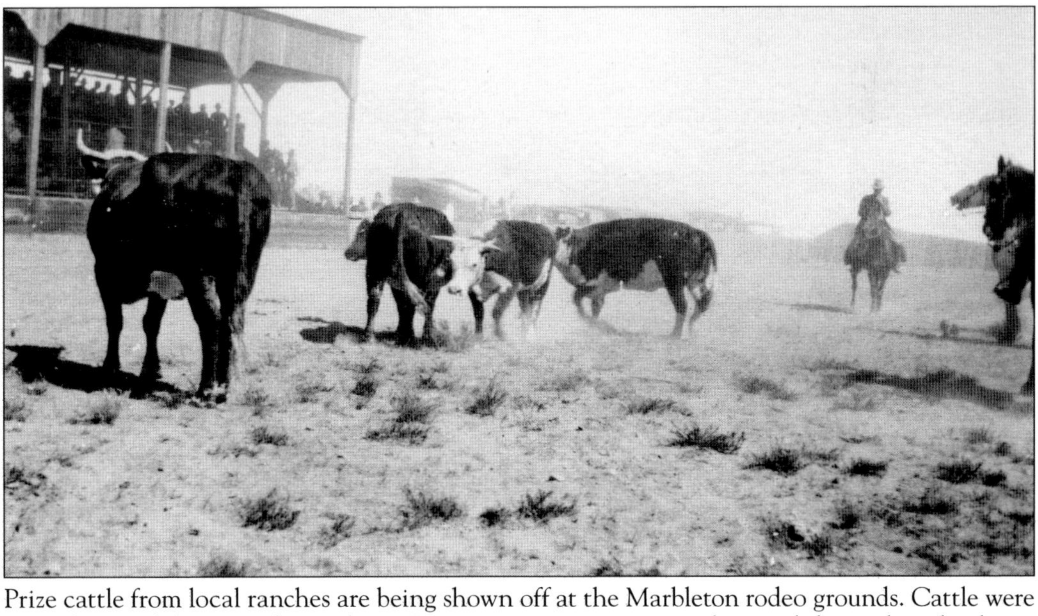

Prize cattle from local ranches are being shown off at the Marbleton rodeo grounds. Cattle were moved around the arena by cowboys. Sometimes steers were roped around the neck with a lariat and then dallied around the horn on the cowboy's saddle. Showing animals was a typical event at the two-day rodeos. (Courtesy of Nancy Budd Espenscheid.)

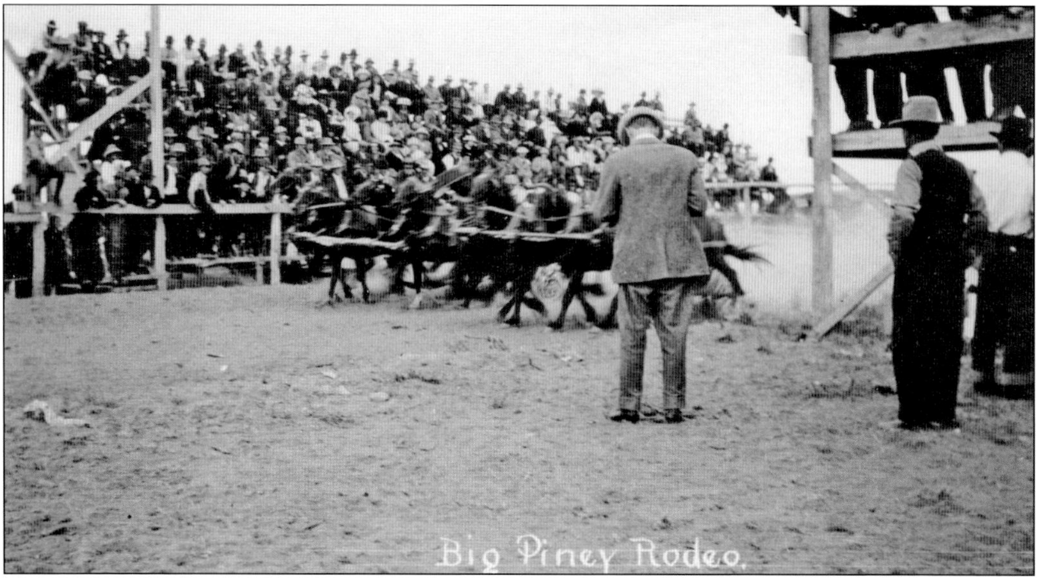

The two teams seem to be neck-and-neck in this chariot race held in Marbleton. Note the size of the crowd in the spectator stands. People came from Kemmerer, Rock Springs, and as far away as Salt Lake City, Utah, to see the Big Piney Rodeo and bet on the chariot race. (Courtesy of Mike and Tara Miller.)

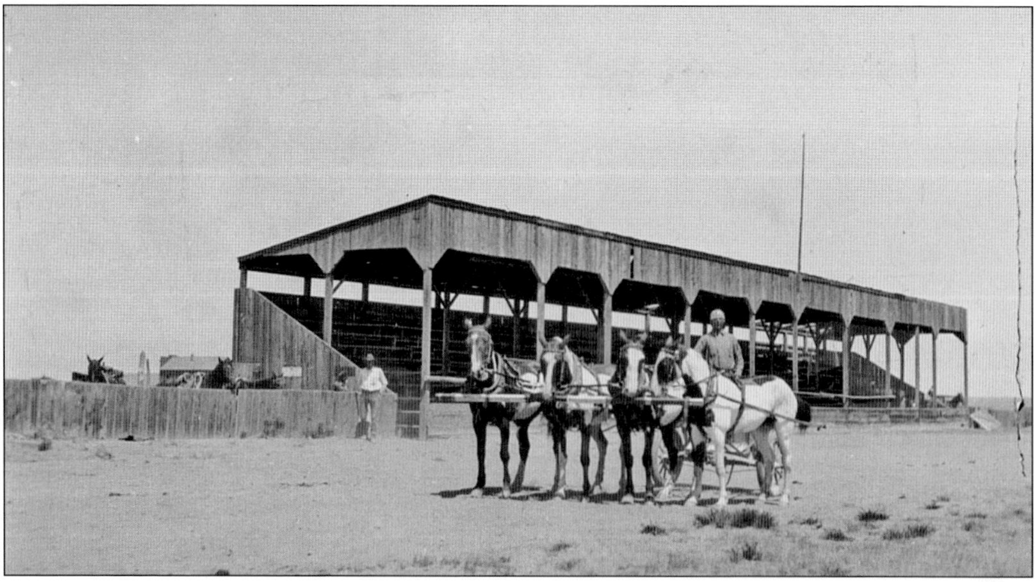

A chariot team of four horses stand in front of the Marbleton grandstand. For the spectators, the chariot race was the most exciting of all the rodeo events. For the two-day rodeo and picnic event held every Fourth of July, the established area ranchers and their families stayed in the local hotels. (Courtesy of Nancy Budd Espenscheid.)

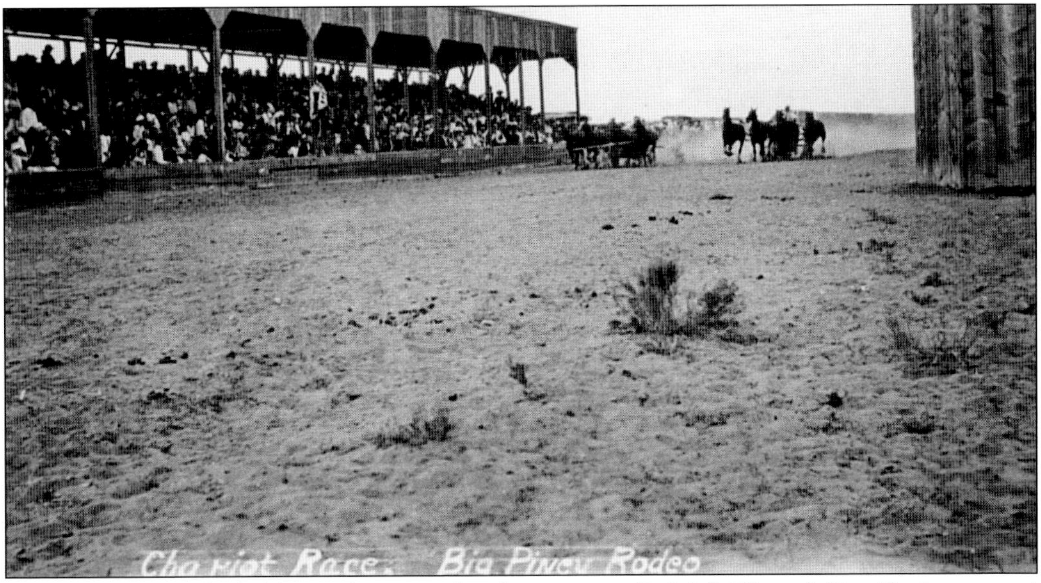

The last event to be held at rodeos was the chariot race. Ralph Mills and Guy Decker started chariot racing in Big Piney with four horses abreast hooked to a two-wheeled cart, shown above. While the event was commonly called the Big Piney Rodeo, it was actually held in Marbleton. (Courtesy of Green River Valley Museum.)

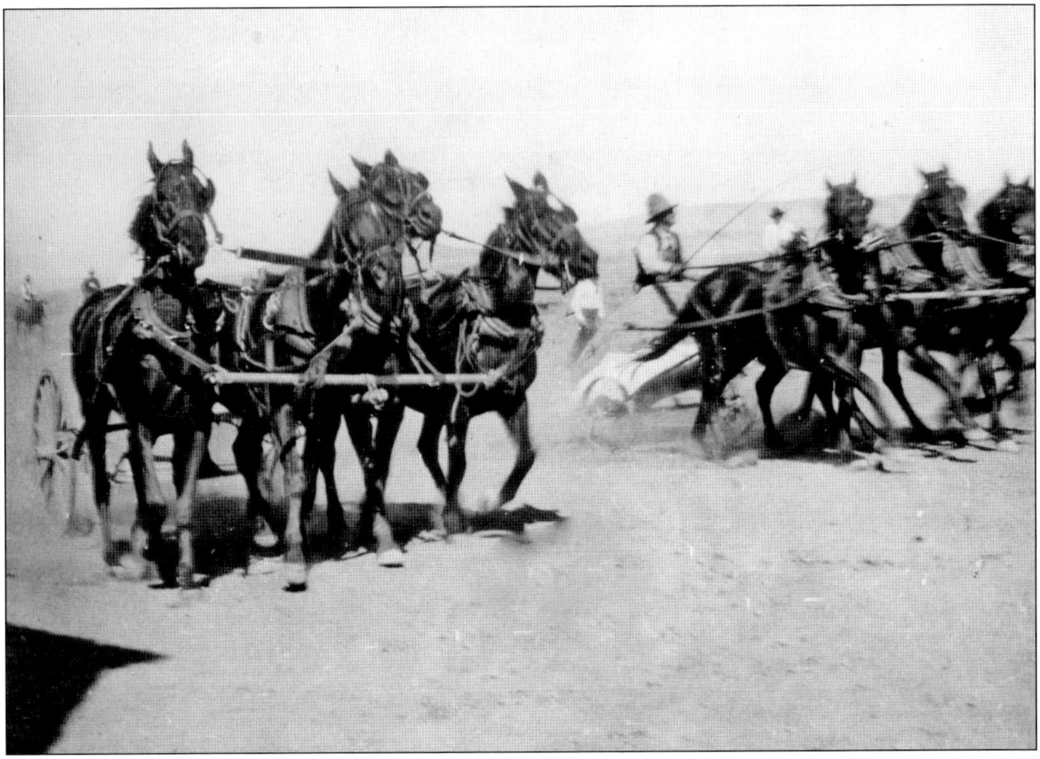

Two teams with four horses each are pulling chariots in this action shot. They are racing in Marbleton in 1916. The competition among the local ranchers and their horses resulted in exciting, action-packed races. (Courtesy of Nancy Budd Espenscheid.)

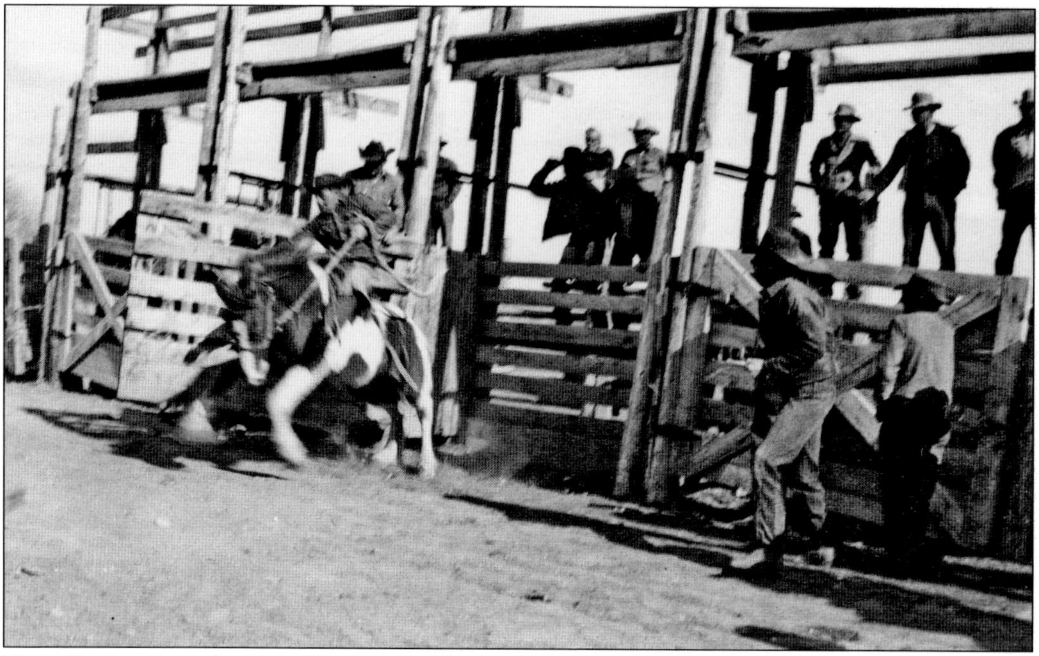

Norm Richie is just leaving the chute on the bucking horse Half and Half at the Big Piney Rodeo in 1953. The bucking horse riding competition could be dangerous, exciting, and financially rewarding. In later years, winners could make good money. (Courtesy of Sommers family.)

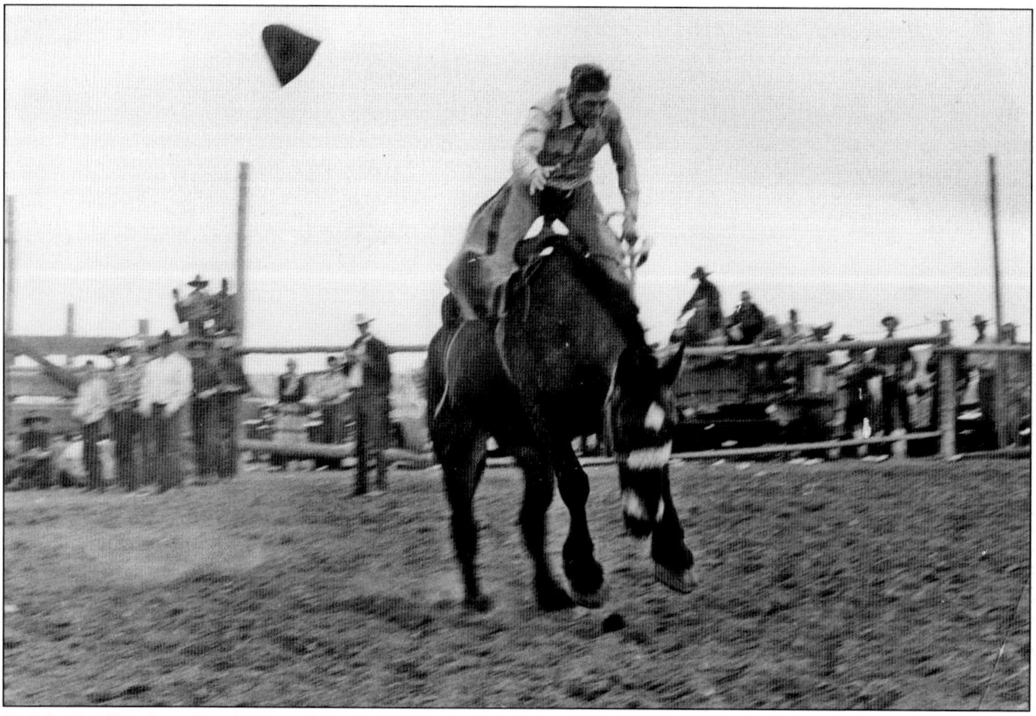

Bobby Miller lost his hat and is about to be bucked off his horse in this Big Piney Rodeo in the 1950s. Rodeos have always been entertaining but dangerous. Most bucking horse rodeo riders were injured at some time. (Courtesy of Mike and Tara Miller.)

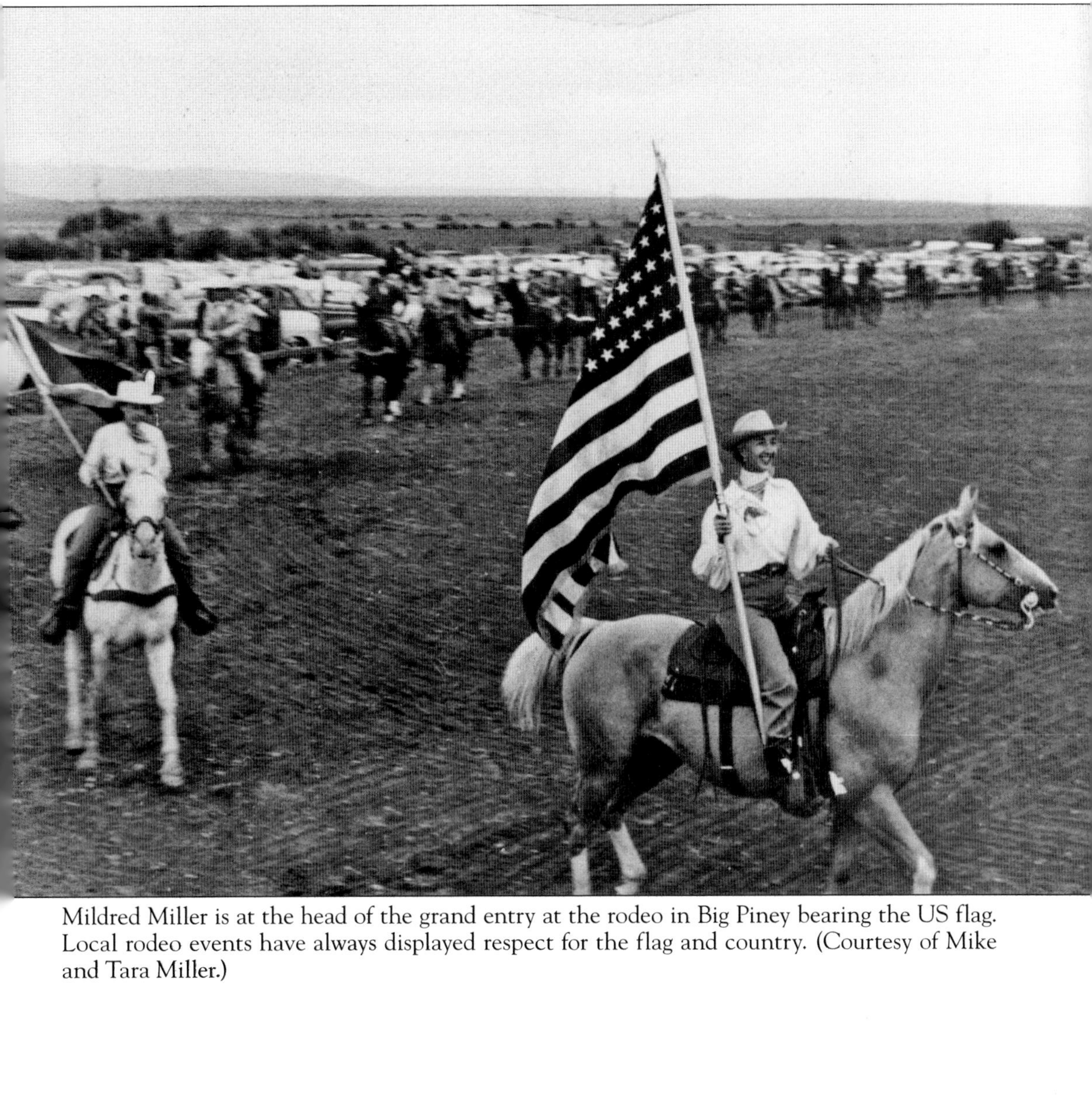

Mildred Miller is at the head of the grand entry at the rodeo in Big Piney bearing the US flag. Local rodeo events have always displayed respect for the flag and country. (Courtesy of Mike and Tara Miller.)

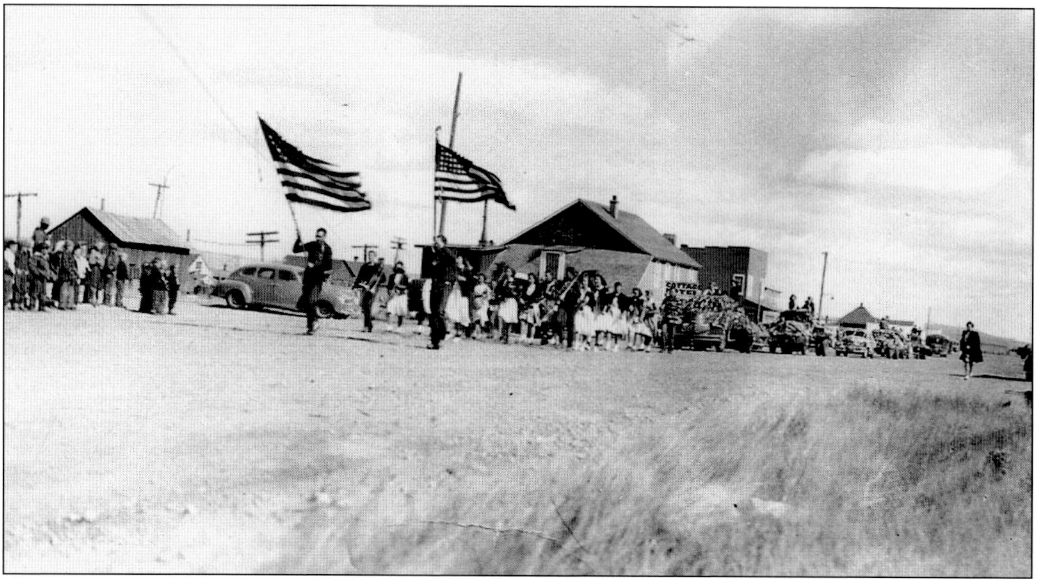

Young men wave the American flag as they lead the school parade down the Main Street in Marbleton. Parades have always been popular in Big Piney and Marbleton. Streets were closed for the events, but the minimal traffic was not inconvenienced. (Courtesy of Green River Valley Museum.)

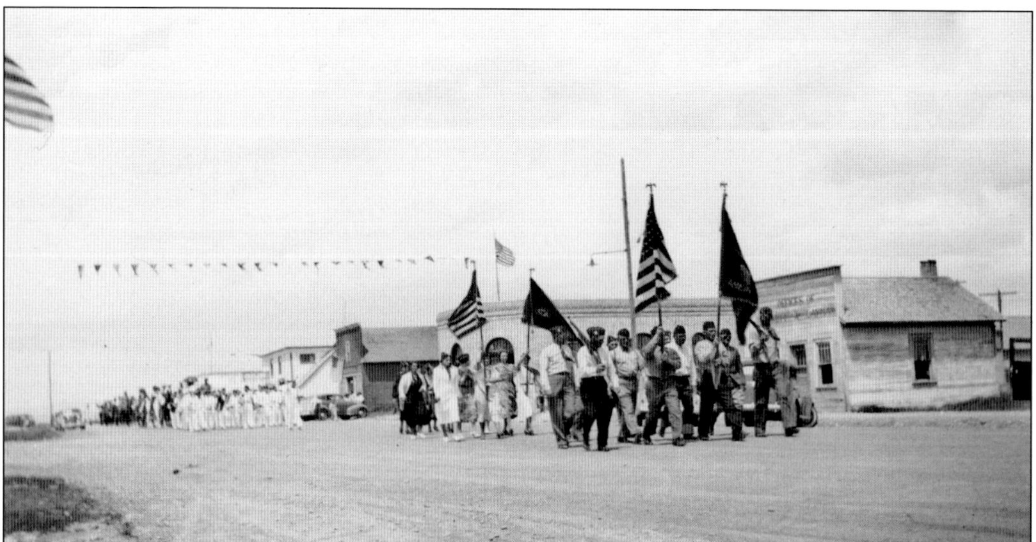

Various veterans and citizens carrying flags marched down Big Piney's Budd Avenue in this 1950s parade. Schoolchildren and different organizations are represented in the town's celebration. (Courtesy of Green River Valley Museum.)

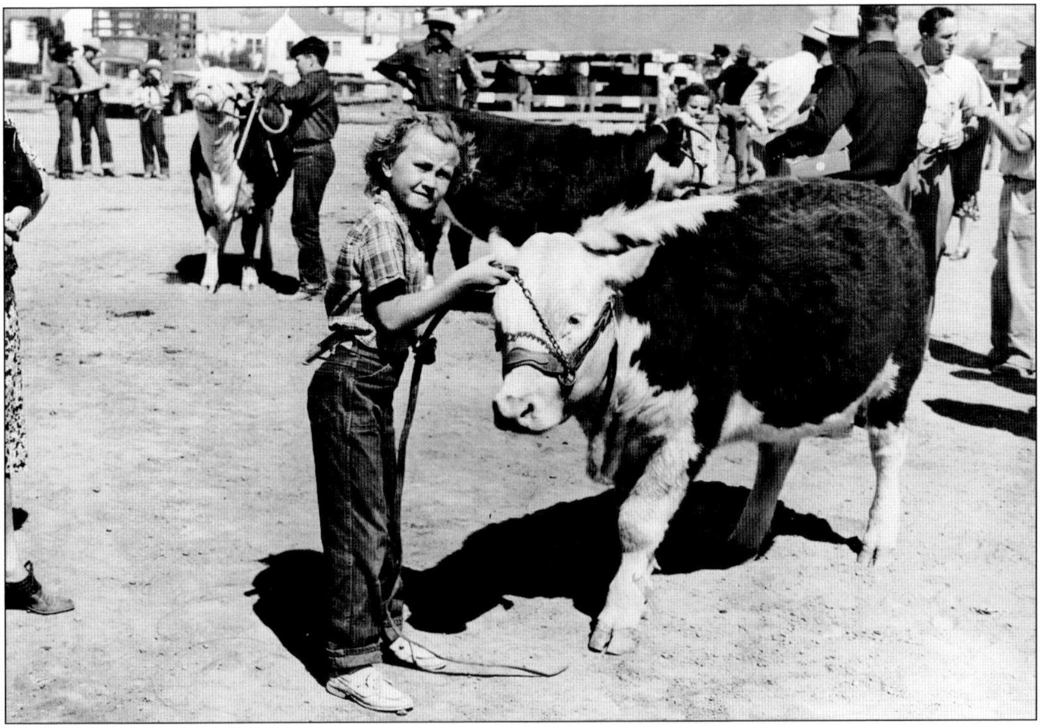

Betty Budd Fear holds her heifer at the local 4-H fair in the 1940s. The fairgrounds were located on the west end of Big Piney by the gazebo built for these types of events. Betty would be parading one of the Budd family's Herefords, well known throughout the West. (Courtesy of Nancy Budd Espenscheid.)

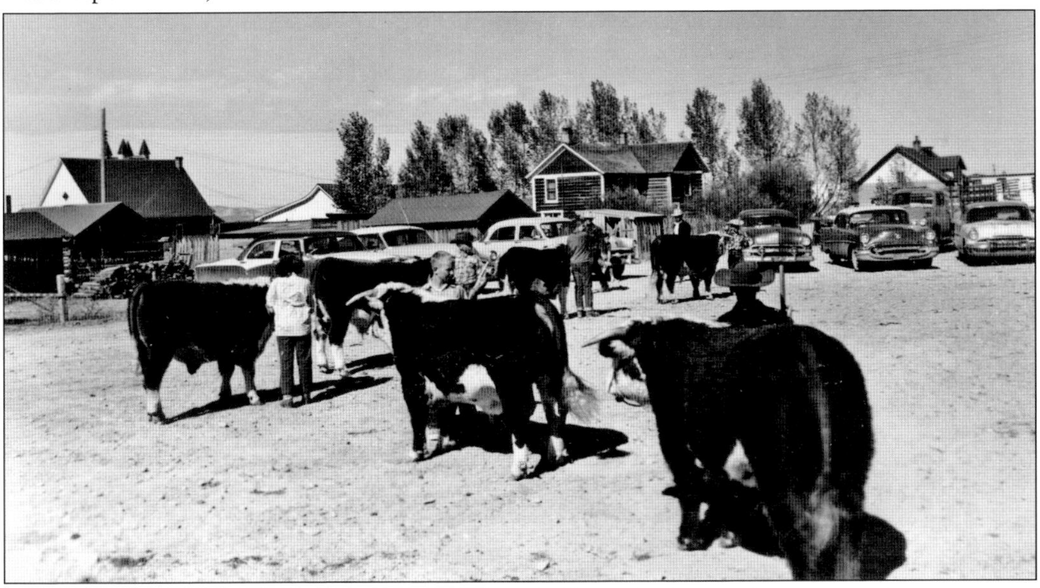

Ranch children from area ranches parade their bulls at this Future Farmers of America event in the 1950s. It was held right in the town of Big Piney, a testimony to a real "cow town." In the center of the photograph is young Jim Miller, surrounded by his competition. (Courtesy of Mike and Tara Miller.)

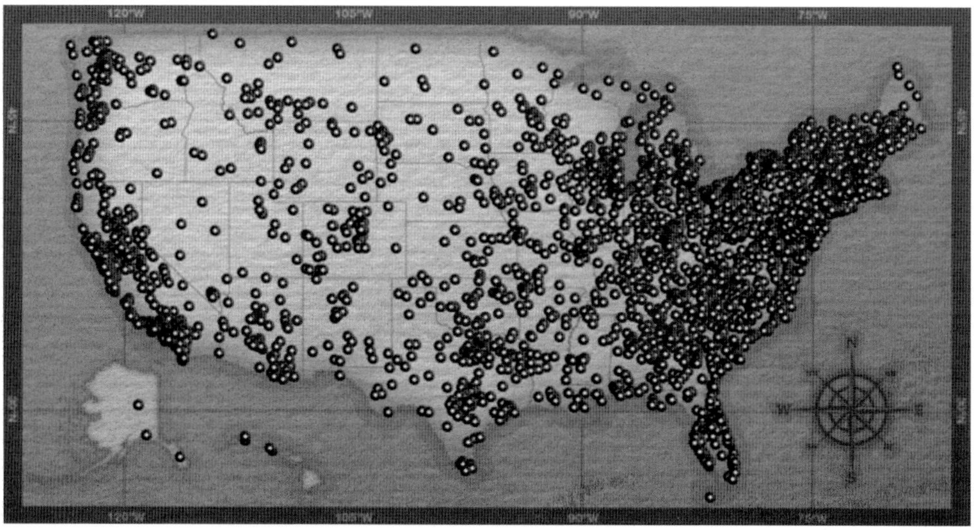